# FI**NANCIALLY**

"Raw. Real. Relatable. For every Latina who has ever wanted more but was told to settle for less. In *Financially Lit!* Jannese takes you on a healing journey where generational poverty ends with you and a new legacy of wealthy Latinas is birthed through you!"

—Rachel Luna, bestselling author of *Permission to Offend: The Compassionate Guide for Living Unfiltered & Unafraid*

"In a world where the financial landscape can be daunting, especially for women and minorities, this book stands as a beacon of hope and a practical, step-by-step guide to mastering your money. *Financially Lit!* is more than a guide; it's a movement. Prepare to be inspired, educated, and motivated."

—Jamila Souffrant, author of *Your Journey to Financial Freedom* and host of the *Journey to Launch* podcast

"*Financially Lit!* is the comprehensive money guide you need to finally get your dinero right!"

—Giovanna Gonzalez, author of *Cultura & Cash* and founder of The First Gen Mentor

"*Financially Lit!* is the book our community has been waiting for! Beyond the basic money principles, it dives deep into essential topics like entrepreneurship and financial independence, illuminating the path to economic freedom and success. It even covers topics we're often hesitant to discuss—like estate planning and financial abuse. This book is bold, honest, and a true game-changer!"

—Cindy Zuniga-Sanchez, author, speaker, and founder of Zero-Based Budget Coaching LLC

"*Financially Lit!* is the complete guide that takes you from surviving to thriving."

—Linda Garcia, author of *Wealth Warrior* and
founder of In Luz We Trust

"An empowering road map to financial freedom that speaks directly to the heart and soul of every modern Latina. This book is not just a guide; it's a revolution, a declaration that financial prowess knows no gender or cultural bounds."

—Erika Cramer, author of *Confidence Feels Like Shit*

"Jannese Torres has written the 'go-to, can-do' manifesto to start today, and light the fire of all things financial in a step-by-step, accessible, and understandable way. What are you waiting for? Go get the dinero, it's ok!"

—Nely Galan, *New York Times* bestselling author of
*Self Made: Becoming Empowered, Self-Reliant,*
*and Rich in Every Way*

"Jannese's voice is what I've been waiting for! She brings so much to the table... not only does she drop knowledge on every page, she does it with wit, humor, and effortless badassery. I can't wait to gift this to everyone I know."

—Mandi Woodruff-Santos, founder of MandiMoney Makers™
Career Coaching Academy and co-host of
the *Brown Ambition* podcast

# Financially

## LIT!

### THE MODERN LATINA'S GUIDE TO LEVEL UP YOUR DINERO & BECOME FINANCIALLY PODEROSA

## Jannese Torres

balance

New York   Boston

Balance
Hachette Book Group
1290 Avenue of the Americas
New York, NY 10104
GCP-Balance.com
@GCPBalance

Originally published in hardcover and ebook in April 2024

First trade paperback edition: March 2025

Balance is an imprint of Grand Central Publishing. The Balance name and logo are registered trademarks of Hachette Book Group, Inc.

The publisher is not responsible for websites (or their content) that are not owned by the publisher.

Balance books may be purchased in bulk for business, educational, or promotional use. For information, please contact your local bookseller or the Hachette Book Group Special Markets Department at special.markets@hbgusa.com.

Library of Congress Control Number: 2023041719

ISBNs: 9781538741672 (trade paperback), 9781538741689 (ebook)

Printed in the United States of America

LSC-C

Printing 1, 2024

To Mami and Papi, we did it! Thanks for not jumping off the deep end when I told you I was quitting my prestigious engineering career to pursue this crazy dream of twerking on the internet to reggaeton music while teaching mujeres about dinero. Ha! Talk about the American Dream! None of this would have been possible if you hadn't taken the chance to start a new life in America.

I know that your decision to leave Puerto Rico, nuestra Isla del Encanto, was the hardest choice you've ever made, but it opened incredible doors for our family. When I reflect on the incredible privilege I've been given to even have the opportunity to write this book, I can't help but reflect on how different my life would be if you had stayed on the island.

I often think about the lyrics from the song "When You're Home" from *In the Heights*, the legendary musical by fellow Boricua Lin-Manuel Miranda: *"When I was younger, I'd imagine what would happen / If my parents had stayed in Puerto Rico / Who would I be if I had never seen Manhattan / If I lived in Puerto Rico with my people?"*

Instead of being born in a modern-day US colony where 57 percent of children live in poverty and where dreams are so often left unrealized, you left your families, your friends, and everything you knew behind to raise me in the shadows of New York City skyscrapers. It was here where I learned book smarts, and street smarts too. This dynamic environment where people from all over the world come to pursue their dreams served as a constant reminder of the limitless potential that exists in the world, and within me. As the saying goes, if you can make it here, you can make it anywhere. And dammit, we made it!

That decision so many years ago made everything possible for me. I have enjoyed privileges that I never would've had access to if you'd stayed.

Because you sacrificed so much, I've been able to dream out loud. I can only hope to repay you by continuing to live out loud...for us and our ancestors. Thank you from the bottom of my heart. Your love, support, encouragement, and understanding have been my rock throughout this journey.

# CONTENTS

# FOREWORD

My foray into the personal finance world began in the summer of 2001. Before TikTok. Before YouTube. Before Roth 401(k)s were a thing.

I scored a coveted college internship at *Money* magazine, where I was tasked with reporting about credit scores, index funds, and private mortgage insurance. Before offering me the gig, the human resources manager called me to be sure I'd applied to the "right" magazine. "You know we also run *Time*, *InStyle*, and *People*?" she said confusedly. Little did she know this was a stepping-stone opportunity, a dream, really, for this nerdy business major with aspirations of becoming a financial storyteller. Plus, it paid $500 a week and included free housing in New York. What fool would pass this up?

For ten weeks, I sat typing away on the thirty-somethingth floor of the prestigious Time & Life Building, the newsroom abuzz with top writers who took the utmost pride in their clever stock columns and profiles of the next issue's "millionaire next door"...usually a suburban fifty-something dad named Howard who'd quietly built a fortune running a pro bike shop or using *his* father's inheritance to buy shares of Amazon soon after it had IPO'd.

But back then, no matter how interesting our coverage was, we—and the vast majority of the personal finance publishers—had a terrible blind spot. I remember my first day on the job when I discovered our target audience: mostly male, mostly white, and mostly soon-to-retire. The face of personal finance in the early 2000s was...how shall I say? *Womp, womp.*

It didn't take long to hit me. Here I was, a young Iranian American woman writing for a national financial journal. Who, despite inheriting her immigrant parents' work ethic and appetite for bargains, had an empty bank account and nothing to show for the thousands of dollars' worth of Visa debt attached to her name. Who was writing for me and my fellow struggling friends? We're the ones who *really* needed the advice, after all. Why shouldn't we also be aspiring millionaires next door? Why shouldn't we become savvy investors like Howard?

If only I could just learn how to live within my means, figure out where to save and why the stock market moved the way it did. If only I could learn how to make more money and build wealth. If only someone would invite me to the money club and tell me how it works—and tell it to me in *my* love language.

So, like any woman who's stood in a room wondering where her seat is, I dragged in my own chair from the outside. I began to write articles, essays, and books and gave talks around the country for young people, women, people of color, children of immigrants, all equally deserving of financial freedom. I hosted financial programs on television, and today I produce and host a long-running podcast, *So Money*, which has earned over twenty-five million downloads.

Throughout the years, one missing ingredient was a fellow financial expert whom I could lean on, look up to, and laugh with when the road to upholding the financial dreams and values of women got rocky—because it did.

If only I'd known Jannese Torres then.

If I'd had the privilege of befriending the wise, talented, and so lovable Jannese all those years ago, I'm certain that we'd have been attached at the hip and that we'd have had a lot of fun. When we met a few years ago through the recommendation of a financial editor friend, I was instantly drawn to this radiant woman. I remember watching her live on Instagram in 2020 when she announced quitting her full-time job to pursue her podcast and financial education business. I remember thinking I could watch Jannese all day. "She needs her own show," I texted that same editor friend who was mutually in awe of Jannese's ability to summon an audience, instill confidence, and show us the way forward.

What can I say? I'm a gushing superfan. A deep admirer. Jannese and I both understand the financial plights of the underrepresented—although she can break it down and serve up the facts better than anyone I know. She and I understand and respect the importance of building community and how when women make money, when they make more—we all win. *The world truly becomes a better place.*

Perhaps what I love most about Jannese is the depth and honesty with which she speaks and shares. She doesn't mince words, as you'll discover throughout these pages. Whether she's offering a key story from her own rich and layered life or encouraging us to earn up and close gender pay gaps, whether she's teaching us how to exceed (expel, even) cultural expectations, invest wisely, or unapologetically forge our own rich paths, Jannese has our backs. She is our guide with big plans for us. She is our woman.

With this book, I am excited to learn and be inspired once more by Jannese. My chair is in the front row—and happily, alongside yours.

Farnoosh Torabi
Host, *So Money*
Author, *A Healthy State of Panic*

# Financially
# LIT!

# INTRODUCTION

**S**he's carrying the heavy weight of her ancestors and their sacrifices.

*She's crumbling under the pressure of being the first in her family to do things they could have only imagined.*

*She's trying to navigate this unfamiliar world where, for the first time, she's seeing that women can earn more than men.*

*She's focused on thriving and building wealth, so she doesn't have to repeat the cycle of working until she can't work anymore.*

Who is this woman? *She is me* and, if you're a first- or second-generation Latina, she is likely you, too.

I'm guessing that, if you picked up this book, there is a good chance that somewhere deep down you feel like building wealth is for other people, but not for you. I believe this is because it is very difficult to aspire to what we don't see. Representation in the Latino community about what wealth looks like is scarce, especially for women. We don't have many examples of financially powerful Latinas to aspire to, other than the actresses and singers who grace the covers of magazines. I love J.Lo. But I also don't wanna *be* J.Lo, ya feel me? Where are the normal women like us who just want *more* in life and want to learn how to use money to achieve that?

When I began my own journey into understanding the world of money, I couldn't find voices like mine, mujeres who are talking about dinero in an unapologetic way. So I created an award-winning personal finance podcast called *Yo Quiero Dinero*. I'm on a mission to help women of color like you level up their lives by becoming FINAN-CIALLY UNFUCKWITHABLE. What does it mean to be financially unfuckwithable? Here are some examples, all of which we'll cover in this book:

- You have moved beyond a scarcity mindset and invited abundance into your life at all times.
- You have a clear vision of your overall financial picture and your game plan for hitting all of your goals.
- You are investing in your future while living your best mutha%$&#@$ life NOW.
- You're making it rain with multiple income streams, because ain't nobody got time to leave your financial security in the hands of an employer.
- You're so financially independent that your spirit cannot be irked by a toxic boss or someone's dusty-ass son.
- You know how to negotiate pay raises, client contracts, bills, and interest rates *like it's your fucking business...because it is!*
- You are a generational-wealth-building badass who's changing the legacy of your familia with the power of money.
- You have a trusted team of professionals in your back pocket who are helping you achieve Rich Tía status.

# The System Wasn't Built for Us

Before we start getting real with your dinero, we need to take a moment to acknowledge what the challenges are for us as Latina women intent on building wealth. Here's the truth. This whole fucking financial system wasn't built for us. Don't believe it? Let's dive into the evidence.

## We Are Paid Less Than White Men and White Women

On average, Latinas in the United States earn 43 percent less than white men and 28 percent less than white women.[1] Per data collected in 2020, Latinas earned just 57 cents for every dollar that a white American man made. This pay inequity amounts to over $1 million[2] in lost lifetime wages. This discrepancy doesn't just affect you today, it can affect your ability to build wealth long-term, too.

There's a common myth that this discrepancy is simply because Latinas tend to be employed in lower-paying professions—but the data shows otherwise. Licensed clinical social worker Caridad Garcia's experience in the healthcare industry is a case in point.[3] After working in the inpatient mental health field for three years at one of the largest inpatient psychiatric units in Miami, Garcia discovered from talking to a new hire that there was a $16,000 pay disparity between the two. The new hire was a white male. When Garcia was hired in 2008 during the economic crash, the hospital had frozen salaries for two years, and then, when they reinstituted them, had only given Garcia a 2 percent increase versus the 5 percent maximum possible. She was essentially still making the same amount of money as when she had first been hired three years prior. To make matters worse, she'd been in charge of seventeen patients on one floor but had

---

1. https://iwpr.org/wp-content/uploads/2021/09/Gender-Wage-Gapm-in-2020-Fact-Sheet_FINAL.pdf.
2. https://nwlc.org/resources/the-lifetime-wage-gap-state-by-state/.
3. https://wearemitu.com/fierce/latina-case-worker-calls-out-healthcare-industry/.

recently been tasked with caring for half the patients on another floor and doing insurance reviews for any patients with HMOs (a job unto itself!).

When Garcia discovered while training the new hire that his salary was $16,000 more than hers, she decided to speak with two other social workers she worked with. One, a white woman, told her the new hire's salary was $7,000 more than hers. The other, a Latina woman, confided that he was making $10,000 more than she was. The new hire had less experience than any of them, so there was zero justification for the pay gap. Unfortunately, when Garcia approached first her manager and then HR, both told her there was nothing that could be done about it. So she left. But before she did, she let them know that it wasn't just about money, it was about respect. Damn right! By the way, Caridad Garcia now runs her own successful food blog at fatgirlhedonist.com. We love to see it!

As Garcia's story reflects, often Latinas are paid less than white men even in the same job. For example, Latina nurses earn 27 percent less than white male nurses, on average. Think that higher education is enough to bridge the gap? Latinas are going to college at higher rates than ever before. But education doesn't eliminate the pay gap either. Latinas with a bachelor's degree earn an average of 35 percent less than white men.

Mainstream personal finance media ignores the realities of the rapidly growing Latina population. As Latinos, community is at the center of who we are. We aren't just building wealth for ourselves. We are trying to overcome generations of systemic oppression, poverty, and struggle. The "pull yourself up by your bootstraps" bullshit that is spewed by ignorant figureheads in political spaces is old, tired, and frankly, racist.[1] We need real change on many fronts, but we also can't afford to wait for the government, policy makers, or corporate America to give a shit about fixing the systemic inequities that exist. We're going to have to learn how to build wealth, despite this big-ass mess. That's where I come in.

---

1. https://www.nytimes.com/2020/02/19/opinion/economic-mobility.html.

As a first-generation Latina, my mission is to provide you with specific advice that addresses the unique challenges that we Latina women face. We will discuss the systemic and cultural barriers that have kept the Latino community from building wealth in the United States despite the fact that we are the largest minority group in America, and together we'll find a way to move forward and come into our power.

The problem is clear. Latinas are paid less than everyone else due to several factors, including discrimination, systemic biases, and economic inequality. As mentioned, studies have shown that Latina women earn significantly less than their non-Hispanic white male and female counterparts, even when they have similar levels of education and experience. This wage gap is often referred to as the "Latina wage gap" or the "Hispanic wage gap."

One reason for this wage gap is outright discrimination. Latinas face discrimination based on our gender, ethnicity, and race. This means that we may be overlooked for job opportunities or promotions, or may be paid less than our non-Latino white counterparts for doing the same job. Systemic biases also play a role in the Latina wage gap. The US workforce is often structured in a way that disadvantages women, and particularly women of color. For example, Latinas are disproportionately overrepresented in lower-paying jobs, such as domestic work or service industry jobs, that offer fewer opportunities for advancement.

Finally, economic inequality also contributes to the Latina wage gap. Latinas are more likely to live in poverty or low-income households, which can limit our educational and career opportunities. If you're a recent immigrant who is still learning English, you may face language barriers or lack access to resources that could help you succeed in the workforce.

To address the Latina wage gap, it is important that we work toward eliminating discrimination, addressing systemic biases, and reducing economic inequality. We must become active participants in changing the legacy of struggle that is pervasive in our community. Change must start with us.

## Money = Options

We are the first generation of women who have access to financial security and autonomy in ways that our mothers could only imagine. Up until the early 1970s, a woman's application for credit could be denied if a husband didn't co-sign, which often created obstacles for both married and single women. It wasn't until the Equal Credit Opportunity Act (ECOA) was passed in 1974 that women were able to get their own credit cards in their own name. This is one generation ago, amiga! It's our duty to create the abundance in our lives that they were denied. It must be our mission to reclaim all that has been lost, so that we may honor the enormous sacrifices they made for us to be here today.

The very fabric of your DNA is made up of generations of survivors. We come from a lineage of people who have survived colonization, oppression, corruption, discrimination, and more, and yet, *we are still here.* We know how to fight, and we damn sure know how to survive. We've had to fight for everything for so long just to make it to this very moment in history, where we are beginning to see our true potential. It is my hope that, with the knowledge in this book, you will finally be able to shift from surviving to thriving. Because when you're thriving, you have an unlimited number of options for what your life can become. Money provides you with the opportunity to be an active participant in shaping your world, instead of being a victim of circumstances beyond your control. It provides you with the choice to say no to an abusive employer, or a controlling spouse or family member. It gives you the ability to ensure that your loved ones have access to good healthcare, safe schools, and reliable caregivers. It empowers you to support those who advocate for the causes that you believe in and dismantle those that would seek to keep us divided. And most importantly, money helps you live the life that you deserve.

Mujer, you are powerful. You are capable. You are so fucking worthy of living a life beyond scarcity. And it is my hope that you can begin to create that life.

## My Journey

Being a Latina personal finance educator and podcaster was never on my life goals list. But as I've learned, life has a way of unfolding in magical ways when you start doing scary shit. My journey as a serial entrepreneur began by puro accidente. Hell, I didn't even know WTF entrepreneurship was as a teenager. That wasn't even a word in my vocabulary. As the eldest child in a Puerto Rican family, my instructions were very clear: "Go to school, get a good job, and work there until you're ready to retire." That was the road to achieving the American Dream for my traditional Latino parents—and I'm guessing it might be the same message that you got, too.

When you grow up Latino, you have three career options: doctor, lawyer, or engineer. That's it. We don't do entrepreneurship. That's for "other people." The only Latino-owned businesses that I had ever seen growing up were mom-and-pop stores like bodegas, salons, or restaurants—so I never even considered it. Working twelve-to-fourteen-hour days was not what I wanted to do with my life. I thought being a business owner was just another negative consequence of not having an education or, worse, having some sort of criminal record or legal issue that made you traditionally unemployable. No one who owned a business in my community was wealthy. Hell, from what I could see, they were struggling all the time. They worked a lot, were never home, and, if they got sick, weren't able to work and the bills didn't get paid. Listen, ain't *nobody* got time for that!

I grew up watching my parents struggle financially until I was in high school, so I knew early on that I wanted the complete opposite of that hardship. I wanted a cushy title, a six-figure salary, and a 401(k) with a match. And I definitely didn't want a man telling me shit about what I could do with my life. I was determined to become an independent woman with a big-ass house, a bougie car with leather seats, fancy purses, a fluffy dog that I could put in said fancy purses, and lots of money in the bank. Then I'd be happy. I just knew it.

So, I followed in my dad's footsteps as an engineer and became the first ingeniera in my familia. In 2007, I graduated from college with a degree in molecular biology and chemistry, and I pursued a career in the highly sought-after biotechnology industry. After five years of job hopping and climbing the white male–dominated corporate ladder, I found myself making $75,000 a year in my twenties. I was making more money than either of my parents. And…I was FUCKING miserable.

I was always the only Latina in the room, and usually the only woman. I felt so lonely and depressed, yet I also wrestled with feelings of guilt because I felt like I should be happy and grateful for what I had. For many first-gen Latinas, this feeling is all too familiar. I've spoken to so many mujeres who've encountered the exact same emotions, and I'll bet you have too. This American Dream was turning out to be a damn nightmare.

My anxiety was at an all-time high, I was spiraling into depression, and I couldn't stomach the idea of continuing to do this shit for the rest of my life. I started seriously considering quitting my job and starting over, but then I remembered that Sallie Mae was not gonna give a shit about my existential crisis. My parents were not about to endorse my desire to embark on some whacked-out *Eat, Pray, Love* journey to discover the meaning of my life.

I knew I had to get a little creative. So instead of yelling "YOLO!" and burning down the office telenovela style, I started a passion project to cope with my quarter-life crisis. I figured maybe I could distract myself a little from hating my life by finding something to keep me busy. I made a list of all the things I enjoyed doing that had nothing to do with work—and I landed on food as my favorite. I love to cook, and I love to eat even more. I'm that friend who researches the cuisine of a place that I'm visiting and organizes a culinary tour so that we can eat every iconic food a city or country is known for. It's a serious problem. So, I started to cook and post pictures online—or as I soon discovered, I was doing what people called blogging.

Little did I know I was charting a path to freedom.

I centered on the idea of blogging as a side hustle because it would allow me to combine my love of food and my desire for location independence. Blogging was something I could do from anywhere, it allowed me to be creative AF, and it didn't involve crunching numbers, sitting through boring-ass conference calls, or being mansplained in meetings. Every night after work, I'd race home to cook, shoot food pics, and write up recipes to share with the world. The act of creating something to share with the world was something that I'd never experienced before, and I was instantly addicted. Then came the moment that would change my trajectory forever.

One day in January 2014, I walked into work, got fired, and made the two-hour trek back home in a blizzard with only a severance check, a small box of my belongings, and my tattered dignity. I was shocked at the time, but the panic began to wear off once I realized this was literally the best thing that could have happened to me. After all, I hated that job! I would walk into work every single day at least thirty minutes late, hoping that one day they'd get sick of me and just fire me right then and there. (PS: Manifestation is real! Be careful what you wish for.)

And so here I was, newly unemployed and the lucky recipient of a $12,000 severance check. I was at a crossroads: I finally had the time and a little money to work on my blog without restrictions. This turned out to be the shock to my system that I desperately needed to take a moment to breathe and consider what would make me truly happy. And so, after sulking on the couch for about a day, I put on my big-girl panties and started thinking about how I could turn the blog into a thriving business.

And that's exactly what I did.

I spent the next three months fully immersing myself in learning everything I could about social media, online content creation, search engine optimization (SEO), photography, how to pitch myself to brands, and more—and things started to take off. I had to go back to a few more unsatisfying jobs, but I never stopped building my side hustles after work. I made a dramatic mindset shift: my paychecks would be my angel investors. I spent years working 9-to-5s and building my businesses between 5 and 9 p.m. (and sometimes later), and eventually, my little food blog that started as a passion project became the ticket that allowed me to achieve financial independence at age thirty-five. Side hustles changed my life: They helped me pay off over $39,000 of student loans in seventeen months, build generational wealth, and would provide me with the opportunity to retire from traditional work decades early. By 2021 I was able to walk away from the corporate grind for good—my side hustles are now my main hustle!

## Finding My FIRE

After I was let go from my job, I continued to explore the world of earning money online (something I never learned about in school) even though I had to take another job three months later to keep me going until I was able to make my move. In 2017, I stumbled upon the concept of FIRE (Financial Independence/Retire Early). For the first time, I was introduced to the idea that I could use online entrepreneurship as a tool to escape the rat race. I was HOOKED! I started listening to a ton of personal finance podcasts, devouring everything I could find. I started implementing FIRE concepts into my finances, and in 2021, I achieved financial independence, thanks to my food blog.

Becoming an entrepreneur helped me find a voice I didn't realize I had lost. When I started my blog in 2013, I didn't realize I was creating the foundation of a six-figure business that centers around my Latina heritage. I literally get paid to be myself, something I could NEVER do in corporate America.

As a food blogger, homing in on my Latina heritage is how I started to differentiate my content from others in this very competitive space. Initially, I didn't realize the importance of having a clear niche. At the beginning of my blogging journey, I was creating content and recipes for everyone, and as a result, I was serving no one. After doing some market research and strategizing how to finally get some solid traction, I realized how underserved the Latin recipe space was, especially among the Puerto Rican community that I'm a part of. It turns out there was a large audience of mi gente out there who were looking for creative twists and classic recipes for such Puerto Rican favorites as arroz con gandules and coquito. So I started sharing my Puerto Rican recipes, and that's when things clicked.

Instead of blending in with the crowd, I started to lean in to my unique heritage, and that has made all the difference. As a woman of color in higher education and the workplace, I have often felt the need to code-switch, which is defined as "the practice of alternating between two or more languages or varieties of language in conversation." Being a bilingual Latina from an urban environment, I've often felt like I had to hide my urban accent, straighten my hair, and never be heard speaking Spanish in a professional environment. That made me shy away from being perceived as too Latina for so long.

This is the first time in my life that I don't have to shy away from who I am, and I want that for you too. These macro- and microaggressions that affect so many of us cause us to play it SO SMALL. I'm tired of us trying to blend into the crowd. It's time for you to speak up, ask for what you want, and claim what is rightfully yours. No more hiding, mija. It's your time to fucking shine.

## ¿Qué Va a Decir la Gente?

For many BIPOC first-generation kids, much of our drive to succeed stems from fear—and a lot of that fear is placed on us by our caregivers.

We don't want to be the reason people talk about us and our families. And so, we grow accustomed to being afraid…of everything.

*Afraid of starting that business.*

*Afraid of investing in the stock market.*

*Afraid of failing.*
*Afraid of making a mistake.*
*Afraid of taking a risk.*
*Afraid of bringing shame to the family.*
*Afraid of being judged for choosing a different path.*
*Afraid of speaking up and asking for more.*
*Afraid of disappointing others by choosing ourselves.*

But I want you to know something: Your ancestors did not sacrifice everything for you to settle for the bare minimum. You fucking deserve abundance. You deserve options. You deserve wealth. You deserve to live the life of your dreams, not the life that others dreamed for you. And I want to teach you how becoming poderosa AF with your money can help you get there.

We don't often talk about money in our communities in a way that allows the next generations to build on these skills. That was certainly the case for me. My parents were constantly stressed about money and so, naturally, I was afraid of it for so long. I avoided thinking about it much, and always felt it controlled my life. It wasn't until I became an entrepreneur that I started learning about the true power of money, and for the first time, I felt like I'd unlocked the next level of the game of life. I started learning about financial independence, investing, and building generational wealth—all topics I never learned about growing up.

The more I learned, the more I wanted to talk about it with my amigas. The main response: major side-eye and lots of "WTF are you talking about?!"

"My parents say that investing is gambling," they'd say.

"You can't earn six figures as a business owner."

"You can't quit your job, you'll end up homeless!"

"But what about your degrees?"

"I don't trust Wall Street."

"If you want to be rich, you need to buy a house."

*Sigh.*

I needed to find a place where this was a normal topic of conversation, but I couldn't find it in my peer group. And so, one day, while twerking to the J.Lo and Cardi B song "Dinero" in the shower, the universe planted an idea in my cabeza: **Yo Quiero Dinero˚**—*that's the name of your podcast.* I jumped out of the shower, did some quick Google searches to confirm that no one had come up with that yet, and on April 26, 2019, the *Yo Quiero Dinero˚* podcast was born.

The creation of my personal finance podcast was a direct response to a recurring theme I see in the world of personal finance. I couldn't find anyone telling stories like mine: a first-generation Latina, saddled with student loan debt, stuck in an unsatisfying career, longing for a life that felt more…free. I wanted more time and financial freedom. I wanted the power to create a life that allows me to live and work how and where I want. As an engineer, I was trained to solve problems and see solutions where they don't exist. And so, the mission became very clear to me.

In just four years, my podcast has become my second business to bring in six figures and has been downloaded over one million times in over 145 countries. We've inspired thousands of listeners to get out of debt, start businesses, open investment portfolios, and become the first people in their families to chart a path to generational wealth. We've given a whole generation of mujeres like you the permission to create the life of their dreams, and that's exactly what you and I will do here together in this book.

Remember: No one is coming to save us. We must be the change that we wish to see.

My promise to you is to provide you with smart, specific advice that addresses the unique challenges that we face as Latinas. It is my hope that it encourages you to understand that what makes us different is also what makes us strong—and with the right tools, we can create wealth and financial freedom for ourselves and generations to come.

So let's get started getting poderosa with your dinero—because money is power, mujer.

# CHAPTER 1

# The Struggle Is Real

As a child, I witnessed a dichotomy that so many kids from the hood can likely identify with. The realities of living in a community in which lack was the norm were all around us. I went to a school that greeted us with metal detectors to check if anyone had brought a weapon. We were regularly placed on lockdown, not for active shooter drills, but because of actual gang violence in the area. We'd drive to towns fifteen minutes away and ooh and ah over the million-dollar homes with perfectly manicured lawns. People sitting outside in the spring to enjoy al fresco dining with no worry about being catcalled or mugged. You could walk down the street in the middle of downtown and not once run into someone asking for money on a street corner. It felt like stepping into an alternate universe. It was the first time I realized that there were other options besides struggling. I saw that poverty was the opposite of what I wanted for my life. This is the life I wanted. But how? I got the same message that so many first-gens get: "Go to school and get a good job. Then you'll be set." So off I went to college—on a full scholarship, no less! You can blame my habitual inner overachiever.

After graduating, I spent the next five years job hopping and climbing the white male–dominated corporate engineer ladder, and even though I was making $75,000 a year in my midtwenties, I was utterly miserable. I found myself being the token Latina in the room, and usually the only woman, too. I felt so lonely and depressed, and I seriously considered quitting my job and starting over with a new career entirely. I needed something more, so I started creating content online as a food blogger to cope with hating my entire life (hello, quarter-life crisis!). I thought I was taking on a fun new hobby that let me express my creativity in a way that I couldn't do in a stuffy corporate engineering job. Little did I know I was charting a path to freedom.

Many of us are taught that the only way to earn a decent living is to do what our parents couldn't: Go to school, get an education, and get a good-paying job with benefits. We think that the only way to become a millionaire is by becoming a celebrity or playing the lottery. My family still plays los numeros religiously, convinced that they'll be the next ones to strike it rich.

We're still waiting, and I'm tired of waiting. I'm tired of waiting for our luck to arrive and maybe you are too. We have the power to create our own path to wealth, and it's so much simpler than you think. You just need the right tools to get you there. In this chapter, we'll discuss how to identify our money triggers and how they may be rooted in the financial trauma we experienced during childhood and adolescence. We will work through exercises to uncover common themes around money that have formed the narratives we hold today.

## Rewriting the Story

Why didn't anyone prepare us to become financially powerful mujeres? As kids, we're encouraged to follow our dreams. But then as we grow up, we're told to be realistic. We're told that our passions won't pay the bills. We're taught to contract, stay small, and avoid asking for what we want. We're taught to avoid giving people a reason to talk about us and what we're doing. We're taught that talking about money is uncivilized or taboo. We're taught that we must work ourselves into the ground, and that rest is for the lazy. We're taught that poverty is noble, and that wealth is immoral. We're taught how to live in scarcity. Fuck that. We deserve to have so much more.

Before we get into the nitty-gritty of making money, let's first talk about the systemic and cultural barriers that have kept the Latino community from building wealth in the United States, despite the fact that we are the largest minority group in America. The struggle is real, mujer—but self-knowledge is power. Together, we will reshape your money mindset from scarcity to abundance. We will squash your limiting beliefs around budgeting, investing, increasing your income, and building wealth. We will empower you to be unapologetically poderosa with your dinero. We've witnessed the impact of financial oppression firsthand with our mothers and our grandmothers. It wasn't too long ago that a woman couldn't inherit property, or have her own bank account, or take out a loan to start a business. We've watched so many who came before us give up their dreams, because those dreams seemed impossible. It's time to start rewriting the narrative.

Right now, give yourself the permission you've been waiting for to create a life that no one told you that you could have. If we can acknowledge all the internalized limiting beliefs we've passed down for generations, we can change the story. If you didn't learn shit about money, welcome to the club. None of us did, but that changes here.

## Money and Stress

Generally speaking, Latinos don't typically seek help for mental health issues, including those caused by financial strain. A 2020 study[1] on low-income

---

1. https://newprairiepress.org/cgi/viewcontent.cgi?article=1221&context=jft.

Latinas and the relationship between financial stress and mental health found that Latinas are less likely to receive mental health services than non-Hispanic whites or Black American women. And yet, another study found that it is common for Latinos in general to identify economic strain as a significant factor affecting their mental health. They also noted the lack of coping strategies and emotional support systems available to them.

Money is a stressful subject for many Latinos, but especially for us Latinas. I think it has a lot to do with the financial trauma we are likely to have experienced watching our caregivers navigate financial pressures. When I think back to my own childhood, money was always a source of conflict. I know I am not alone as a first-generation Latina in responding to all the financial challenges I experienced growing up by developing a scarcity mindset, the psychological tendency to fear that there isn't enough (money, resources, etc.). This mindset tells us that, in order to maintain any semblance of security, we must avoid risky behaviors like job hopping, advocating for a salary increase, or investing in the stock market.

My father works as an engineering consultant and has always been the primary breadwinner. When we were growing up, he traveled...a lot. As a result, my mom was perpetually trapped in low-paying jobs without benefits, because she needed a flexible schedule that allowed her to pick us up from school and be there for us while my dad was away Monday through Friday. She gave up decades of benefits like a 401(k) and paid time off in exchange for a flexible schedule. I witnessed her become a prisoner to motherhood in a system that provides little to no help to working parents. I also watched her give up her own hopes and dreams in order to allow me the privilege of pursuing mine, because there was no other choice. It wasn't until I started driving myself to high school that she began to work full time.

Because my mom carried the heavy load of raising my sister and me, there were frequent conflicts over money in our home that I saw and felt firsthand. Seeing this discrepancy as a child taught me that making money meant sacrificing time with your family. It also taught me that, as a woman, I needed to have my own financial safety net because I never wanted to be in a situation where I was dependent on a partner.

The result of all this stress? I became a freaking hustler. I started working at fourteen years old while still keeping up my good grades throughout school. I got a full scholarship to go to college to study biology, and never looked back. I worked my way through college, graduated with a job in biotechnology as a process engineer, and focused solely on making as much money as possible as quickly as possible. I was determined not to repeat the cycle of struggle that I witnessed as a young child. But I realized in my late twenties that I was pursuing a false goal. I didn't actually want money. What I really wanted was the freedom to pursue a life that looked completely different than the one I saw my mother live.

These financial conflicts are traumatic; they stay with you until you decide to do the healing work. My mother has told me stories about her first and only time applying for public assistance, after my dad was injured on the job and subsequently fired because he refused to keep working with a broken hand. Money and steady work were constant stressors for my parents growing up, and, as a result, I began to equate it to my parents' decision to have kids. It took me many years of therapy to realize that one of the reasons I have decided not to become a mother is because I saw motherhood and financial security as completely incompatible. Talk about some deep fucking trauma. Chances are you've seen and experienced some traumatic shit when it comes to money, and so if we're talking about it honestly and openly here, we have to first acknowledge the hard things we likely experienced growing up.

Now, I want to caution you: This is not an invitation for you to judge, criticize, blame, or guilt your caretakers for any hangups you may have around money. As you work through the experiences that impacted your views on money, I encourage you to see this as an opportunity for compassionate inquiry and radical empathy. After all, our parents are not likely to be capable of passing on healthy money beliefs to us unless they have them themselves! When I started to consider the environment my parents came up in as kids in Puerto Rico, I began to stop feeling so much resentment about their inability to pass on financial literacy skills to me. My dad's mother (my abuela Carmen) had seven kids, and only a third-grade education. She was abandoned by her husband when he moved to New York City with their three oldest children while my dad was still in elementary school. She turned to a solution that many people in Puerto Rico resort to, because there is no other option and good-paying jobs are scarce: entrepreneurship. Always savvy with whatever little money she had, she took her small savings and constructed a corner store on the first floor of her elevated home in Mercedita, Puerto Rico, a very poor suburb of the major southern city of Ponce. Selling cigarettes, alcohol, soda, and other bodega staples helped her keep a roof over her head and support the four children who were left behind. She even put two of her kids through college.

That's some legendary shit right there.

Yeah, my grandmother didn't know how to open a 401(k) or buy an index fund, but she taught my dad incredibly valuable lessons that I'm so grateful he was able to pass on to me and that I now want to pass on to you:

- No matter what life throws at you, you can figure shit out.
- You can make opportunities where none exist when you get creative and resourceful.
- You can come from nothing and still make something of yourself.
- You come from an incredible lineage of badass women who survived against all odds.

## Moving from Scarcity to Abundance

We are the first generation of Latina women who have access to financial security and autonomy in ways our mothers and grandmothers could only imagine. It's our duty to create the abundance in our lives that they were denied. It must be our mission to reclaim all that has been lost, so that we may honor the enormous sacrifices they made in order for us to be here today.

Our ancestors survived so that we can soar. You owe it to them to be the brightest, biggest, loudest, most authentic version of yourself, because they couldn't. Their sacrifices are why you must refuse to stay small. It's time for you to bring to life all the dreams that they gave up, just so you could live yours.

So, in order for us to make the switch from scarcity to abundance, we first have to understand and uncover our internalized money beliefs. All of our money stories start at the baseline level of the wealth-building journey: financial dependence. As kids, we experience money through our caretakers. If we see our parents or caregivers experience money in a negative way, that can have a direct impact on our own relationship with money as adolescents and adults. This can manifest into financial trauma. What can we do to counter this? We can build the self-knowledge to understand our history and emotions (including stressful ones) around money. We can name it to tame it.

## PRACTICE: NAME IT TO TAME IT

In this practice, I encourage you to write answers to the following questions in your own journal or notebook. Try as much as possible to record these messages in the specific language with which they were delivered to you. Keep it real, because this practice will help you begin to discover the subconscious narratives you have about money.

1. What are my earliest memories or experiences related to money? How did they shape my beliefs and attitudes toward money?

2. What are my current financial habits and behaviors? How do they reflect my underlying beliefs and emotions about money?

3. What are my core beliefs about money? Are they empowering or limiting? How do these beliefs impact my financial decisions and actions?

4. How do I define financial success? Is it aligned with my values and priorities, or is it influenced by societal expectations or external pressures?

5. What are my fears and anxieties around money? How do they hold me back from achieving my financial goals or taking necessary risks?

6. How does my upbringing and family background influence my relationship with money? Are there any patterns or lessons passed down through generations that I need to examine and potentially change?

## What Is Financial Trauma?

Mujer, you have likely heard much talk about trauma. It's become a buzzword, and the problem with buzzwords is that they begin to get misused. Trauma isn't just anything that causes distress or discomfort. The American Psychological Association (APA) defines trauma as "any disturbing experience that results in significant fear, helplessness, disassociation, confusion, or other disruptive feelings intense enough to have a long-lasting effect on a person's attitudes, behaviors and other aspects of functioning." One type of trauma that isn't getting as much attention is financial trauma. Dr. Galen Buckwater, a research psychologist who studies the psychology of money, defines financial trauma as "the physical, emotional, and cognitive deficits people experience when they cannot cope with either abrupt financial loss or the chronic stress of having inadequate financial resources."[1] The key here is that it is chronic, meaning the stress that you experience around your finances occurs over a long period of time. As is the case with any type of trauma, you may experience emotional responses, cognitive responses (like thought patterns or beliefs), and/or physical responses. Financial trauma has many possible causes:

- Inheriting toxic money beliefs from your caretakers
- Chronic debt
- The sudden loss of a job
- The loss of a home
- Unstable income
- A chronic inability to pay all the bills
- Low-wage work
- Entering the job market during a recession

In communities of color, financial trauma can come from a combination of any number of the above circumstances. Maybe you saw your parents swipe credit cards to treat themselves to material gifts as a result of working a grueling job (or even multiple jobs). Maybe you find yourself doing this too, buying that new pair of shoes or taking yourself out for a spa day only to realize you've actually added to your stress load. Money can become an unhealthy coping mechanism that spirals you further and further into debt, which causes more stress. It's the epitome of a vicious cycle.

---

1. https://goop.com/wellness/career-money/are-you-struggling-with-financial-ptsd/.

Our behaviors with money are a physical manifestation of financial trauma we have experienced, and if you don't learn how to identify those triggers, you will find yourself feeling constantly overwhelmed and powerless over your money.

## Signs of Financial Trauma

Financial trauma can manifest in a number of different ways, so this is by no means a one-size-fits-all list. But if you can relate to anything on this list below, chances are you're experiencing the aftereffects of financial trauma:

- Compulsive or chronic overspending
- Negative thought patterns around money or compulsive budgeting
- Extreme spending deprivation
- Physical stress over social outings or self-isolation out of fear of spending money
- Limiting beliefs around money: "I'll never be able to afford this," "I'll never make more money," "No one would ever pay me that much for this job," etc.
- Hoarding excess amounts of money in the bank
- Refusing to invest because you're scared to lose money
- Feeling excess amounts of guilt when spending money on yourself
- Feeling the need to give away all your money because you "don't deserve it"

If any of the above feels familiar, it's time to understand the root causes in terms of the messages you received around money growing up. But amiga, as you do this personal development work through practices like journaling or therapy, I also want you to remember to be gentle with yourself and practice what I like to call Financial Self-Care.

## PRACTICE: IDENTIFYING YOUR MONEY TRAUMA

Identifying your money trauma involves recognizing and understanding past experiences or beliefs related to money that have negatively impacted your financial behavior and mindset. Money trauma can stem from various sources, such as childhood experiences, family dynamics, societal influences, or significant financial hardships. These questions will help you begin to identify areas in your life that may have contributed to your money trauma.

1. Have I ever experienced a significant financial loss or hardship that still affects me emotionally or psychologically? If so, how has it shaped my current money beliefs and behaviors?

2. What were the messages or beliefs about money that I learned from my family or primary caregivers? How have these messages influenced my relationship with money?

3. Are there any specific events or experiences related to money in my past that still evoke strong emotional reactions or triggers? How do these reactions impact my current financial decisions and actions?

4. How does my money trauma manifest in my current financial habits or patterns? Do I engage in excessive saving, overspending, or avoidance of financial responsibilities?

5. Have I ever experienced feelings of shame, guilt, or worthlessness related to money? Where do these feelings

originate from, and how do they affect my self-worth and financial decisions?

6.  How does my money trauma impact my relationships with others, particularly when it comes to financial matters? Do I experience fear, control issues, or conflicts when discussing or sharing finances with loved ones?

## Taking Power Over Your Dinero

Embracing your truth as a first-generation individual and acknowledging your lack of learning regarding personal finance is the first step toward reclaiming control over your money. It's not about where you start. The most important part is the effort you put into educating yourself and making informed financial decisions.

Take this as an opportunity to break the cycle and rewrite your family's financial narrative. You have the strength to overcome obstacles, the tenacity to learn, and the willpower to take charge of your financial future.

By empowering yourself with knowledge and making mindful choices, you can pave the way for a more secure and prosperous life, not just for yourself, but for generations to come. Let's start by uncovering your current money story by doing a deep dive into your dinero.

**STEP ONE: Tell your money story.** The first step to take control of your dinero is to pinpoint what is causing you stress. Use these journal prompts to home in on what the root causes of your financial stress might be. Answer these questions in your notebook or journal; you can also look back at your answers from the previous practice:

When talking about _____, I feel stressed because _____.

The thought of money makes me feel _____.

My money story from my childhood looked like _____.

Identifying where your money story starts, and where your money stress comes from, is key to a sustainable practice of financial self-care. This will allow you to give yourself the true patience and compassion you need to sustain you on your journey to becoming poderosa with your dinero.

**STEP TWO: Put a "finance date" in your calendar.** Once a month, book a "Finance Date" in your calendar. In your notebook or journal, this is the time to review all of your account balances and revisit your current savings and investing goals (or set some new goals if you haven't started yet). Don't forget to also check in with any debt, noting if you can find a way to put a little bit more money toward paying it off in the following month. Last, be sure to give yourself kudos for staying on top of it and staying real with your dinero situation.

**STEP THREE: Map out your money days.** Step three is to map out your money days. Note any paydays on your calendar and take a moment to practice gratitude for your income stream(s). At the same time, map out any dates in the month when bills are due. Rather than dreading these days as if they will be the final nail in the coffin—as they say—visualize how you will pay these bills; for instance, *If I hold off on buying this new appliance, I can cover this bill.* Remind yourself, *I have enough, it's just a question of timing.*

**STEP FOUR: Identify your *why*.** We often lose sight of why we are doing what we are doing. In order to keep your drive and motivation strong, it's important to regularly remind yourself of your goals. Do you want to change jobs? Will it involve short-term pain (a pay cut)? Identifying your big-picture hopes and dreams can help you stay on track. In your notebook or journal, write a paragraph or two describing your financial goals and how you will achieve them. Be sure to write and rewrite these paragraphs as your journey evolves. You got this, amiga!

## PRACTICE: DEFINING YOUR WHY FOR WEALTH

Defining your why for wealth involves understanding the deeper motivations and reasons behind your desire to accumulate wealth. It goes beyond the mere pursuit of money and encompasses the core values, aspirations, and purpose that drive your financial goals. Defining your why for wealth is a personal and introspective process. Take the time to reflect on what truly drives you, align your financial goals with your values, and ensure that your pursuit of wealth supports a meaningful and purposeful life. It's essential to strike a balance between material wealth and overall well-being, as true wealth means more than just money. It's about having the options to choose what your life looks like.

- **What does wealth mean to me personally?**
  Understanding your personal definition of wealth is crucial. Is it about financial security, freedom, or the ability to pursue your passions? By clarifying what wealth truly means to you, you can align your efforts with your core values and motivations.
- **What are my long-term goals and aspirations?**
  Consider the goals and aspirations you have for your life. Do you want to retire early, travel the world, start your own business, or support causes you're passionate about? Building wealth can provide the means to achieve these dreams, so it's essential to identify and connect with your long-term goals.

- **How will wealth enhance my life and the lives of my loved ones?**

  Reflect on how wealth can positively impact your life and the lives of those you care about. Will it provide greater security, opportunities, or the ability to support your family? Understanding the potential benefits of wealth can help you stay motivated and focused on your financial journey.

- **What values and principles guide my approach to building wealth?**

  Consider the values and principles that guide your financial decisions. Are you driven by integrity, generosity, or a desire to make a positive impact on the world? Reflecting on your values will ensure that your pursuit of wealth is aligned with your beliefs and ethics.

- **How will building wealth contribute to my overall well-being?**

  Explore how building wealth can contribute to your overall well-being. Will it provide peace of mind, reduce stress, or increase your sense of empowerment? Understanding the holistic benefits of wealth can help you maintain a healthy perspective and prioritize your well-being along the way.

- **How can I use my wealth to create a meaningful legacy?**

  Think beyond your own lifetime and consider how you can use your accumulated wealth to create a lasting impact. Can you support causes you care about, establish scholarships, or leave a positive mark on your community? Reflecting on the legacy you want to leave behind can add a deeper sense of purpose to your wealth-building journey.

Remember, building wealth is a personal endeavor, and the answers to these questions will vary for each individual. By exploring your motivations and aligning them with your goals, values, and aspirations, you can build a solid foundation for your financial journey and create a meaningful and fulfilling relationship with wealth.

## Embrace Your Inner Hustler

This means unleashing the power that's inside of you. It's about harnessing the power of your ancestors and owning your ambition to slay the game of wealth creation without losing your sparkle. It's about tapping into your Latina power, breaking barriers, and hustling smart to make those dollar bills rain. It means recognizing and celebrating the unique qualities, strengths, and cultural values that empower you to strive for success and overcome challenges. It involves embracing your heritage, embracing your identity as a Latina, and utilizing those aspects to fuel your ambitions and goals. Because, amiga, you are a badass!

As a Latina, you have likely faced and overcome numerous obstacles and adversities. Embracing your inner hustler means acknowledging your resilience and using it as a driving force to pursue your dreams, no matter the setbacks or challenges that may arise. Honey, we don't let obstacles bring us down. We bounce back stronger and show the world that we can handle anything that comes our way! Embrace challenges with a confident strut, knowing that setbacks are just fabulous opportunities for personal growth. Failures? They're your stepping-stones to greatness, amiga. Keep that head held high and let that mindset slay.

We don't just embrace our heritage; we rock it! We bring that fiery Latina spirit, with values like hard work, familia, and comunidad, and use them as our secret sauce for success. I want you to celebrate your cultural heritage and the values instilled in you. Embracing your inner hustler means leveraging these values and incorporating them into your personal and professional pursuits.

The ability to adapt, think outside the box, and find innovative solutions is a common trait among Latinas. We are resourceful AF. We can turn any situation around with our quick thinking, innovation, and those incredible skills to find solutions where others see roadblocks. Embrace your resourcefulness and creativity to navigate challenges, identify opportunities, and find unique ways to achieve your goals.

We don't settle for average; we dream big, and we go after those dreams like nobody's business. We've got that fuego in our souls that keeps us hungry for success and constantly pushing ourselves to new heights. Embracing your inner hustler means recognizing and embracing your ambition and drive for success. It involves setting high goals for yourself, pushing beyond your comfort zone, and continuously striving for personal and professional growth. Take strategic risks that make your heart race with excitement. Dare to go beyond your comfort zone, bella, and remember that fortune favors the bold.

As a Latina, you have the opportunity to uplift and empower others within your community. We lift each other up because that's how we roll! We share our knowledge, experiences, and successes to inspire our fellow Latinas, showing them that they have the power to achieve greatness too. Connect with powerhouses who can uplift and inspire you on your path to greatness. Surround yourself with a squad of fabulous individuals who lift you higher. Find mentors who can guide you with their wisdom and strut alongside peers who share your ambition. Collaborate and conquer together, reina. When we rise together, the world can't help but bow down.

Embracing your inner hustler also means taking ownership of your narrative and defying stereotypes or societal expectations that may limit your potential. We don't fit into anyone's boxes or stereotypes. We own our stories, break those barriers, and shatter expectations. Flaunt your unique talents, skills, and that sizzling Latina charm. Embrace your cultural heritage, baby, and let it shine as your secret weapon in your financial journey. Own your unique story, experiences, and perspectives, and use them to create your own path to success. We're unapologetic about who we are, and we're out to show the world what we're capable of!

But most of all, make sure that you remind yourself that you don't always need to be hustling. Part of breaking generational curses means using the power of money to build a life that gives you ample time to rest and enjoy the soft life that our ancestors didn't get a chance to experience. The fact is that you can't conquer the world if you're burned out and tired AF. It's so important that you establish boundaries that scream "I'm a boss" to protect your precious time and energy. Don't feel guilty about indulging in self-care practices that make you feel like the fierce queen you are. Remember that even the baddest badasses need (and deserve) a break. Work hard but play harder.

Embracing your inner hustler is all about unleashing your confidence, fierce ambition, and sassy charm to create wealth like a true queen. Remember, you were born for greatness, mi amor. So put on your corona, strut your stuff, and let the world know that you're on a mission to break generational curses once and for all!

## CHAPTER 2

# When Jenny from the Block Becomes Jenny with the Bag

You know that feeling of being able to afford anything you want in life? Swiping your credit card knowing "I got this!"? Yeah, me neither. Or at least, I didn't know what that felt like as a kid growing up in Elizabeth, New Jersey, in the shadow of Newark International Airport. As a kid from the hood, I got my back-to-school clothes on layaway from discount big box stores. I watched my parents host yard sales with items they'd scavenged from nearby ritzy neighborhoods during trash days. And don't you dare ask for something if it's not on sale. If there wasn't a coupon for it, fuhgetaboutit.

You can imagine that when I found myself at age thirty with two degrees to my name, working as a high-powered Latina engineer at a Fortune Top 50 healthcare company, making more than either of my parents, I'd be fucking ecstatic, right?

# We Made It—Didn't We?

All the sacrifices finally paid off. The American Dream achieved. We did the things, we got the degrees, we got the dinero, it's time to celebrate!! Eh, well, for me that's not exactly how it went. In fact, some really shitty feelings started to come up. It wasn't joy, elation, or pride. It was straight-up guilt. Why me? Why should I be able to make more money than anyone in my family has ever made? Who am I to deserve this level of success? What if everything I've built suddenly disappears? Does this now mean *I* have to become everyone's financial safety net? All these thoughts and more are hallmarks of what I like to call financial survivor's guilt.

Why didn't anyone tell me that getting the bag would come with so much *baggage*?! As a first-generation Latina and the oldest sibling, the message I received was very clear, like we talked about in the previous chapter: To achieve the American Dream, you must go to school, get a good (meaning GREAT) job with some bomb-ass benefits, and make a shit ton of money. Got it! But what happens when you follow those instructions and actually start doing better than the people around you? Why did I feel so shitty about "making it" when so many I knew were still struggling to make ends meet? No one warned me about the relentless guilt that comes from being the one who made it out.

What happens when Jenny from the block doesn't live on the block anymore? We're told to work hard so we can make it "out"—out of the barrio. Out of the hood. Out of the very place that made us. But no one tells us where we're supposed to go, or why it feels so lonely when we get there. No one mentions how much angst we'll feel about those we had to leave behind. No one tells us that the further along we get, the less we'll see of who and what made us who we are. No one mentions how people will call you unrelatable because "you live in the burbs now," or because "you went to that fancy college," or because "you talk like a white girl."

*"You don't know the struggle anymore."*

*"You've got white people problems now."*

*"Must be nice."*

Your friends may start to treat you like a stranger. Going to your hometown may trigger negative emotions. Your family may talk shit about that new car you're driving.

No one talks about the grief that comes from growth.

No one prepares you for what it feels like to be on the other side of the struggle, when so many of the people you love are still there and you feel powerless to help them all.

## You Are So Worthy

Thanks to years of working on my money mindset and traumas through therapy, personal development work, working with coaches, and after talking to so many first-gens like myself through my podcast and social media, I've come to realize that this "why me" feeling can be quite common.

For many of us who are the first in our families to go to college, the first to make more than our parents, the first to invest, start a business, build wealth, achieve financial independence and more...I've uncovered a common theme: Many of us feel inherently unworthy of what we've been able to achieve, because we grew up thinking it just wouldn't be possible for us. *Have you felt this way?*

And when we do achieve the upward mobility that our families want for us, it becomes both a blessing and a curse: On one hand, you're no longer in survival mode. Your bills are paid, you've got savings, and even fun money. Life doesn't feel so hard anymore. On the other hand, you feel an enormous sense of responsibility to make up for the sacrifices that your caretakers have made to put you in a position that you were able to achieve this level of financial security. So you work even harder, you feel like you haven't made it "enough." You won't let yourself rest until you have reached a degree of certainty about your level of success. It's time to pause and take stock of all that you have accomplished and give yourself kudos for making it this far.

---

### Journal Exercise

List five things you've accomplished in your life that you are proud of. It doesn't matter if it's in your professional or personal life—anything that you have worked hard to achieve. Now is the time to acknowledge your success.

---

## Money Is the Root of All Evil ... or Is It?

Individual success is something that feels very counterintuitive in our culture, which emphasizes community over the individual self. As Latina women, it's not uncommon for us to grow up in multigenerational households where we learn to rely on each other for physical, emotional, and financial support. So the idea that we're just supposed to save ourselves and leave everyone else behind doesn't sit right with me, and maybe you've thought the same thing.

Ironically, though, many of us can come from households and communities where pursuing wealth is seen as a morally corrupt endeavor, oftentimes due to religious beliefs. For example, "poverty gospel" is a term often used to describe a religious perspective or belief system that emphasizes poverty as a virtue and sees material wealth as inherently sinful or indicative of spiritual corruption. This perspective suggests that true spirituality and closeness to God can only be achieved through a life of poverty and self-denial.

Those who follow the poverty gospel often argue that material possessions and wealth can distract individuals from their spiritual journey and lead to greed, selfishness, and a lack of focus on God. They may advocate for a lifestyle of simplicity, detachment from worldly possessions, and a strong emphasis on serving the poor and marginalized.

Critics argue that these beliefs can create a negative and judgmental attitude toward wealth and prosperity. They claim that this perspective overlooks the potential for wealth to be used for positive purposes, such as supporting charitable causes, creating employment opportunities, and improving living standards. Critics also argue that it can perpetuate a cycle of poverty by discouraging individuals from pursuing economic growth and personal success.

On the flip side, there's the prosperity gospel, also known as the "health and wealth gospel" or "name it and claim it theology," a religious belief system that emphasizes financial prosperity, physical well-being, and success as signs of God's favor and blessings. It is commonly associated with certain branches of Christianity, particularly within charismatic and Pentecostal movements.

Followers of the prosperity gospel believe that faith, positive confession, and financial giving can lead to material abundance and blessings from God. They teach that God desires believers to be wealthy, healthy, and successful in all areas of life. According to this teaching, if a person has enough faith and adheres to certain spiritual principles, they can expect God to provide them with material wealth, good health, and a life of abundance.

Critics of the prosperity gospel argue that it oversimplifies the Christian message that through belief in and acceptance of the death and resurrection of Jesus, sinful humans can be reconciled to God and thereby are offered salvation and the promise of eternal life, and that it places an excessive focus on material wealth and personal gain. They assert that it can promote a shallow understanding of faith and spirituality, where God is viewed primarily as a means to achieve financial success and physical well-being. Critics also point out that this teaching often ignores the reality of suffering, inequality, and the biblical call to care for the poor and marginalized.

If you come from a religious household, as many of us do, you may have deep-seated beliefs about what it actually means about YOU if you want to make money, be wealthy, drive a fancy car, etc. I want to assure you, wanting money doesn't make you a bad person. Money simply amplifies who you are. If you're a shitty person, money just helps you be even shittier. And if you're a good person, you can do more good in the world when you have access to more resources. Money's true power is in what it allows you to do. It gives you options and flexibility to prioritize the things that are most important to you. And who doesn't want that?

Bernadette Joy, Filipina American money coach and founder of the money media company Crush Your Money Goals*, told me a story that really resonates (tune in to episode 150 of the podcast to hear the whole story). The eighth of nine kids in her family, Bernadette had built financial security while many of her siblings were struggling financially. She used to feel guilty that she didn't have to struggle nearly as much compared to her brothers and sisters, but then a day came that shifted her perspective. Sadly, she received a call that her father was nearing the end of his life, and because of her financial independence she was able to be the first one on a plane to be with him. Many of her siblings weren't able to make it so quickly due to their existing obligations. She told me, "It was a real wake-up call...I saw that I had worked to become financially free so that I could do what I wanted to do in this kind of moment, to be there for my family. Before this, I felt guilty that I had wealth while many of my siblings did not, but in this moment, I saw that I had the time to do what I wanted to do for my family, and this meant a great deal to me."

## PRACTICE: HOW DO YOU FEEL ABOUT WEALTH?

The following prompts are designed to help you explore your feelings and attitudes toward wealth. It's essential to approach this process with self-reflection and honesty, allowing yourself the space to uncover any underlying beliefs or emotions that may be influencing your relationship with wealth. Take some time to answer these questions in your journal:

Wealth, to me, represents _____.

When I think about having a substantial amount of money, I imagine myself _____.

My relationship with money is influenced by my upbringing in the sense that _____.

If I were to acquire significant wealth, I believe it would impact my life by _____.

I often associate wealth with _____.

One fear I have about pursuing wealth is _____.

I feel most confident and empowered when it comes to money when _____.

My current financial situation makes me feel

_____.

If I were to achieve financial abundance, it would allow me to

_____.

The role of money in my life is _____.

When I imagine myself having significant wealth, I feel

_____.

The idea of pursuing financial abundance makes me feel _____ because _____.

If I were to become extremely wealthy, I worry that

_____.

The thought of having more money than I currently do makes

me feel _____.

When I see others who are wealthy, I tend to _____.

My current beliefs about wealth are influenced by

_____.

## When Enough Is Never Enough

If you have a negative relationship with money, you're likely operating from a scarcity mindset, the perpetual feeling that "there will never be enough" time, money, energy, resources, security, etcetera. This belief system can become a self-fulfilling prophecy; you become so focused on what you lack that it paralyzes you from making any decisions that can change your situation. Often, our feelings of unworthiness are rooted in being raised in households in which our caregivers operated in a scarcity mindset. The scarcity mindset believes that there isn't enough, and that there will never be enough.

It's common to feel this way when you've witnessed your parent(s) struggle financially, or if you witnessed or experienced financial abuse, which we'll talk about later in the book. This isn't a moment to blame anyone for raising you in this environment, as our caregivers were only capable of providing the type of environment that they could with the skills, resources, and emotional intelligence they possessed. I invite you to take a few moments to acknowledge the role your environment played in promoting a scarcity mindset. This includes reflecting on your familial and social circle to determine if you are surrounded by people who exemplify this mentality.

## QUIZ: ARE YOU LIVING IN SCARCITY OR ABUNDANCE?

1. When faced with a challenge or setback, do you tend to focus on the limitations and potential losses, or do you look for opportunities and possibilities? (Scarcity = limitations, Abundance = opportunities)

2. How do you view competition? Do you believe there is only a limited amount of success available, and someone else's success means less for you (scarcity), or do you believe that there is enough success and abundance for everyone (abundance)?

3. When you receive a compliment or recognition, how do you respond? Do you feel a sense of scarcity, thinking it was just luck or a one-time thing, or do you embrace it and believe it's a sign of more good things to come (abundance)?

4. How do you feel when others around you succeed or achieve their goals? Are you genuinely happy for them and believe their success doesn't diminish your own opportunities (abundance), or do you feel envy, comparison, or a sense of scarcity thinking it's taking away from your own chances?

5. How do you approach giving and generosity? Do you give freely, believing that there is enough to share (abundance), or do you hold on to things tightly, feeling a scarcity mindset that giving means losing something?

6. When it comes to learning new skills or expanding your knowledge, how do you approach it? Do you believe that there are limitations to what you can learn or achieve (scarcity), or do you have a growth mindset and believe that there are endless possibilities for growth and development (abundance)?

7. How do you handle setbacks or failures? Do you see them as permanent and define your worth based on them (scarcity), or do you see them as temporary and opportunities for growth and learning (abundance)?

8. How do you feel about asking for help or seeking support? Do you believe that asking for help is a sign of weakness or scarcity, or do you see it as a way to expand your resources and create abundance through collaboration?

9. How do you approach financial decisions? Do you often feel anxious or worried about money, thinking there is never enough (scarcity), or do you have confidence in your ability to attract and manage money, believing there are abundant opportunities for financial well-being?

10. When faced with a new opportunity, how do you respond? Do you tend to hesitate or hold back, fearing scarcity and potential loss, or do you embrace the opportunity and believe in the abundance of possibilities?

## Scoring:

Count the number of times you chose the abundance mindset option (Abundance).

Count the number of times you chose the scarcity mindset option (Scarcity).

Whichever mindset option has a higher count reflects your dominant mindset.

Remember, this quiz provides a general understanding, and it's important to reflect on your mindset beyond these questions. Developing an abundance mindset is an ongoing process, and with awareness and practice, you can shift your mindset toward abundance.

## Secure Your Own Mask First

Let's talk about the ways you can navigate the complex feelings that come with outgrowing your existing environment. Ever heard the saying "You can't pour from an empty cup"? When you're building your own financial safety net, it's easy to allow guilt about the fact that you're even able to do so. What a privilege! It can be very difficult to say no to friends or family members who solicit help, especially if they're used to receiving it from you already. But managing wealth guilt requires you to get into the habit of practicing financial self-care.

When you think of self-care, you probably think of eating a healthful diet, getting your nails done, getting a massage, or taking a bubble bath. That's not what we're talking about. Financial self-care is not about spending a bunch of money on spa visits, scented candles, or healing crystals. It is not about having a high net worth, nor is it about obsessing about money. Financial self-care means putting your own finances first.

## What Financial Self-Care Looks Like

So what does financial self-care look like? As you begin to allow yourself to really focus in on what your own financial needs are in order to feel safe, secure, and ready to focus on your personal financial goals:

- You're taking deliberate action and making conscious choices to manage and improve your financial well-being.
- You're adopting healthy financial habits and putting them into practice.
- You're healing your money wounds and maintaining a positive relationship with money.
- You're prioritizing your long-term financial goals.
- You're cultivating a mindset of financial responsibility.
- You're building your resilience to navigate financial challenges.

Sounds great, right?! So, what do you need to do to practice financial self-care? It requires you to take a holistic approach with your dinero. We'll be diving into these fundamental financial self-care topics throughout this book:

**BUDGETING:** Creating and following a budget helps you understand your income, expenses, and spending patterns. It enables you to allocate your money wisely, prioritize your needs, and plan for the future. (chapter 4)

**SAVING AND INVESTING:** Setting aside a portion of your income for savings and investments is essential for building financial security. Saving for emergencies, retirement, and other financial goals is an act of self-care that provides you with a safety net and promotes your long-term financial well-being. (chapters 2, 4, and 6)

**DEBT MANAGEMENT:** Taking steps to manage and reduce debt is an important part of financial self-care. This includes creating a repayment plan, consolidating high-interest debt, and seeking professional guidance if needed. (chapter 4)

**MINDFUL SPENDING:** Practicing mindful spending involves being intentional about your purchases and avoiding impulsive or emotional spending. It means aligning your spending with your values and goals, and making conscious decisions about how you use your money.

**GETTING EDUCATED:** Continuously learning about personal finance and improving your financial literacy is an act of self-care. It empowers you to make informed decisions, understand financial concepts, and navigate the complexities of the financial world. *(You're already here, by picking up and reading this book! YAY!)*

**ASKING FOR HELP:** If you feel overwhelmed or uncertain about your financial situation, seeking guidance from a money coach (like me!), a financial advisor, or financial planner can be a form of self-care. A financial professional can provide personalized advice, help you create a financial plan, and offer strategies for achieving your goals. *(This is one of the ways I work with my clients. We work together one-on-one to create customized plans to achieve their goals in money and business. To learn more, visit yoqui erodineropodcast.com/work-with-me.)*

**PRIORITIZING YOUR WELL-BEING:** Ultimately, financial self-care is about recognizing that your financial health is interconnected with your overall well-being. It involves finding a balance between your financial goals and your physical, emotional, and mental well-being. This might include setting boundaries around work, practicing real self-care routines, and nurturing healthy relationships.

Financial self-care is a long-term process that requires consistent effort and adjustment. By taking care of your finances, you can reduce stress, increase your financial security, and create a foundation for a healthier and more fulfilling life. This won't be an easy journey, but it will be worth it when you've secured your own finances and can now extend help to those around you.

## Emergency-Proofing Your Life

Achieving financial security requires a bit of forward planning. You want to make sure the current you is prepared to help future you in an emergency, because life is gonna life. You can't possibly know what unforeseen events will occur in life, but stashing away some cash will help you weather those unpredictable storms. Whether it's a job loss, an illness, a flat tire, or even burnout, having money that is earmarked for those moments when things happen is key to your own financial well-being. You can't help anyone else if you can't help yourself first. This is why you need an emergency fund (EF).

An emergency fund is...basically what it sounds like. It is a designated pool of money that is easily accessible and specifically set aside for unforeseen circumstances such as medical emergencies, car repairs, a job loss, or other unexpected events. With an emergency fund, you can ideally cover these expenses without relying on credit cards, loans, or other forms of borrowing, which can lead to debt and financial stress long after the emergency is over. That's not a vibe, y'all! Defining what an emergency looks like is up to you, but overall, you want to make sure you're only dipping into this money for the essentials.

### Examples of Valid Emergencies
- You lose your job, get furloughed, or your work hours are reduced.
- You get sick and need to take time off work.
- You lose your prescription glasses on vacation.
- Your car breaks down and you need to tow it to the nearest mechanic.
- A friend or family member gets sick or passes away and you need to travel.
- Your business has a slow month, and you didn't make enough to cover all your bills.
- One of your household appliances stops working.
- Your dog swallows a sock and ends up needing emergency surgery.
- You need to get out of an unsafe or abusive relationship.

### These Are Not Emergencies
- Your friend plans a last-minute destination wedding on New Year's Eve in Hawaii.
- You want to upgrade to the latest iPhone that does the exact same thing that your current phone does.
- Your favorite store is having their semi-annual sale and you just have to be there.

Not sure if something qualifies as an emergency? Before using your emergency fund, it's important to ask yourself a few questions to assess the situation and determine if dipping into the fund is the appropriate course of action. Here are some key questions to consider:

**Is it truly an emergency?** Evaluate the nature of the situation and determine if it qualifies as a genuine emergency. Using the fund for non-essential expenses or purchases could deplete your safety net and leave you vulnerable in a true crisis.

**Can the expense be covered through other means?** Explore alternative options before tapping into your emergency fund. Can the expense be covered by insurance, warranties, or other benefits? Are there any non-essential expenses you can temporarily cut back on to free up funds?

**What are the potential consequences?** Consider the short-term and long-term implications of using the emergency fund. Will it leave you with an insufficient amount for future emergencies? Will it disrupt your financial goals or plans? Understanding the consequences can help you make an informed decision.

**Can the expense be delayed or reduced?** Evaluate if the expense can be postponed or if there are ways to minimize the cost—for example, negotiating a payment plan, seeking discounts or alternatives, or finding other resources to address the situation.

**How will it impact your overall financial stability?** Assess the impact of using the emergency fund on your financial well-being. Will it jeopardize your ability to meet essential living expenses or other financial obligations? Consider your current income, savings, and future financial needs.

**How quickly can you replenish the fund?** Evaluate your ability to replenish the emergency fund after using it. Determine how long it will take to rebuild the fund and ensure that you have a plan in place to resume regular contributions.

By asking these questions, you can make a thoughtful and informed decision about whether using your emergency fund is the best course of action in a given situation. It's essential to prioritize the fund for genuine emergencies to maintain your financial security in the long run.

## How Much Do You Need?

The ideal size of your emergency fund of course depends on your personal circumstances, but a general rule of thumb is to aim for three to six months' worth of living expenses. This amount should be able to cover your essential expenses such as rent or mortgage payments, utilities, food, transportation, and other necessary expenses during a period of financial uncertainty. To determine your goal, you first have to calculate your monthly expenses. Start by collecting your bank statements, credit card statements, receipts, and any other relevant financial documents that can provide information about your expenses. Next, create categories to organize your expenses. Common categories will include housing, utilities, transportation, food, healthcare, debt payments, insurance, entertainment, personal care, and miscellaneous expenses. Remember, your emergency fund should cover only essentials, so no, you don't include your $200 monthly brunch expense in this calculation. #sorrynotsorry. Don't forget to take into account irregular or annual expenses, such as insurance premiums, vehicle registration, or property taxes. Divide these expenses by the number of months they cover to estimate the monthly amount. Finally, tally up the expenses in each category to determine the total amount spent in each area. Also calculate the total of all expenses combined. This number will help you determine your emergency fund goal. Based on your analysis, make adjustments to your budget and spending habits as needed. Identify areas where you can cut back or allocate more funds to align with your financial goals and priorities.

**Emergency Fund Savings Formula With Examples**

| Monthly Expenses x 6 = 6 month Emergency Fund<br>Monthly Expenses x 3 = 3 month Emergency Fund | | |
|---|---|---|
| **Monthly Expenses** | **Emergency Fund** | |
| | **3 month** | **6 month** |
| $1,500 | $4,500 | $9,000 |
| $2,500 | $7,500 | $15,000 |
| $3,500 | $10,500 | $21,000 |
| $4,500 | $13,500 | $27,000 |
| $5,500 | $16,500 | $33,000 |
| **Monthly Expenses** | **Save Monthly for 3 years** | |
| | **3 month** | **6 month** |
| $1,500 | $125 | $250 |
| $2,500 | $208 | $416 |
| $3,500 | $291 | $583 |
| $4,500 | $375 | $750 |
| $5,500 | $458 | $916 |

## Where to Keep Your Emergency Fund

You need to be able to deploy your emergency fund money rapidly when needed, so you'll want to be intentional about where you store this fund. Although you may be tempted, I don't recommend having this money stored in cash at home. There are too many risks, like theft, a fire, or even forgetting where you put it! Luckily, you've got more solid options besides hiding your EF under the mattress (despite Abuela's advice). These are:

**High-yield savings account (HYSA):** A high-yield savings account is a popular choice for emergency funds. These accounts are typically offered by banks and online financial institutions, and they offer higher interest rates compared to traditional savings accounts. Sometimes it can be 25 times the national average! A HYSA provides you with easy access to your funds while also earning some interest. I love me some free dinero!

**Money market account:** Money market accounts are similar to savings accounts but may offer a slightly higher interest rate. They often have minimum balance requirements and limited check-writing capabilities. Money market accounts are relatively low-risk and provide liquidity.

**Certificate of deposit (CD):** CDs are time-deposit accounts where you deposit a specific amount of money for a fixed period at a predetermined interest rate. Essentially, your funds are locked up for a specific time period in exchange for some interest at the end of that term. While CDs may offer higher interest rates than savings accounts, they have a fixed term, and accessing the funds before maturity (aka the end of the fixed time period) may result in penalties. Consider using shorter-term CDs or those with no penalties for early with-drawal if you choose this option for your emergency fund.

**Traditional savings account:** You can also keep your emergency fund in a traditional savings account provided by a brick-and-mortar bank. While interest rates may be lower compared to online banks or high-yield accounts, they generally provide you with convenient access to your funds.

**Cash management account (CMA):** A type of account offered by brokerage firms and robo-advisors. These accounts typically pay interest just like a high-yield savings account, while offering flexible access to your money, just like a checking account.

Building an emergency fund requires consistent saving over time. Once you've determined your EF goal, it's time to decide how much you can con-sistently contribute until you reach your targets. Once your emergency fund is established, make sure you're regularly reviewing and replenishing it as needed to account for inflation or any withdrawals that you've made during emergencies.

---

## INFLATION 101

Inflation is the increase in the cost of living that we experience over time. When you were little, the price of a movie ticket was maybe $5. Now it's $20 or more! This rise in the cost for the products and services we need to live, such as groceries, rent, health insurance—everything!—is inflation at work. In order to build wealth *now* that will work for you in the years to come, you need to account for inflation. We'll talk about what this looks like in terms of investing (the key to growing your nest egg!) in chapter 6. When it comes to your emergency fund requirements, it's a good idea to review your expenses on an annual basis to see if your EF needs adjustment. For example, it's not uncommon for your rent or mortgage to go up each year, so make sure to account for these and other rising costs when calculating your desired emergency fund amount.

## Extending Help in a Sustainable Way: The Family Emergency Fund

So, by now it's (hopefully) crystal clear to you that an emergency fund is an essential part of your financial self-care tool kit. But what if one of your loved ones has an emergency? As a first-gen kid, you've probably seen your parents send money back to the motherland. Many of our parents face the pressure to help family members who were left behind with living expenses or financial emergencies—even when it means putting a financial strain on themselves. Maybe you're feeling the pressure to "pay back" your parent(s) for these sacrifices. Maybe you just want to be able to help when things come up. The truth is that for many of us, one emergency fund might not cut it. This is where the family emergency fund comes into play.

I was first introduced to the idea of having a separate family emergency fund by my certified financial planner Anna N'Jie Konte. I was talking to her about my desire to be able to provide financial support to my parents without totally draining my own emergency fund. My mind was blown by the concept. It's such a simple idea, but so impactful!

Now, I know what you may be thinking…Jannese, the idea of having to build not one but two emergency funds is overwhelming, how the eff am I supposed to do this and manage my own expenses and financial obligations? But as with anything, proper preparation can take some time and it doesn't need to be done all at once.

When it comes to planning for two emergency funds, it's the same idea as being on a plane and putting your oxygen mask on first. Take care of yourself, then you can figure out how much assistance you can comfortably extend to your family. Get creative! If the idea of doing this alone feels like more than you can handle, talk to your family about possibly collaborating with you on building their emergency fund. Explain to them what the funds can be used for (medical expenses, a car repair, etc.), and that you want to work together to prepare for these types of emergencies so that everyone can sleep better at night, knowing that there's a plan in place. Don't be afraid to start small. Just $5 a week will add up to hundreds of dollars at the end of the year, especially if several of you are contributing at the same rate! This also helps you empower your family members to take an active role in financial planning and can help relieve the pressure of having to shoulder their financial emergencies on your own.

## Setting Money Boundaries: Extending Financial Support Without Drama

First things first. Giving money to your familia requires careful consideration and communication. Lending money can be a great way to destroy a relationship. The reality is that when someone is asking you for money, they're often not in a great financial position, and are unlikely to be able to repay the funds they're asking to borrow. Never give money to family—or anyone, really—if you expect to get it back. If you can't afford to give it away, then say so. Otherwise, consider any financial support that you extend to a loved one as a gift. Here are some suggestions to help you navigate an ask for financial support:

**Assess your own financial situation:** Before giving money to a loved one, evaluate your own financial stability and ensure that you can afford to provide the assistance without compromising your own financial well-being. Consider your expenses, savings goals, and any other financial obligations you have. While supporting family is important, it's crucial to prioritize your own financial stability. Avoid putting yourself in a difficult financial situation by overextending yourself or sacrificing your own needs and goals.

**Set clear boundaries and expectations:** This is important to do when dealing with family members regarding the financial assistance you're providing. Clearly communicate the purpose, amount, and duration of the assistance to avoid misunderstandings and unrealistic expectations. Establish a schedule or budget that works for you and your family, so they can have a clear expectation of when and how much support they can anticipate.

**Determine the purpose of the financial assistance:** Understand the specific needs of your family members and discuss how the money will be used. Assess if it's a one-time emergency situation or an ongoing need, as this may influence the amount and frequency of your financial support.

**Communicate openly:** Engage in open and honest conversations with your family members about their financial situation and explore alternative ways to offer support. Help your family members understand any financial limitations or challenges you may face. This could include expenses such as debt repayments, savings goals, or other financial obligations that may impact your ability to send money regularly or in large amounts. Encourage them to share their challenges and aspirations so that you can provide guidance and assistance accordingly.

**Consider non-monetary forms of support:** Sometimes, non-monetary assistance can be just as valuable. Offer your time, skills, or resources to help your family members address their needs. This could include providing guidance on budgeting, offering career advice, or assisting with specific tasks.

**Maintain balance and fairness:** If you have multiple family members in need of financial assistance, strive to maintain a fair and balanced approach. Consider establishing a system or criteria to ensure that you're distributing your resources equitably among your family members.

**Encourage financial independence:** Instead of providing ongoing financial support, encourage your family members to work toward financial independence. Offer guidance on budgeting, saving, and finding opportunities for earning more income. Consider assisting them in developing skills or exploring educational or vocational programs.

**Keep records and track the assistance provided:** Maintain clear records of the financial assistance you provide to your family members. This can help you keep track of the support you're offering and enable you to assess the impact on your own finances.

**Seek professional advice if needed:** If you're unsure about the best approach or feel overwhelmed, consider consulting with a financial advisor or a professional who can provide guidance tailored to your specific situation.

Remember, it's important to strike a balance between supporting your family and maintaining your own financial well-being. Open communication, transparency, and realistic expectations are key! It's natural to immediately want to help your family cover large emergency expenses. But emptying your own bank accounts to save everyone else could put you in a terrible situation if you wind up with a surprise expense of your own. This is why having a personal emergency fund and a family emergency fund can allow you to help your parents and siblings while still planning for your own future emergencies.

There are many ways you can go about executing this idea, but the worst thing you could do is think that you won't ever have an unexpected expense. Having an emergency fund can give you that much-needed wiggle room to breathe a little easier.

Amiga, you have worked very hard to get where you are, and you are so worthy of all that you have achieved. Wealth guilt is real, but don't let it dominate your life. Shift your perspective and see that money can open the door to living the life you always dreamed of, as well as enable you to offer support to your family and community.

# CHAPTER 3

# Know Your Worth, Mujer

M ujer, you can change the world, but you're gonna need money to do it. Increasing your income has the power to transform your life. It can help you pay off debt faster, invest in education or career development, start a business, save and invest your way to an early retirement, and so much more. It can also allow you to help friends and family who may come on hard times—and it can even enable you to leave a toxic relationship or workplace that is no longer serving you. If we're gonna be the most badass versions of ourselves, we have to take the stress of not having enough money off the list of shit we gotta worry about. It's time for us to stop settling for scraps.

During my fourteen-year corporate career, I made sure to job hop every two to three years, and, as a result, I went from a starting salary of $42,000 at age twenty-two to a $100,000 salary by age thirty. That's an 81 percent increase in eight years! With the average annual salary increase being around 2 to 3 percent, that jump never would have happened if I'd stayed loyal to the same job and employer. I'm here to tell you that if you want to make sure you're getting paid what you're worth, LOYALTY DOESN'T PAY!

If you're a first-gen Latina, you're likely facing a financial crisis or a potential financial crisis down the road. It's a reality that many of us are all too familiar with. You might be staring at an uncertain future where you want to retire before you're sixty-seven or even sooner, but you also have the responsibility of providing financial support to your parents. Maybe you have children, and you want them to start their lives with a stronger financial foundation than you had growing up. It's a lot of pressure, and it's going to require a lot of money to make it all happen. We already know we're paid less than other groups, and without federal legislation that mandates equal pay, we need to learn how to be our biggest advocates for getting paid what we deserve. So how do we begin?

First, you've gotta get comfortable doing something that most of us don't do—that's right, we're talking about salary negotiation. Did you know that 60 percent of women have never attempted to negotiate their salaries? Ay Dios mío! If this is you, know that you're not alone. In our culture, we aren't taught about money and we don't talk about money—so how the hell can we get comfortable asking for money? Evie Prete, former rocket engineer turned salary negotiation coach and founder of the personal finance platform La Mala Mujer, told me, "Many times as Latinas we are fearful of appearing ungrateful. I tell my clients that it is important to remember that you are only asking for what you deserve."

So how do you start? Well, for one, it starts with opening up the dialogue. Here's a challenge for you: Next time you're at brunch with amigas, ask them, "Girl, how much do you make at your job?" It might sound like an insane question to ask, but if you're comfortable talking about your latest hookup from a dating app, you can definitely muster up the cojones to talk about your salaries.

Why is this important? Not researching if you are being paid fairly and negotiating for the higher pay you deserve is not just about leaving money on the table. Learning how to advocate for yourself ensures that you are paid fairly for the work you do. You deserve to be paid fairly based on your skills, experience, and job responsibilities, regardless of your gender, race, ethnicity, or any other factor. Equal pay can provide financial stability, which can lead to a better quality of life for you and your family. It can help you save for retirement, pay off debt, and meet your financial goals. We're talking generational wealth, baby—and we need all the help we can get to make that happen!

It's normal to feel fear about negotiation, just like Gabriela. She had worked tirelessly to build her career as a nurse practitioner and had achieved success through her hard work and dedication. However, there was one area where Gabriela felt a deep sense of insecurity: negotiation.

Whenever Gabriela found herself in a situation that required negotiating, her confidence would plummet, and fear would grip her tightly. She worried about appearing greedy, being rejected, or damaging her relationships. As a result, she often settled for less than she deserved, both personally and professionally. Determined to overcome her fear, Gabriela decided to attend a workshop on negotiation skills. She wanted to learn the art of confidently advocating for herself and expressing her worth. Little did she know, this decision would change her life forever.

At the workshop, Gabriela met an extraordinary woman named Elena. Elena was a successful Latina professional with a reputation for exceptional negotiation skills. Gabriela was immediately drawn to her confidence and poise. Inspired, she mustered the courage to approach Elena and share her struggles. Elena, with a warm smile, reassured Gabriela that her fears were common and conquerable. She understood the internal battles Gabriela faced, having experienced them herself earlier in her career. Elena became Gabriela's mentor, guiding her through the intricacies of negotiation and helping her build the confidence she so desperately sought.

Under Elena's mentorship, Gabriela embarked on a journey of self-discovery and skill-building. They practiced various negotiation scenarios, role-playing conversations, and strategizing approaches. Elena taught Gabriela the importance of preparation, understanding one's value, and the art of effective communication. With every negotiation practice session, Gabriela's confidence grew. She realized that negotiating was not about being aggressive or selfish, but about asserting her worth and creating mutually beneficial outcomes. Through Elena's guidance, Gabriela began to understand that negotiation was an essential tool for personal and professional growth.

Armed with newfound knowledge and confidence, Gabriela fearlessly entered negotiation conversations. She advocated for fair compensation, spoke up for her ideas, and negotiated favorable terms in business dealings. To her surprise, Gabriela discovered that the more she embraced negotiation, the more doors of opportunity opened for her. Negotiation not only improved Gabriela's financial situation but also transformed her mindset and relationships. It elevated her self-worth and empowered her to set boundaries and express her needs in all areas of her life. Gabriela's newfound confidence and assertiveness positively impacted her personal relationships, leading to stronger connections and healthier dynamics.

As time went on, Gabriela's reputation as a skilled negotiator spread throughout her professional network. She became a mentor herself, helping other Latinas and individuals overcome their fears and realize the power of negotiation. Gabriela's journey from fear to confidence became a beacon of inspiration for those longing to break free from the shackles of self-doubt.

From that day forward, Gabriela lived a life transformed. Negotiation became her superpower, a tool that increased her confidence, improved her life, and allowed her to navigate both personal and professional spheres with grace and determination. Gabriela's story is a powerful reminder that embracing negotiation can lead to personal growth, empowerment, and the realization of one's true worth.

# Advocate!

Negotiating for equal pay can even help you advance in your career. When you are paid fairly, you are more likely to be satisfied with your job, which can lead to increased job performance and opportunities for advancement. Advocating for yourself can help build your confidence and assertiveness. When you stand up for yourself, you are sending a message that you value your work and your contributions. And that's a message that we must learn to fully embody as women of color.

This is why I cannot stress enough the importance of knowing your worth and advocating for higher pay in your career. While the burden of fixing this issue can't and shouldn't fall entirely on us (because this is a complex systemic issue with many layers like implicit bias, stereotyping, a lack of representation in leadership roles, and outward racism), there are plenty of ways that we can fight back, speak up, and ask for our worth.

## Know Your Worth

One of the most important things you can do when negotiating for a salary increase or promotion at your current job or negotiating your salary for a new one is to know your worth. By researching industry standards for salaries and benefits, as well as the qualifications and experience required for the compensation at your current job or for a new role you're seeking, you'll be prepared with data rather than a random number out of nowhere. With this information in hand, you'll be much better prepared to communicate your value to the company and demonstrate how your skills and experience uniquely align with the position.

Start by identifying the job title you are interested in, or one similar to your current title. It's important to ensure you have the correct job title, as this can impact salary ranges. By knowing the market rate for your job and industry, you can establish a baseline for your negotiation. You can begin your research process by using salary aggregation websites like Salary.com, PayScale.com, or GlassDoor.com. These sites will give you a range to start with, but to get an even more accurate idea of salaries at a specific company, consider reaching out to industry professionals to get an idea of what the salary range is for the position you are researching. This could include colleagues, recruiters, or mentors. LinkedIn is a great platform to use for this.

Keep in mind that salary ranges can be impacted by several factors, such as education level, years of experience, industry, location, and company size. Make sure to take these factors into account when researching salary data. You can also check job postings for the position you are researching to get an idea of the salary range. In 2021, Colorado became the first US state to require employers to list salary ranges on job advertisements for work that could be done in the state. Since then, several other states (California, Rhode Island, and Washington) and cities (NYC, Cincinnati, and Toledo) have enacted their own similar laws, while others have laws that say employers must disclose the minimum and maximum pay to job seekers during the hiring process. These new laws are intended to protect job seekers during the hiring process, and prevent employers from asking candidates about their salary history (which can perpetuate a pay gap).

## Prepare Ahead

Negotiating your salary or other benefits requires preparation. Before entering a negotiation, make sure to identify your goals and priorities, as well as any concessions you're willing to make. For instance, if it's a job offer situation, determine your minimum salary requirement so you know going in the absolute minimum you will accept. If it seems like your potential new employer is standing firm on less than you were hoping for, consider suggesting that they give you a signing bonus or an offer of equity in the company in lieu of salary. Another consideration is paid time off—perhaps if you aren't getting to the number you're looking for in terms of salary, you can ask for more vacation time.

Next step: Practice your negotiation skills by starting small, like calling up your cell phone carrier and asking for a lower rate or negotiating less of an annual rent increase on the lease for your apartment. Just like any other skill, learning how to negotiate takes practice, so the more, the better. And who knows, if you're successful, you may even save a little money on your bills!

During this preparation process, you'll want to identify and anticipate potential objections, and come up with responses to address them. Consider taking negotiation courses or workshops to learn new strategies and techniques and to practice with others. You can practice in front of a mirror or by recording yourself on your phone, and enlist a friend or family member to help you do a mock interview. This will help you identify any areas you need more practice in. Take turns playing each role to gain different perspectives.

## It's Time to Talk Yourself Up!

When seeking a new job or a promotion, it's important to highlight your accomplishments and the value you've brought to the organization (either the one you're leaving, or the one you're already a part of). Be prepared with data and evidence that demonstrates your value, and be ready to provide specific examples of your achievements and how they've contributed to the company's success. The more you can tie your accomplishments to the company's overall mission and vision, the better. Your goal is to demonstrate how your skills and experience make you an asset to the team and to the company as a whole.

Even armed with all your accomplishments, do you find yourself feeling a little nervous before an important meeting to discuss advancement at your company or in a job interview situation? Welcome to the club! A great way to prepare is to make a list of your key accomplishments and successes. If it's a job interview, talk about your previous role or roles and consider how these accomplishments relate to the position you are interviewing for. Make sure to tie those two things together.

Terrified that you might ramble versus hitting all the points you want to hit? Prepare ahead of time using the STAR (Situation, Task, Action, Result) method. This interview technique can help you structure your responses to questions and ensure that you provide a complete and compelling answer. Instead of just describing your responsibilities or tasks, focus on the specific results you achieved. Quantify your accomplishments where possible, such as by citing specific numbers or percentages. Here's how it works:

- **Situation:** Quickly set the scene, making sure to give only the necessary details.
- **Task:** Make it really clear up front exactly what your role or responsibility was in that situation.
- **Action:** Explain exactly what steps you took to address it (be sure not to give too many of the steps, just the crucial ones!).
- **Result:** Share what outcomes your actions achieved. For example, did your actions lead to a change in the company's way of handling a common situation? Did you solve a business problem they were having?

Remember to provide context (Situation) around your accomplishments (Results) to help the interviewer understand the impact of your work. Explain the challenges you faced (Task) and how you overcame them (Action). When discussing your accomplishments, highlight the skills you used to achieve them.

For example, profits at your company were down one year (Situation) and your manager asked you to look for ways to increase sales (Task). You took a look at all of your accounts with an eye toward how you could provide better service while at the same time offering targeted discounts to bring in more business (Action). Voilà, you increased sales by 20 percent (Results)!

Explain how you used your communication and negotiation skills to achieve this result. Demonstrate how your accomplishments had a positive impact on the company or team. This shows that you are results-driven and can make a meaningful contribution to the organization. Keep your responses concise and focused on the most important points. Avoid going into too much detail or getting sidetracked by tangential information. Using this method, you can effectively showcase your accomplishments during an interview and demonstrate your value as a candidate for the position.

Often, at the end of an interview you'll be asked, "What are your salary requirements?" Evie Prete cautions against feeling pressured to answer right there on the spot. She advises her clients to give themselves the time they need to answer so that they don't undervalue themselves. "You can say something like, 'I'd like more time to think about this. Can I follow up with you in an email?'"

### Be Confident and Assertive

As a woman of color, you bring a unique perspective to the workplace that adds value to the company. Use this to your advantage and highlight how your diverse background can contribute to the success of the company. Confidence is the key to successful negotiation. Be strong and clear in describing your abilities and the value that you bring to the company. Use confident body language and speak with conviction to convey the faith you have in yourself to your employer.

## Seek Out Allies and Mentors

For years, Lucia poured her heart and soul into her career as a marketing manager, dedicating long hours and hard work. However, as time went on, she began to feel a growing sense of dissatisfaction and frustration. One evening, after a particularly challenging day at work, Lucia found herself scrolling through social media, searching for inspiration and a glimmer of hope. In her feed, she stumbled upon an article featuring the stories of successful career "transitioners" who had found fulfillment and happiness in new professional paths.

Intrigued by the idea of reinventing her career, Lucia decided to take a leap of faith. She attended a local networking event designed to connect professionals seeking guidance with experienced mentors who had successfully transitioned their own careers. As Lucia entered the event space, she felt a mix of nervousness and excitement. She knew that this gathering held the potential to change her life. As she mingled with fellow attendees, she caught sight of two mujeres engaged in a lively conversation. Lucia sensed an immediate connection with their energy and approached them hesitantly.

The women, named Carmen and Sofia, greeted Lucia with warm smiles and open arms. They were both accomplished Latinas who had navigated their own career transitions with grace and success. Carmen had left the corporate world to pursue her passion for entrepreneurship, while Sofia had transitioned from a finance career to become a renowned life coach. Over cups of coffee and heartfelt conversations, Carmen and Sofia became Lucia's pillars of support and guidance. They listened intently to her frustrations, fears, and aspirations, providing a safe space for her to express herself. Carmen shared her journey of overcoming self-doubt and taking the leap into entrepreneurship, while Sofia provided insights into finding one's true calling and aligning values with a new career path.

With their mentorship, Lucia embarked on a journey of self-discovery. Carmen and Sofia encouraged her to reflect on her passions, strengths, and the kind of work that would bring her fulfillment. They helped her identify transferable skills and explore different industries that aligned with her values and interests. Armed with newfound clarity and a strong support system, Lucia began to take intentional steps toward her career transition. Carmen and Sofia introduced her to relevant networks, recommended courses and workshops, and shared valuable resources to sharpen her skills. They acted as cheerleaders, reminding her of her worth and potential during moments of doubt.

Months passed, and Lucia blossomed. She gained confidence and clarity, discovering her true passion for social impact and community development work. With the support of Carmen and Sofia, she crafted a new career path that combined her skills in project management with her desire to make a positive difference in the world. When the day finally arrived for Lucia to embark on her new journey, she stood tall and proud. Surrounded by Carmen and Sofia, she delivered a heartfelt speech at her farewell gathering. Lucia expressed her deep gratitude for the incredible mentors who had believed in her and guided her to career transition success.

From that day forward, Lucia dedicated herself to uplifting others who were yearning for career fulfillment. She became an advocate for mentorship and a beacon of hope for those seeking change. Lucia's story reminds us that with the right mentors and unwavering determination, one can navigate the path of career transition and find immense joy and purpose on the other side.

Allies and mentors can be valuable sources of support and guidance throughout the negotiation and promotion process. By connecting with women of color in your field and building a network of support, you can gain much-needed guidance and encouragement during this process. Look for people in your field, or the field you want to be in, who have experience and expertise in the areas where you need help. This could be someone in your current or previous workplace, a professional organization, or at an industry event. Many organizations and professional associations offer mentorship programs. Seek out programs that match your interests and career goals, and apply to participate.

You may even already have people in your network who can assist you. Reach out to your current and former colleagues, professors, and alumni from your school. Let them know that you are looking for a mentor and ask if they know anyone who might be a good fit.

When you approach potential mentors, be sure to be respectful of their time and expertise. Be clear about what you are looking for and what you hope to gain from the mentorship, set realistic expectations, and be grateful for any time they are willing to give you. After you meet with a potential mentor, follow up with them to thank them for their time and any advice they provided. Keep them updated on your progress and continue to ask for their guidance when needed.

## PRACTICE: Salary Negotiation Script

If you're ready to start advocating for yourself at work but don't know where to begin, here's a script you can use to help frame your discussion with your boss. Start by scheduling a meeting with your manager to discuss your compensation.

**You:** Hi [manager's name], I would like to request a meeting to discuss my current compensation. I believe it's important to have a conversation about my contributions to the company and the value I bring to my role.

**Manager:** Of course, [your name]. I appreciate your initiative. Let's find a time that works for both of us. How about [suggested date and time]?

**You:** That works for me. Thank you, [manager's name]. I look forward to discussing this further.

*On the day of the meeting, enter with confidence and be prepared to make your case.*

**You:** Thank you for taking the time to meet with me, [manager's name]. I wanted to discuss my performance and the value I've added to the company since my last compensation review.

**Manager:** Yes, [your name]. What specifically would you like to discuss today?

**You:** I'd like to talk about my current salary and explore the possibility of a salary increase. Over the past [specific time period], I have consistently demonstrated my dedication, achieved notable results, and contributed to the success of the team and the company as a whole.

**Manager:** I understand your perspective, [your name]. Can you provide me with more information about your contributions and the reasons you believe a salary increase is warranted?

**You:** Certainly, [manager's name]. Let me share some highlights of my accomplishments since our last compensation review. [Mention specific achievements, such as exceeding targets, leading successful projects, receiving positive feedback from clients or colleagues, or taking on additional responsibilities.]

**Manager:** I appreciate your efforts, [your name]. Let me review your performance and the current budget. I'll assess what can be done in terms of a salary adjustment.

**You:** Thank you, [manager's name]. I also want to express my continued commitment to the company's success and growth. As my responsibilities have increased, and I have consistently delivered results, I believe a salary increase would reflect my dedication and the value I bring to the organization.

**Manager:** I understand your perspective, [your name]. Let me consider this and discuss it with the relevant stakeholders. I will get back to you with a response as soon as possible.

**You:** Thank you, [manager's name]. I appreciate your consideration and look forward to hearing back from you. I'm confident that an adjustment in my compensation would not only recognize my contributions but also motivate me to continue delivering exceptional results.

*End the conversation with professionalism and express gratitude for the opportunity to discuss the matter.*

It might help to get a friend or family member to help you practice. Remember, every negotiation is unique, and it's important to tailor the script to your specific situation and company culture. Be prepared to answer any questions or concerns your manager may have, and approach the conversation with confidence, backed by your performance and the value you bring to the organization. Good luck, babe!

## You Didn't Receive the Pay Increase or Promotion...What Now?

If you got the job or the promotion—YAY! Time to pop open the champagne! But what if it doesn't go as planned? What happens if they don't offer you the job or give you that pay increase or promotion? Receiving a "no" can be disappointing, but it's important to remain professional and respectful in your response. And it's important to know that hope is not lost, amiga. There are many more jobs out there, and many things you can negotiate for besides a pay increase.

First, you have to decide if you're willing to go back to the negotiation table, or if you're going to pursue another opportunity elsewhere. Here are some steps you can take if you've received a no during the negotiation process.

First, thank the employer for their time and consideration. Even if you're disappointed with the outcome, it's important to thank them for taking the time to consider your request. Next, ask if they can provide any feedback on why they were unable to grant your request for a promotion and/or salary increase. It could have been your presentation, or it could have absolutely nothing to do with you, like companywide budget cuts. If you're unsure about any aspects of your employer's decision, be sure to ask for clarification. This can help you better understand their perspective and what you can do to improve your chances in the future.

## What If It's Still a No?

If your employer is unable to provide a salary increase or promotion, consider asking about alternative forms of compensation. Here's a list of things you can potentially negotiate for besides a pay increase.

**Health and wellness benefits:** Consider negotiating for health and wellness benefits, such as medical, dental, and vision insurance, as well as wellness programs, gym memberships, or mental health resources. If these are already provided to you, try asking for better options in your plan.

**Retirement benefits:** If they are not already provided to you, negotiate for retirement benefits, such as a 401(k) plan or a pension, as well as employer contributions or matching.

**Time off:** Negotiate for additional or better vacation time, sick leave, or personal days. You can also consider asking for flexible scheduling or the ability to work from home.

**Professional development:** Consider negotiating for opportunities for professional development, such as training or education programs, tuition reimbursement, or mentorship opportunities.

**Stock options or equity:** Equity refers to ownership in the company. When an employee is granted equity, they become a partial owner of the company, and are entitled to a share of its profits and assets. Equity can be granted in the form of actual stock in the company or as an ownership interest in the company's profits. Stock options, on the other hand, give an employee the right to purchase a certain number of shares of the company's stock at a predetermined price, known as the exercise price. The exercise price is usually set at the fair market value of the stock at the time the options are granted. The employee can exercise their options at any time before the options expire, which is usually several years after the options are granted. If the stock price increases, the employee can purchase the shares at the lower exercise price and sell them at the higher market price, making a profit. Both equity and stock options can be valuable forms of compensation, as they give employees a stake in the company's success and potential for financial gain. However, they also come with risks, as the value of the equity or stock options can decrease if the company does not perform well. It is important for you to carefully consider the terms and conditions of the equity or stock options being offered, and to consult with a financial advisor or tax professional before making any decisions.

**Relocation assistance:** If a new job requires you to relocate, consider negotiating for relocation assistance, such as reimbursement for moving expenses or temporary housing.

**Commuter benefits:** These are a type of employee benefit that some companies offer to help offset the costs of commuting to work. These benefits can come in a variety of forms, such as:

**Pre-tax deductions:** Some companies allow employees to use pre-tax dollars to pay for eligible commuting expenses, such as public transportation or qualified parking.

**Transit subsidies:** Employers may offer transit subsidies or reimbursement programs to help cover the cost of public transportation, such as bus or train passes.

**Parking subsidies:** Some employers provide subsidies or reimbursements for parking expenses, such as fees for parking garages or lots.

**Bicycle benefits:** Employers may offer benefits for employees who commute by bike, such as reimbursement for bike maintenance or equipment, or access to bike-sharing programs.

**Bonuses:** If you are negotiating compensation for a new job and your new employer won't budge on salary, you may be able to ask for a signing bonus as a one-time payment or an increase in your overall percentage for performance-based bonuses. Ditto if your employer is saying "not at this time" to a promotion or pay increase: Ask about the possibility of a performance bonus based on agreed-upon achievements—for instance, if you're in sales, how many new customers you will bring in by year's end.

# An Open Letter to Corporate America

Now that we have explored how important it is that you know and truly own your worth, it's time to take a step back and remember that you are not alone! As Latinas, we have struggled for centuries for fair compensation. The time for equal pay is now. We can no longer ignore the necessary systemic changes and we can't do this work alone. We must join together in this fight. I want to share a letter I wrote as a rallying cry to American companies to start acknowledging our worth and making equitable compensation for Latina women a priority. Feel free to pass it along to anyone who is joining us in the struggle!

*To the Powers That Be,*

*We can rally day and night in the streets for equal pay for all, but let's be honest…truly eliminating the gender wage gap is going to require a multi-pronged approach that addresses the systemic barriers and cultural biases that can make it difficult for us to negotiate for higher salaries. Basically, WE NEED YOU TO FIX THIS. Many women of color may not even be aware of the factors that contribute to wage disparities, or how to negotiate for higher pay. If you want to play an active role in dismantling the disparities you've created, we need you to be proactive in providing training on these topics so that we can develop the skills and confidence we need to advocate for ourselves.*

*Women of color deserve wage transparency. We need you to keep it real when you're talking about all things pay and promotions to your employees, in order to reduce the likelihood of wage disparities. Make sure that all employees are aware of the criteria for promotions and salary increases and that they understand the process for requesting a raise.*

*Women of color face biases and discrimination in the workplace that make it more difficult for us to negotiate for higher pay. We need you to lead by example by actively working to educate people managers on DEI (Diversity, Equity & Inclusion) topics, like cultural sensitivity and unconscious bias. And please stop treating DEI like a trendy social media hashtag. Develop real policies and programs that actually create opportunities for underrepresented groups, and actively promote diversity and inclusion within your organizations. Addressing these issues through training and policy changes can create a more inclusive and supportive environment that rewards people equally for their hard work and skills.*

*Finally, we need you to stop funding politicians who are ok with the status quo. We need you to advocate for policy changes at the local, state, and federal level that address wage disparities and promote pay equity. This includes advocating for stronger equal pay laws, supporting initiatives that promote diversity and inclusion, supporting paid parental leave and affordable childcare, and pushing for greater transparency around pay and promotions. Because alone, we can do a little, but together, we can do a lot.*

*In Solidarity,*
*Jannese*

Mujer, your journey to becoming Financially Lit begins with truly knowing your worth. Please never forget that you are 100 percent worthy and deserving of achieving your dreams.

# CHAPTER 4

# Stop Chasing "The Dream" and Start Getting Real with Your Dinero

**I** bought a home to pursue the American Dream. It landed me in therapy.
Let me tell you a story. My twenties were filled with lots of mindless spending. I didn't have a budget, just a loose idea of what my bills were and when they were due. Budgeting felt tedious—the thought of having to track how much I spent on a Starbucks coffee felt so...extra. I didn't have the time for it, and I was sure no one else did either. I didn't set or even think about any real financial goals. And it showed.

Newly independent and living on my own, I tried to replicate the lifestyle I grew up with. By the time I was in high school, my parents were both working full-time jobs, they had bought their first home, and our overall quality of life had improved dramatically. We started taking more family trips, going out to eat, and getting newer cars. Life was good. So as soon as I had my first full-time job after graduation, I started doing the same thing.

I splurged on expensive trips (three to four times per year), moved into my first place, bought a brand-new car, spent $50,000 on a lavish wedding and honeymoon, added another $30,000 of student loan debt to get a master's degree. I was living the American Dream (or so I thought). In reality, I was living paycheck to paycheck. I thought all I needed was to make six figures, and then I wouldn't need a budget and credit card debt wouldn't ever be an issue again! It made sense to me at the time.

So began my six-figure pursuit. Exactly fifty-one days after my thirtieth birthday, I finally secured my first six-figure job offer, more money than I'd ever had before. Making six figures meant I'd never have to worry about money again...except it didn't actually make a difference. At all. I quickly learned that you can't actually outearn your crappy spending habits. I was still spending money recklessly. I just had more of it to spend.

I had finally checked off a big box, but instead of getting real with my financial situation, I moved on to the next big "dream" slash expectation. In my thirties everyone around me was adulting like it was their business, getting married, buying homes, and so on. I set out to take what felt like the next logical step for me, too. I bought a house, because "renting is wasting money." It's one of the narratives we're all force-fed, especially in the Latino community. If you want to build wealth, you buy a house. So I did. After all, that's what adults with six-figure jobs do, right? But no one prepared me for what came next.

In July 2016, I closed on a two-family home using the US Department of Housing & Urban Development's FHA (Federal Housing Authority) program for first-time home buyers, saddling myself with a $3,000-per-month mortgage for the next thirty years. Instead of just buying a single-family home, I figured that purchasing a multifamily unit and renting the unused portion would allow me to afford a more expensive home than I could otherwise buy on my own. If buying a home equals success, then isn't becoming a landlord the ultimate boss move?

As a first-time homeowner, I thought I had covered all my bases. After closing costs, I still had a few thousand dollars left in our emergency fund. It was a well-kept home built in the 1930s, owned by the same family for multiple generations, and the downstairs unit (where I would be living) was recently renovated. The home inspection didn't reveal any major issues, and the seller even had a new heating system installed as part of the purchase.

Everything seemed great, at first. Dios mío, was I in for a surprise!

The first bad sign came when I set about renting the second apartment. My real estate agent anticipated that I could rent the two-bedroom unit on the second floor for $1,600 per month—if so, it would cover over half of the mortgage. As it turned out, the second-floor unit was too small to fetch the $1,600 in monthly rent that I had hoped (and planned) for, and so I had to lower the rent to $1,300. I figured I'd be ok, though.

This was just the beginning of the fuckery to come. Two weeks after moving in, I came home from work and was met by the stench of raw sewage. It turns out that during the DIY renovation of the home, someone had poured cement down the main sewage line, resulting in a 95 percent blockage. The basement was flooded with six inches of filthy water.

Despite showing no signs of water damage during the inspection, the basement started flooding every time it rained. Price tag for a French drain system with two sump pumps: $15,000. The main cast-iron sewer line had to be replaced: another $4,000. All told, the sewage issues cost me about $17,000 more than I had in the small $2,000 emergency fund I had set aside when I bought the house.

The damage was more than financial. From the beginning, I was hemorrhaging money, and my mental health began to suffer. Two weeks after moving in, I was already ready to sell it. Stressed out and anxious, I would lie in bed crying for hours, trying to figure out how to undo the nightmare of my own making.

Eventually, full-blown depression set in. With help from a psychiatrist, I realized I'd been making major life decisions that weren't aligned with the actual amount of dinero I had in my bank account. I had let societal expectations pressure me into believing that if I didn't own a home, I was throwing away money as a renter. But remember, chica, what's best for everyone else isn't always what's best for you.

Less than three years later, I sold the house (at a loss of $10,000), and I went back to renting after relocating from New Jersey to Florida in 2018. I wanted a fresh start, and decided to focus on my own financial goals instead of those that had been imposed on me. Over the next two years, I dedicated myself to paying off my student loans and credit card debt using money I was making with my side hustles (more on that later) and was able to become debt free in February 2020, right before the pandemic. Talk about good timing! I couldn't be more at peace with my decision to go back to renting after taking a chance at homeownership. I had to come to terms with the fact that I just wasn't ready, and that's ok! I do plan to purchase a primary home eventually, but when I do, it won't be because "it's a good investment," it will be because I'm ready to settle down in one place and I'm in a position to manage the financial responsibility that comes with it.

In this chapter we'll talk more about the decision to buy a home and other traditional markers of financial success and stability that might be great for you to achieve…at some point…but maybe not right *now*. Or maybe never. And that's all right. In order for you to sort out what's right for you, let's take a quick look at a list of some other common dreams and their accompanying financial realities. We'll address the pros and cons of these in more depth later in the chapter.

| THE DREAM | THE REALITY |
| --- | --- |
| The "Safe" Job | No job is safe. That was true before the COVID-19 pandemic, but it's even more evident now. |

| The Big Happily Ever After | 50% of first marriages, 67% of second marriages, and 73% of third marriages end in divorce. Make sure you're getting married for the right reasons, not just because you have been made to believe you are "supposed" to. |
| --- | --- |
| The Wedding Extravaganza | The average wedding in 2023 cost $29,000. That's a serious chunk of change! Maybe think about what really matters when planning your "big day," because in a few years it's not the extra-extra-large flower arrangements you'll remember, it's marrying the person you love. |
| The Creds—MA, MFA, MBA, CPA, PhD, etc. | About 9% of Americans have master's degrees, but it increases their employability by less than 3%. Mujeres, think long and hard about taking time (and money) out to get those extra creds! |
| The Dream Home | More than a fifth of all American homeowners (almost 17 million households) are considered "house poor," meaning they spend more than 30% of their total income on housing-related costs. |
| Having Kids | According to the US Department of Agriculture (USDA), it costs $233,610 to raise a child to age 18. Adjusted for inflation, that figure is likely closer to $288,094. If you plan on having kids, start saving! |

Chica, please, before you plunge into achieving your dreams, take a moment to figure out what they actually are! This is known as **value-based spending**.

Practicing value-based spending involves being intentional and thoughtful about your purchasing decisions. By adopting these practices, you can develop a more intentional and mindful approach to spending money, ensuring that your financial resources are directed toward what truly matters to you. So, where can you start? Establish a budget that reflects your income, expenses, and financial goals. By tracking your income and expenses, you can allocate your money intentionally toward your priorities and avoid impulsive purchases. In order to begin to practice value-based spending, you need a budget.

# Budgeting Basics

First, let's get one thing straight. The word "budget" can feel like a negative word in the English language, but I think it's because budgets have gotten a really bad rap. The word has become associated with restriction, constriction, and deprivation. In reality, a budget can (and should) be your BFF! I like to think of my budget as a spending plan. It's a way of giving your money a job, instead of letting it go buckwild and hoping it does what you want it to do. Instead of wishing and praying for our dollars to take care of us, let's give our dinero specific instructions for how to love us back. Let your budget be the love language for your money. With a solid plan, you'll find it easier to reach your goals and stay on track. How to get started? Let's review some common strategies for creating a budget.

## Budgeting for Beginners: The 50/30/20 Budget

This system gives you a basic template for allocating your expenditures to different categories so you can pay down debt, cover current costs, and save for future expenses. It splits your income across three major categories: 50 percent goes to necessities, 30 percent to wants, and 20 percent to savings and debt repayment. You can use these percentages as a suggestion rather than a hard-and-fast rule, as they are entirely dependent on your income and expenses.

It's not unusual for someone in a high-cost-of-living area to spend 50 percent or more of their income on housing and transportation. In these cases, your ratios will fluctuate, but the important part of budgeting is determining where you can build in wiggle room. That may require you to move to a cheaper apartment while you pay off debt, and then you can redirect money that was going toward debt payoff to upgrade to a nicer home once you're debt free.

The idea with the 50/30/20 budget is to set your percentages and then observe where there are pain points and where there is possible wiggle room so that you can get closer to achieving your financial goals. After doing the 50/30/20 budget for a few months, Sonia noticed that childcare was taking up half of her "necessities" budget, leaving her with barely any wiggle room in her "wants" and "savings" categories. Knowing that her mom had expressed a desire to spend more time with her daughter, Sonia asked if she'd be willing to look after her a couple days of the week. Her mom was delighted. It was a win-win situation for everyone!

## The 50/30/20 Budget Rule

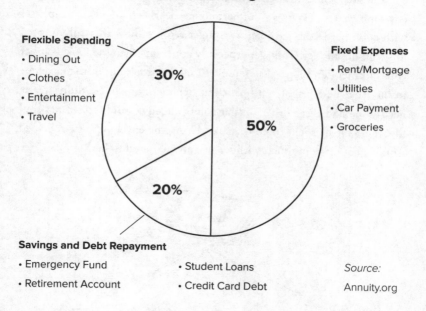

**Flexible Spending**
- Dining Out
- Clothes
- Entertainment
- Travel

**30%**

**Fixed Expenses**
- Rent/Mortgage
- Utilities
- Car Payment
- Groceries

**50%**

**20%**

**Savings and Debt Repayment**
- Emergency Fund
- Retirement Account
- Student Loans
- Credit Card Debt

*Source:*
Annuity.org

## Control Your Spending: The Envelope System

If you need a rigid system to help you reduce frivolous spending or stay out of debt but don't want to track every purchase, try this cash-based approach. You set a spending limit for each expense category—like groceries, utilities, rent, and entertainment—and fill envelopes with the allotted cash, then use only that money for purchases. Once an envelope is empty, you can't spend any more money on that particular category for the month.

Goodbudget is a digital budgeting app based on the envelope system, and it's perfect for those who like the method but don't want to deal with carrying around lots of cash in paper envelopes. By using this app and others like it, you will be able to allot certain amounts of cash to virtual envelopes that you can see on your phone or laptop anytime. You can also share information with your partner or family so that you can all stay on track together.

Zoraida, a client, discovered an interesting thing when she tried the envelope system. Having all of her money clearly "marked" for expenses with cold, hard cash gave her a stronger sense of how she truly wanted to spend her money. This was especially apparent when she looked at her entertainment envelope. The same $20 bill she took out of the envelope to buy that new bright red lipstick at Sephora, which she didn't really need—she had three other similar colors already!—didn't feed her soul like the $20 she spent to go dancing. Using the envelope system helped Zoraida get more in touch with what truly mattered to her.

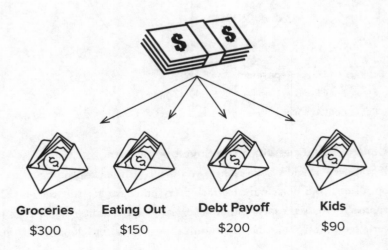

| Groceries | Eating Out | Debt Payoff | Kids |
|-----------|------------|-------------|------|
| $300 | $150 | $200 | $90 |

**Started with $300**

**-$235**

**Groceries**    **Money left over $65**

## The Anti-Budget: Pay Yourself First

Designed to align your spending habits with your financial goals and values, this "anti-budget" budget puts priorities such as saving more money for retirement, an emergency fund, or a down payment on a house before immediate expenses. With this system, you decide how much to set aside from your monthly income to realize your goals before you pay your bills. You don't have to crunch every number each month; you simply work with what you have left over after you have addressed your number one financial goal.

Here's how to create a pay-yourself-first budget:

**Step 1: Make a list of your expenses.** To make this budget successful, you need to start with a realistic sense of how much you can afford to set aside for your financial goal each month. Take a look at your bank accounts and credit card statements and make a list of the regular expenses you have each month, big (i.e., rent) and small (i.e., that very expensive shampoo you can't live without). Next, determine a reasonable amount you could save each month without coming up short.

**Step 2: Figure out how much to pay yourself.** Pinpoint a realistic amount using the 50/30/20 approach. This method allocates 20 percent of your monthly income to savings and debt repayment, 50 percent to necessities, and 30 percent to wants. With a $4,600 monthly income, for example, you'd reserve no more than $920 for savings and debt repayment, $2,300 for needs, and $1,380 for wants.

**Step 3: Automate your deposits.** Automation is the key to making this system work for you. Relying on manual transfers can make it hard for you to prioritize your savings and investment goals. Set up an automatic transfer for some of each paycheck to go directly into a savings account, retirement account, investment, or other savings vehicle, based on your overall goals.

**Step 4: Adjust as needed.** Ideally, you have enough money coming in to cover your needs, wants, and financial goals. But if you find yourself coming up short, look for ways to scale back. That might mean focusing on one savings goal at a time or finding ways to trim expenses from your needs and wants categories, or all of the above. You can also explore supplementing your income with side gigs. Selma C., personal finance content creator and founder of the social media platform Bitch I'm Budgeting, was able to pay off $41,000 in debt in two and a half years by doing a series of side gigs. For example, she earned $4,000 in one month working for Instacart a couple hours a day—more than she earned in a month from her salary working as a special needs teacher.

### Give Every Dollar a Job: The Zero-Based Budget

This budget suits over-spenders and meticulous planners alike. It makes monitoring your spending 100 percent clear. You take your monthly income

---

**Budgeting Concept Comparison**

| Typical Savings Habits | | Pay Yourself First ✔ | |
|---|---|---|---|
| | **Paycheck** | | **Paycheck** |
| MINUS | **Bills** | MINUS | **Savings** |
| MINUS | **My Spending** | MINUS | **Bills** |
| | **Leftover** | | **My Spending** |
| THEN MAYBE | **Savings** ↩ | | |

and use every dollar in a deliberate way—like saving a certain amount for a trip and paying for utilities and groceries—until there are zero dollars left to spend. But if you don't strictly use cash as with the envelope system, you'll have to log each expense in a spreadsheet or tracker to make sure you're on budget. Budget apps such as YNAB (You Need A Budget) and EveryDollar can help you follow a zero-based budget digitally.

| HOW TO CREATE A ZERO-BASED BUDGET | |
|---|---|
| Total Monthly Income: $3,250 | |
| Rent | $1,200 |
| Utilities | $120 |
| Groceries | $400 |
| Phone Bill | $80 |
| Gas | $250 |
| Insurance | $100 |
| Clothes | $100 |
| Entertainment | $150 |
| Charity | $100 |
| Travel Fund | $100 |
| Emergency Fund | $150 |
| Retirement | $200 |
| Loans | $200 |
| Misc. | $100 |
| Amount Left Over $0 | |

When choosing a budget method, it's good to consider how much time and effort you're willing to dedicate to creating and managing your budget. Some of these methods, like the zero-based budget, will require detailed daily or weekly tracking. The pay-yourself-first system and apps that sync to your financial accounts require little upkeep.

How often should you budget? There's no set rule, so go at your own pace. If you're confident in your financial situation, you can probably get away with reviewing your information once a month or a couple of times a year. However, if you feel like you are still figuring out how to handle your money well, you may want to check in weekly or after every purchase you make.

Determine whether you want to take a DIY approach to budgeting or seek technological assistance. Personal finance software like Mint or Empower (formerly Personal Capital) can be convenient if you want to access and update your information on the go. Apps like Digit can automate your savings, which can help you kick-start your budget. If it doesn't automatically input and categorize your purchases or it's hard to use, it might not add much value. For some, a hands-on approach with old-fashioned pen and paper is best. Writing things down can help you retain information and feel connected to your budget.

Most budgeting apps have special security features to protect your financial data from getting into the hands of hackers. However, that doesn't mean you should totally let down your guard when using financial apps to budget. Hackers may still be able to access your financial data by stealing your password. If you're not comfortable linking your bank accounts to an electronic budgeting service, a physical method can save you worry, too. Note that popular peer-to-peer cash platforms like PayPal, Venmo, and CashApp aren't actually banks, and any funds in those accounts are not FDIC insured (learn more about the FDIC on page 106).

If you're still not sure, let me reassure you that you do not need to follow a specific budgeting system, as long as you're aware of important details like your income, debts, goals, and general spending. If you live within your means and know you're on track to reach your goals, then tracking every penny is probably overkill. The most important thing is to find a system that works for you and that helps you achieve your goals!

## Tackling Debt: Your Gateway to Financial Freedom

Debt is your biggest obstacle to achieving financial freedom, and if you're currently in debt, you're definitely not alone. The average American has $90,460 in debt.[1] The average millennial in 2023 owes $56,538 in student loans. About 70 percent of millennials are currently living paycheck to paycheck.[2] If you're gonna build serious wealth, your debt has got to kick rocks, honey! Carrying this amount of debt impacts your credit score, your access to different financial products, your ability to purchase big-ticket items, and your mental health. The longer you carry this debt, the more you end up paying—depending on the interest rate, you could end up paying more in interest than the actual principal. Without a debt payoff strategy, financial freedom will be out of reach. Let's talk about the best ways to tackle debt so you can live your best life.

### Debt Avalanche

Debt avalanche is a method for paying off multiple debts, typically credit cards or loans, in a strategic and efficient manner. It involves prioritizing debts based on their interest rates and paying off the debt with the highest interest rate first while making minimum payments on the other debts. Once the highest-interest debt is paid off, the same approach is applied to the debt with the next highest interest, and so on. It's important to note here that, for any debt payoff method to be effective, you have to actively

---

1. https://www.cnbc.com/select/average-american-debt-by-age/#:~:text=While%20the%20average%20American%20has,loans%2C%20mortgages%20and%20student%20debt.
2. https://www.realestatewitch.com/millennial-debt-2023/.

work to avoid increasing existing debt. Here's how to implement the debt avalanche method:

- **List all your debts:** Make a comprehensive list of all your debts, including the outstanding balance, interest rate, and minimum monthly payment for each.
- **Order debts by interest rate:** Arrange the debts from highest to lowest interest rate. This step is crucial because the goal is to pay off the debt with the highest interest rate first to minimize the total interest paid over time.
- **Make minimum payments:** Pay the minimum monthly payment on each debt except for the one with the highest interest rate. Ensure you meet all minimum payment obligations to avoid penalties or fees.
- **Allocate extra funds:** Allocate any additional money you can afford to put toward debt repayment each month. This can be achieved by cutting back on expenses or finding ways to increase your income.
- **Target the highest-interest debt:** Direct all your extra funds toward the debt with the highest interest rate while continuing to make minimum payments on the other debts. This approach reduces the overall interest accruing on your debts.
- **Repeat the process:** Once the first debt is fully paid off, take the total amount you were paying toward it (minimum payment plus the extra funds) and apply it to the debt with the next highest interest rate. Continue this process until all your debts are paid off.

By following the debt avalanche method, you can save money on interest payments over time and potentially pay off your debts faster.

However, it's essential to stay disciplined and committed to the process, as it may take time to see significant progress, especially with larger debts.

## The Debt Snowball Method

The debt snowball method is another popular strategy for paying off multiple debts. It focuses on psychological motivation and involves paying off debts in order of the smallest balance, regardless of the interest rates. Here's how the debt snowball method works:

- **List all your debts:** Make a list of all your debts, including the outstanding balance, minimum monthly payment, and interest rate for each.

- **Order debts by balance:** Arrange the debts from smallest to largest balance. Ignore the interest rates at this stage and focus solely on the amount owed.

- **Make minimum payments:** Pay the minimum monthly payment on each debt, ensuring you meet all the minimum payment obligations.

- **Allocate extra funds:** If you have any additional money available for debt repayment, allocate it toward the debt with the smallest balance. This can come from cutting expenses, increasing income, or reallocating funds from other areas of your budget.

- **Pay off the smallest debt:** Direct all your extra funds toward paying off the debt with the smallest balance while continuing to make minimum payments on the other debts. By focusing on the smallest debt, you can achieve a quick win and gain motivation to tackle the remaining debts.

- **Snowball payments:** Once the smallest debt is paid off, take the total amount you were paying toward it (minimum payment plus the extra funds) and apply it to the debt with the next smallest balance. This "snowballs" the payments, as you progressively have more money available for each subsequent debt.

- **Repeat the process:** Keep repeating the snowball payments by rolling over the funds from paid-off debts into the next one until you have paid off all your debts.

The debt snowball method emphasizes the psychological benefits of gaining momentum and motivation by paying off smaller debts first, even if they have lower interest rates. While it may not save you as much money on interest compared to the debt avalanche method, the psychological boost can help you stay motivated and committed to your debt repayment journey.

## The Debt Lasso

One of the newer strategies for paying down debt is the debt lasso method, which was created by David and John Auten-Schneider—aka the Debt Free Guys. This method helped them tackle $51,000 in credit card debt in less than three years. The debt lasso method is the act of "lassoing" all of your debt into as few locations as possible at the lowest interest rate possible.

This method is similar to the debt avalanche method in that it requires you to tackle your highest-interest-rate debt first. However, it has additional steps, which the Debt Free Guys maintain is the quickest, easiest, and most cost-effective method to pay off credit card debt that also will help improve your credit score. This is the method I used to pay off over $10,000 of credit card debt in less than a year.

Before you get started with the debt lasso method, the first thing you should do is commit to not spending any more money using credit cards, and if possible, pay off any small credit card debts within the first month or two. Here's how it works:

- Create a spreadsheet and list all your credit cards, with columns for current balance, minimum payment, and current APR.

- Total up the minimum payment column, and then decide on an additional lump sum you are willing to commit toward your debt each month without fail. This will be the bonus payment that you'll pay toward your credit card debt with the highest APR.

- Look for balance-transfer cards with a 0% APR or a low APR to eliminate or lower the interest you are currently paying. If you are unable to get approved for a balance-transfer card, consider a personal loan from your bank or credit union.

- Transfer your balances or pay off your debts with a personal loan, if applicable.

- Set up automatic payments for all your credit card accounts to avoid missing due dates, acquiring late fees, and dinging your credit.

- Add the bonus payment to the minimum payment for the credit card with the highest APR, and pay the minimum payment toward all your other debts.

- Create a reminder for two months before any balance transfer offers are set to expire. This will allow you to find another balance transfer offer or loan if you won't be able to pay off the balance before the offer expires.

- Each time you pay off a credit card, add the amount you were paying to the bonus payment. And once you pay off the credit card with the highest APR, start applying the growing bonus payment to the account with the next highest APR until all your credit cards are paid off.

## Accelerate Your Debt Payoff: Debt Consolidation & Refinancing

Debt consolidation and refinancing are two different approaches to managing and restructuring debt. While they both involve combining multiple debts into a single payment, they have distinct characteristics and purposes.

**Refinancing** is the process of replacing an existing loan with a new loan that offers better terms. It typically involves finding a lender who can provide a loan with a lower interest rate, more favorable repayment terms, or other benefits. When considering refinancing, you should assess your current loan and compare it with available options from different lenders. If you find a loan that suits your needs, you can apply and, if approved, use the new loan to pay off your existing loan. Refinancing can be a smart move in various situations. For example, if interest rates have dropped since you obtained your original loan, refinancing can help you secure a lower rate and reduce your monthly payments. Additionally, if your creditworthiness has improved or you need to adjust your loan terms due to changes in your financial circumstances, refinancing may be a viable option. It can also be useful for consolidating multiple loans or accessing equity in assets like a home.

Debt **consolidation** can help simplify your finances and potentially save you money. It involves combining multiple debts, such as credit card balances or personal loans, into a single loan or credit line. By doing so, you streamline your debt payments into one monthly payment to a consolidation lender. This can make it easier to manage your debts and stay organized. Additionally, debt consolidation may allow you to secure a lower interest rate, which can help reduce the overall cost of your debt. It can be particularly beneficial if you have high-interest debts or if you're struggling to keep up with multiple payments each month. Debt consolidation provides an opportunity to regain control over your financial situation and work toward paying off your debts more efficiently.

## Got Student Loans?

To be eligible for student loan consolidation, you must have federal student loans that are in repayment, in the grace period, or in default. Private student loans are not eligible for federal consolidation. Note that some types of federal loans, such as Perkins Loans, may have specific requirements or limitations for consolidation. The US Department of Education's Direct Consolidation Loan program allows borrowers to consolidate eligible federal student loans into a single loan. To apply for consolidation, you'll need to complete the consolidation application, which can be done online through the Federal Student Aid website (studentaid.gov).

### Things to Know Before Consolidating Your Student Loans

Before you move forward with consolidating your student loans, it's important to be aware of the following and to ask for more information if you need it.

- Your monthly payment may go down, but you may have to pay it down over a longer period of time.
- If you have unpaid interest, your principal balance will go up.
- Your new consolidation loan will generally have a new interest rate.
- You can lose credit for your payments toward income-driven repayment (IDR) forgiveness.
- You don't have to consolidate all your federal student loans.
- You can't undo your consolidation.

In order to apply for student loan consolidation, you'll provide the required information about your loans and personal details, and choose a repayment plan for the consolidated loan. When applying for student loan consolidation, you'll have the opportunity to select a new repayment plan for the consolidated loan. Federal student loans offer several repayment plans to accommodate borrowers with different financial situations and repayment preferences. Here are the main types of federal student loan repayment plans:

**Standard Repayment Plan:** This is the default repayment plan for federal student loans. It has a fixed monthly payment amount over a 10-year term.

*Eligible Loans:* Direct Subsidized Loans, Direct Unsubsidized Loans, Subsidized Federal Stafford Loans, Unsubsidized Federal Stafford Loans, all PLUS loans (Parent PLUS and Graduate PLUS), and Consolidation Loans (excluding Parent PLUS Consolidation Loans).

**Graduated Repayment Plan:** This plan starts with lower monthly payments that gradually increase every two years over a 10-year term.

*Eligible Loans:* Direct Subsidized Loans, Direct Unsubsidized Loans, Subsidized Federal Stafford Loans, Unsubsidized Federal Stafford Loans, all PLUS loans (Parent PLUS and Graduate PLUS), and Consolidation Loans (excluding Parent PLUS Consolidation Loans).

**Extended Repayment Plan:** This plan offers fixed or graduated monthly payments over a repayment term of up to 25 years.

*Eligible Loans:* Direct Subsidized Loans, Direct Unsubsidized Loans, Subsidized Federal Stafford Loans, Unsubsidized Federal Stafford Loans, all PLUS loans (Parent PLUS and Graduate PLUS), and Consolidation Loans (excluding Parent PLUS Consolidation Loans) with a total balance of at least $30,000.

**Income-Driven Repayment Plans:** Income-driven plans set monthly payments based on a percentage of your discretionary income and family size, offering more affordable payments for borrowers with lower income. There are some variations:

**Income-Based Repayment (IBR):** Generally, payments are 10–15% of discretionary income, and repayment period is up to 20 or 25 years depending on when you borrowed.

**Pay As You Earn (PAYE):** Payments are 10% of discretionary income, and repayment period is up to 20 years.

**Revised Pay As You Earn (REPAYE):** Payments are 10% of discretionary income, and repayment period is up to 20 or 25 years depending on the type of loans being repaid.

**Income-Contingent Repayment (ICR):** Payments are either 20% of discretionary income or a fixed amount over a 25-year repayment period.

***Eligible Loans:*** Most federal student loans, including Direct Subsidized Loans, Direct Unsubsidized Loans, Direct PLUS Loans made to graduate or professional students, and Direct Consolidation Loans (including Parent PLUS Consolidation Loans).

**Income-Sensitive Repayment Plan:** This plan sets monthly payments based on your annual income, with payments adjusted annually. The repayment term is typically up to 10 years.

***Eligible Loans:*** Federal Family Education Loan (FFEL) program loans.

It's important to note that eligibility and specific terms can vary based on the loan program, consolidation, and when the loans were disbursed.

I recommend contacting your loan servicer or visiting the Federal Student Aid website (studentaid.gov) for more information and to determine the repayment plan that best suits your needs. Once your application is approved and the consolidation process is complete, your previous federal student loans will be paid off and replaced by the new consolidated loan. You'll start making payments on the consolidated loan according to the chosen repayment plan. It's important to note that student loan consolidation is different from refinancing. Consolidation is available only for federal student loans and combines them into a new federal loan.

Student loan refinancing involves obtaining a new loan from a private lender to pay off existing student loans, potentially with different terms and interest rates. Federal student loans come with several protections and benefits that are designed to assist borrowers in managing their loan repayment, such as the PSLF (Public Student Loan Forgiveness) program, income-driven repayment plans, deferment and forbearance if you lose your job, and student loan discharge for Total and Permanent Disability. These protections and benefits apply specifically to federal student loans. Private student loans generally have different terms and may not offer the same level of borrower protections. If you have private student loans, it's advisable to review the terms of your loan agreement or contact your lender to understand the specific options available to you.

Paying off debt isn't fun, but it will grant you the freedom you're looking for. When you don't owe other people money, you can use the money you're earning to save and invest. That's how wealth is built, so when you're feeling overwhelmed around creating a debt payoff plan, remember that you're actually creating a life freedom plan. That's got a nice ring to it.

## Ready, Set, Dream!

Now that you have gotten real with your dinero by figuring out how much you actually have and how you can use it more effectively with a good budget, let's take a look at how to set your financial goals, another key part of practicing value-based spending. It's so important that your goals align with your values and aspirations, because really, WTF is the point of building a life made up of goals that aren't even yours?! These goals can include saving for a specific purpose, building an emergency fund, or investing for the future. Having well-defined goals provides you with a clear sense of purpose for your dinero and helps guide your spending decisions.

Start by really getting clear on your values and priorities in life. Consider what truly matters to you—whether it's financial security, home-ownership, education, travel, retirement, starting a business, or supporting a cause. This self-reflection will help you set goals that are meaningful and aligned with your core values. Ensure that your goals are realistic and achievable within your financial capabilities. Consider your current income, expenses, and financial obligations when setting your goals. Unrealistic goals can lead you to feeling frustrated and unmotivated, while pursuing achievable goals will provide you with a sense of accomplishment and progress.

It's important to make your goals specific and measurable so that you can track your progress. Instead of a vague goal like "save more money," specify the exact amount you want to save and by when. For example, "Save $5,000 for a down payment on a house within two years." Assigning timeframes helps create a sense of urgency and gives you a clear target to work toward. Consider how long it will realistically take to achieve each goal, and break them down into smaller milestones if necessary.

Once you have your goals defined, break them down again into actionable steps. Identify the specific actions you need to take to work toward each goal. For instance, if your goal is to pay off credit card debt, your actions may include creating a budget, reducing discretionary spending, and making regular extra payments. Regularly monitor and track your progress toward your goals. This can be done monthly, quarterly, or annually. Use tools like spreadsheets, budgeting apps, or personal finance software to keep track of your income, expenses, savings, and debt repayment. Tracking your progress helps you stay accountable and make adjustments as needed.

Be OK with things not always going according to plan! Your life circumstances and priorities can change over time. It's important to periodically review and adjust your goals to ensure they remain relevant and meaningful. Revisit your goals annually or whenever a major life event occurs, such as a job change, marriage, or having children. Remember, financial goals are personal, and everyone's circumstances are unique. Customize your goals to fit your individual situation and aspirations. With clear goals in place, you'll have a road map for making financial decisions and working toward a more secure and fulfilling financial future.

## Sinking Funds

A sinking fund is a financial strategy in which you save money for a specific future expense or goal. It involves setting aside funds over time to accumulate a designated amount needed for a particular purpose. They're a great way to set aside money for your specific money goals, especially large, anticipated expenses or financial obligations that may occur periodically but are not part of regular monthly budgeting. Some examples of sinking funds you can set:

- Security deposit for a new apartment fund
- Vacation fund
- Back-to-school fund
- Holiday/birthday gift fund
- New car fund
- Down payment for a new home fund
- Insurance deductible fund
- Vet bill fund
- Bad Bunny concert tickets fund

Sinking funds are one of my favorite saving strategies. They allow you to plan and save for future expenses, reducing the need to rely on credit cards or loans when the time comes. By making regular contributions, you spread out the financial impact over time, making the expense more manageable. Sinking funds also promote financial discipline and help you prioritize your financial goals.

Before implementing sinking funds into my budget, I used to keep all my money in a single savings account. This made it almost impossible to see the progress I was making on different savings goals, like building my emergency fund or saving money for a cruise to Mexico. When you use sinking funds, you can literally watch your savings goals in real time.

To get an even bigger bang for your buck, use a high-yield savings account or a cash management account to save your dinero. A high-yield savings account, or HYSA, is a type of savings account offered by banks and financial institutions that typically offers a higher interest rate compared to traditional savings accounts. HYSA accounts are designed to help you earn more on your savings while maintaining easy access to your funds.

A cash management account (CMA) is a type of account that combines some features of checking and savings accounts, and is offered by brokerage firms and robo-advisors. It is designed for people with large cash holdings who want to keep their money safe but easily accessible. Cash management accounts offer much of the flexibility of checking accounts, which often don't pay interest, and they often pay higher interest rates than traditional checking and savings accounts at many banks and charge little to no fees.

## Some Cool Features of HYSAs and CMAs
### HYSA

- **Higher interest rates:** HYSAs generally offer higher interest rates compared to regular savings accounts, sometimes as high as 25 times the national average. The exact interest rate can vary at different banks and institutions, and it's important to compare rates to find the best option available. This is literally free money for keeping your funds at the bank. We love passive income!

- **FDIC insurance:** Like regular savings accounts, most HYSAs are FDIC-insured up to $250,000 per depositor, per bank. This means that even if the bank fails, your funds are protected by the Federal Deposit Insurance Corporation.

---

The Federal Deposit Insurance Corporation (FDIC) is an independent agency created by the Congress to maintain stability and public confidence in the nation's financial system. The FDIC insures deposits; examines and supervises financial institutions for safety, soundness, and consumer protection. The standard insurance amount is $250,000 per depositor, per insured bank, for each account ownership category. The FDIC provides tools, education, and news updates to help consumers make informed decisions and protect their assets. They also offer an Electronic Deposit Insurance Estimator (EDIE) that helps you calculate how much of your bank deposits are covered by FDIC deposit insurance and what portion of your funds (if any) exceeds the coverage limits. You can also use their BankFind Suite to search FDIC's records for information on insured banking institutions, including to verify if a company does have deposit insurance.

---

- **Easy access to funds:** HYSAs typically provide the flexibility to access your funds whenever needed. You can make withdrawals or transfers online, through ATMs, or by visiting a branch, depending on the bank's policies.
- **No minimum balance requirements:** Many HYSAs do not require a minimum balance, allowing you to open an

account and start earning interest with whatever amount you have available to deposit.

- **No or low fees:** Most HYSAs have no monthly maintenance fees. However, it's always advisable to review the terms and conditions to ensure you understand any potential fees associated with the account.
- **Online banking:** HYSAs are often offered by online banks or as part of online banking services. This allows for easy management of your account through online platforms, mobile apps, and electronic transfers.

I'm a big fan of Ally Bank, which offers savings buckets as a free feature of their online high-yield savings accounts.

## CMAs

- **Cash storage:** A CMA acts as a hub for your cash, allowing you to deposit and withdraw money as needed. It typically offers a higher interest rate than a regular checking account from a big bank, which usually doesn't pay any interest.
- **Investments:** Many CMAs offer the ability to invest in a range of financial products, including stocks, bonds, mutual funds, and exchange-traded funds (ETFs). This integration allows you to easily move funds between your cash balance and investment portfolio.
- **Check writing:** CMAs often come with the option to write checks from the account, which can be useful for paying bills, making large purchases, or simply accessing your funds.
- **Debit card:** Some CMAs provide a debit card that can be used for everyday spending, ATM withdrawals, and online purchases. The card is linked to your CMA's cash balance.

- **Bill pay services:** Many CMAs offer online bill payment services, allowing you to pay bills directly from your account. This can streamline your finances by consolidating bill payments in one place.
- **FDIC insurance:** If your CMA is held at a bank, the funds in the cash portion of the account are typically FDIC-insured up to certain limits, providing a level of security for your deposits.
- **Sweep accounts:** CMAs often have an automated feature called "sweep accounts" that moves excess cash from your CMA into higher-yielding investment options, helping you maximize your returns while keeping your funds readily accessible.
- **Financial planning tools:** Some CMAs provide financial planning tools and analytics to help you manage your finances effectively and make informed decisions.

Cash Management Accounts are a flexible and convenient way to manage your money, combining the features of a traditional checking or savings account with investment options. You can find them at major brokerage firms like Fidelity and Charles Schwab or robo-advisors like Betterment or Wealthfront.

## Be Mindful with Your Money

It's super easy to fall prey to the "tyranny of the shoulds." This ominous phrase was coined by psychoanalyst Karen Horney in the 1950s. She believed we split ourselves between our idealized self and our real self. We bounce between what we are and what we believe we "should be." We're forever beating ourselves up when we remember our failings, weaknesses, and foibles, bumping into the same "shoulds" like a fish in a bowl with a short memory. It's an eternal battle for perfection. Am I the only one feeling triggered here? Sheesh. This also applies to the beliefs you may have about what you should be doing with your money. I definitely fell victim to the shoulds when I decided to buy my first home, and I learned some very valuable yet expensive lessons because of it. We're told nonsensical things about money, like "being in debt is normal," "renting is a waste of money," "credit cards are dangerous," and "investing is only for rich people." This type of toxic money messaging can lead you to make all kinds of money mistakes, and I don't want that for you. That's why it's so important to learn about how money works, so you can be in the driver's seat.

## The Complicated World of Credit

My parents instilled the fear of God in me when it came to credit cards. They told me credit cards were the devil and never to get one, because they would, and I quote "definitely ruin my life." They rightfully had this opinion, as they got into debt early on in their marriage and ended up having to file for bankruptcy because of credit card debt. So when I got my first credit card at eighteen, I didn't tell them anything. I started using my credit card for very small bills, like my cell phone bill or for a quick grocery trip, as I was terrified to make a mistake, but looking back, there was no reason to be. I want to assure you: Credit cards are not the devil. When used responsibly, credit cards are actually pretty fucking awesome.

A credit card is a financial account that allows you to make purchases on credit, aka by borrowing money from a card issuer, often a bank, to acquire goods and services. The process of using a credit card begins with an application to a bank or credit card issuer, which assesses your financial history, income, and other factors to determine your creditworthiness. If approved, you receive a credit card with a predefined credit limit, which is the maximum amount you can borrow. When you make a purchase using the credit card, you essentially take a short-term loan from the card issuer to cover the transaction. Transactions made during a billing cycle, which generally lasts about a month, are recorded, and at the end of the cycle, you receive a statement summarizing your purchases, fees, and the minimum payment due. While you have the option to pay your bill in full, you can also choose to make a minimum payment, typically a small percentage of your outstanding balance. However, this is usually not advisable, as it can lead to high-interest charges and long-term debt. Interest charges, in the form of the Annual Percentage Rate (APR), apply to any balance carried beyond the billing cycle. Credit cards also typically offer a grace period during which interest charges can be avoided if the balance is paid in full by the due date.

Credit cards can give you access to some freakin' awesome perks. Common benefits include cashback rewards, where a percentage of your purchases is returned to you as cash or statement credits, providing a small discount on your overall spending. Many credit cards also offer rewards points or miles, which can be redeemed for travel, merchandise, or gift cards. Additionally, credit cards may provide purchase protection, extending warranties, and covering you against theft or damage for items bought with the card. Some cards offer introductory 0 percent APR periods, allowing you to make purchases or transfer balances without incurring interest for a specified time. Other perks can include travel benefits like airport lounge access, travel insurance, or rental car coverage. And as if that's not enough, credit cards often provide fraud protection, helping you avoid liability for unauthorized transactions.

I actually use credit cards for every purchase I make. I don't even touch my debit card unless I'm taking cash out of an ATM at this point. Thanks to credit card rewards, I've been able get free flights, hotel rooms, upgrades, and more. I'll never use cash to make a purchase unless I have to, but it's taken me years to get good at taking advantage of credit cards, instead of them taking advantage of me. Before becoming debt free in 2020, I used credit cards like most people do. I bought things I wanted, didn't make a plan for paying them off, and found myself constantly in and out of credit card debt. Now, I make sure I only spend what I can afford, my credit cards are on autopay, and I don't worry about paying interest, because they're being paid in full every month. Using credit to your advantage requires both discipline and knowledge, so let's talk about basic credit terminology that you've probably seen but have no idea WTF it means.

Let's start off with APR (Annual Percentage Rate) and APY (Annual Percentage Yield). These are both important financial terms used to represent the interest rate or return on financial products, but they are calculated and used differently.

## APR (Annual Percentage Rate):

APR is typically used to represent the interest rate on loans, credit cards, mortgages, and other borrowing products. APR represents the interest rate you'll pay or earn on a financial product over the course of a year, expressed as a percentage. It includes only the interest rate and any associated fees or costs required for obtaining the loan or credit, such as origination fees or points. APR does not take into account the effects of compounding, which means it assumes that interest is calculated only once at the beginning of the year (which isn't the case, more on that in a sec). APR is useful for comparing the cost of borrowing between different lenders or credit card offers.

## APY (Annual Percentage Yield):

APY is typically used to represent the interest rate on savings accounts, certificates of deposit (CDs), and other investment products. APY represents the effective annual interest rate you'll earn or pay on a financial product, taking into account compounding. It considers not only the interest rate but also how often that interest is compounded (e.g., monthly, quarterly, annually). APY reflects the actual growth or return on an investment over a year, considering both interest and the effects of compounding. It is always higher than the nominal interest rate, assuming interest is compounded.

APY helps investors or savers understand how much their money will grow or accumulate over time, taking into account compounding.

So to recap, APR is used for borrowing products and represents the interest rate and associated fees, while APY is used for investment and savings products and represents the effective interest rate that considers compounding. When comparing financial products or evaluating the cost of borrowing or the potential return on an investment, it's essential to consider both APR and APY to get a comprehensive understanding of the true cost or benefit.

Let's illustrate the difference between APR and APY in a simple savings account example:

### Scenario:

Imagine you have $1,000 to put in a savings account, and the bank offers the following two options:

### Option 1:

APR: 5%

Compounding: Annually (once a year)

### Option 2:

APY: 5%

Compounding: Quarterly (four times a year)

Now, let's calculate how much you would have in each account after one year.

### Option 1 (APR):

The APR is 5%, and it compounds annually.

So, after one year, you'd have:

$1,000 + (5% of $1,000) = $1,000 + $50 = $1,050

**Option 2 (APY):**

The APY is also 5%, but it compounds quarterly. This means that your interest is calculated and added to the balance four times during the year.

After the first quarter, you'd have $1,000 + (1 + .05/12) x 3 = $1,000 + ($4.17 x 3) = $1,012.50.

After the second quarter, you'd have $1,012.50 + (1 + .05/12) x 3 = $1,000 + ($4.22 x 3) = $1,025.16.

After the third quarter, you'd have $1,025.16 + (1 + .05/12) x 3 = $1,000 + ($4.27 x 3) = $1,037.97.

Finally, after the fourth quarter, you'd have $1,037.97 + (1 + .05/12) x 3 = $1,000 + ($4.32 x 3) = $1,050.95.

So, with Option 2 (APY), you would have $1,050.95 in your account after one year.

In this example, the difference between APR and APY becomes obvious when compounding is taken into account. Even though both options offer a 5% rate, the account with quarterly compounding (APY) yields more because it allows your money to earn interest on the interest it has already earned. APY reflects the actual growth of your money more accurately when compounding is involved.

Now, when we're talking about how your interest is calculated on a credit card, it's a bit different. Interest on a credit card is typically calculated using a method called the Average Daily Balance method. Here's how it works:

**Daily balance calculation:** First, the credit card company calculates your daily balance for each day in your billing cycle. They do this by adding up the outstanding balance on your card at the end of each day.

**Average daily balance:** After calculating the daily balances, they add them up for the entire billing cycle and then divide by the number of days in the billing cycle. This gives them the average daily balance.

**Daily periodic rate:** Next, they determine your daily periodic interest rate, which is your annual interest rate (APR) divided by the number of days in a year (usually 365).

**Interest Calculation:** Finally, they multiply your average daily balance by the daily periodic rate to calculate the daily interest charge. They sum up these daily interest charges to get the total interest for the billing cycle.

Here's a simplified example:

Let's say you have a credit card with an APR of 18%.

Your billing cycle is 30 days.

You started the month with a balance of $1,000.

First, they calculate the average daily balance:

(0 (day 1) + 10 (day 2) + ... + 1,000 (last day)) / 30 =

Average Daily Balance

Then, they calculate the daily periodic rate:

18% / 365 = Daily Periodic Rate

Finally, they calculate the interest for the billing cycle:

(Average Daily Balance) x (Daily Periodic Rate)

x (Number of days in the billing cycle)

So, in this example, if the average daily balance is $800, the daily periodic rate is approximately 0.0493% (0.18 / 365), and the billing cycle has 30 days, you would be charged around $11.84 in interest for that month.

It's important to note that credit card companies may use slightly different methods for interest calculations, and some may also offer a grace period during which no interest is charged if you pay your balance in full by the due date. Always check your credit card agreement or statement to understand the specific terms and conditions for interest calculation on your card.

A great way to avoid worrying about any of these calculations is to pay off your credit cards in full each month instead of paying the minimum payment. As long as you do that, how much your credit card charges in interest doesn't matter. If you can't afford to pay off the card in full each month, then I recommend using cash or your debit card instead. Credit card interest adds up quickly, so much so that you could end up paying almost as much interest as the thing you originally purchased. Let's see this in action.

Credit Card Balance: $2,000

Annual Interest Rate (APR): 27%

Minimum Payment: 3% of the balance or $25,

whichever is greater.

## Scenario 1: Paying Off in Full

If you decide to pay off the entire $2,000 credit card balance in full,

you won't incur any interest charges.

You'll simply owe $2,000.

## Scenario 2: Paying the Minimum Payment

If you choose to pay only the minimum payment,

which is 3% of the balance or $25 (whichever is greater),

here's how it would work:

### Month 1:

Starting Balance: $2,000

Minimum Payment: $60 (3% of $2,000)

Remaining Balance: $1,940 ($2,000 – $60)

Interest Charged: $45.50

(27% annual interest divided by 12 months)

**Month 2:**

Starting Balance: $1,940

Minimum Payment: $58.20 (3% of $1,940, since the

balance decreased)

Remaining Balance: $1,941.30 ($1,940 - $58.20)

Interest Charged: $45.28

This process continues each month with the minimum payment decreasing as the balance decreases. It would take approximately 4 years and 11 months to pay off the $2,000 debt, and you'd pay a total of around $1,827.42 in interest. Woof. This emphasizes the importance of managing credit card debt and paying it off as quickly as possible to avoid excessive interest charges.

## Understanding Your Credit Score

A credit score is a numerical representation of your creditworthiness and is used by lenders to assess the risk of lending to you. While specific credit scoring models may vary, the most widely used credit scoring model is the FICO score. FICO stands for Fair Isaac Corporation, the company that developed this scoring system. Your FICO credit score is made up of the following factors:

**Payment history (35%):** This is the most significant factor in your credit score. It assesses your history of making on-time payments for credit cards, loans, mortgages, and other debts. Late payments, defaults, and accounts sent to collections will negatively impact your score.

**Credit utilization (30%):** This factor evaluates how much of your available credit you are using. It's calculated by dividing your credit card

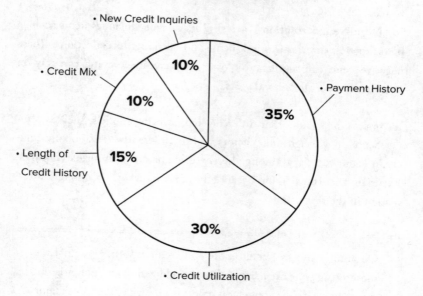

## % of Credit Score

- New Credit Inquiries — 10%
- Credit Mix — 10%
- Length of Credit History — 15%
- Payment History — 35%
- Credit Utilization — 30%

balances by your credit card limits. It's essential to keep your credit utilization low, ideally below 30% of your available credit.

**Length of credit history (15%):** This considers the age of your credit accounts. A longer credit history can have a positive impact on your score. It takes into account the age of your oldest account, the average age of all your accounts, and the age of your newest account.

**Credit mix (10%):** Credit scoring models like to see a diverse mix of credit accounts, such as credit cards, installment loans (like auto loans or personal loans), and mortgages. Having a mix of credit types can be beneficial if managed responsibly.

**New credit inquiries (10%):** Each time you apply for new credit, a hard inquiry is placed on your credit report. Multiple recent inquiries can suggest higher risk and negatively impact your score. Soft inquiries, like those from checking your own credit or pre-approval offers, do not affect your score.

**Negative information (varies):** This category includes items such as bankruptcies, foreclosures, tax liens, and accounts in collections. These negative items can significantly lower your credit score and can stay on your credit report for several years.

It's important to note that different credit scoring models, such as VantageScore, may weigh these factors slightly differently. Additionally, your credit score can vary among the three major credit bureaus (Equifax, Experian, and TransUnion) because they may have slightly different information in their reports.

---

Obtaining your free credit score and credit report is essential for monitoring your financial health and addressing any potential issues. You can access your credit report from each of the three major credit bureaus (Equifax, Experian, and TransUnion) for free once a year, thanks to the Fair Credit Reporting Act (FCRA). Here's how to get your free credit score and report:

**AnnualCreditReport.com:** The most straightforward way to get your free credit report is through AnnualCreditReport.com, the official website authorized by the US government. It's the only website that provides free annual credit reports from all three major credit bureaus. Here's what you need to do:

Visit AnnualCreditReport.com.
Click on "Request your free credit reports."
Fill out the required information, including your name, address, Social Security number, and date of birth.

Select the credit bureaus (Equifax, Experian, and TransUnion) from which you want to request reports. You can choose to get all three reports at once or stagger them throughout the year.

Complete any additional verification steps as prompted.

Review and save or print your credit reports for your records.

**Through Each Credit Bureau:** Alternatively, you can request your free credit report directly from each credit bureau's website. Keep in mind that this method allows you to access one report at a time, so you may want to stagger your requests every few months to monitor your credit throughout the year. Here's how to do it:

**Equifax:** Visit the Equifax website (www.equifax.com) and navigate to the "Free Credit Report" section. Follow the prompts to request your free report.

**Experian:** Go to the Experian website (www.experian.com) and click on "Free Credit Report." Follow the instructions to obtain your report.

**TransUnion:** Visit the TransUnion website (www.transunion .com) and locate the "Get Your Free Credit Score" section. You can request your free report from there.

**Credit Monitoring Services:** Some credit monitoring services and financial apps offer access to your credit score and report for free. While these services often provide your credit information, they may also offer additional features and credit-related tools. Be sure to review the terms and conditions to understand any potential limitations.

**Credit Card Statements:** Some credit card issuers provide free access to your credit score on your monthly statements or through your online account. Check with your credit card company to see if this service is available.

Remember that you're entitled to one free credit report from each of the three major credit bureaus once every twelve months. Regularly reviewing your credit reports is an essential part of monitoring your financial health and detecting any errors or fraudulent activity.

To maintain and improve your credit score, focus on making on-time payments, keeping your credit card balances low, and avoiding excessive new credit applications. Regularly monitoring your credit reports for errors and inaccuracies is also essential, as inaccuracies can negatively affect your score. Finally, remember that building and maintaining good credit takes time, so be patient and responsible with your credit management.

Being mindful of your credit is so important due to its profound impact on your financial well-being and future prospects. First, it grants you access to a multitude of financial opportunities, ranging from loans and credit cards to mortgages and favorable interest rates. A strong credit history serves as a financial passport, making significant life events like homeownership, entrepreneurship, and higher education more affordable. Moreover, it plays a pivotal role in reducing borrowing costs, as lenders assess the risk of lending to you based on your credit score. A high credit score translates to lower interest rates, potentially saving you substantial sums over time.

Beyond borrowing, your credit health extends its influence into various aspects of life. It can sway rental applications, making it easier to secure that new waterfront apartment you've been eyeing, while poor credit may lead to rejections or higher security deposits. Your employment opportunities may also be affected, as some employers conduct credit checks, particularly for roles involving financial responsibilities. Furthermore, how much you pay for insurance premiums, utilities, and even your cell phone bill can be impacted by your credit profile. Lastly, maintaining good credit is crucial for realizing your long-term financial goals, such as homeownership, retirement savings, and entrepreneurial endeavors. Being vigilant about your credit can help you detect identity theft or fraudulent activity, safeguarding your financial reputation.

Being mindful of your credit involves a conscientious approach to managing your financial health and creditworthiness. It begins with regular monitoring of your credit reports from the major credit bureaus, ensuring that the information is accurate, and promptly addressing any errors or signs of fraud.

Paying your bills on time is critical, as your payment history significantly influences your credit score. To avoid negative consequences, consider setting up reminders or automatic payments. Additionally, managing your credit utilization by keeping credit card balances low relative to your credit limits is essential for maintaining a healthy credit profile.

Exercise caution when taking on new debt, only borrowing what you can afford to pay off in full. It's wise to steer clear of opening multiple new credit accounts in a short span, which can raise concerns among lenders. Routinely reviewing your credit statements helps you spot inaccuracies or unauthorized transactions, ensuring that your financial records remain reliable. Building an emergency fund is another key aspect of credit mindfulness, serving as a financial safety net and reducing the need for credit in emergencies.

In cases where you require guidance on improving your credit or face financial challenges, seeking advice from certified credit counselors is a solid move. You can find certified credit counselors through several reputable sources and organizations.

- **National Foundation for Credit Counseling (NFCC):** NFCC is a nonprofit organization that connects consumers with accredited and certified credit counseling agencies across the United States. You can visit their website (www.nfcc.org) and use their locator tool to find a nearby NFCC member agency.
- **Financial Counseling Association of America (FCAA):** FCAA is another nonprofit organization that provides a directory of certified credit counselors and financial counselors. Their website (www.fcaa.org) allows you to search for counselors by location.

Practicing self-discipline and patience in your financial life is probably the best advice I can give you when it comes to managing your credit (and your money in general). Remember that your personal finance journey is a marathon, not a sprint and you're going to make mistakes along the way. The key is to learn from those mistakes, stay committed to your goals, and make steady progress over time. So, amiga, work on keeping that credit score high and that debt low and you'll be well on your way to being a financial baddie.

## The Hidden Costs of Homeownership

There are so many hidden costs that come with homeownership that I was *not* ready for when I bought my first house, and if you're not prepared for a major financial decision like this one, you can quickly find yourself swimming in debt and hating your life. When the toilet starts flooding, you can't call your landlord. I don't know about you, but I have no interest in becoming an amateur plumber...or electrician, or roof installer. On the other hand, owning a home means that you control rent increases. If you rent, your landlord can raise your rent, sometimes by a lot, when your lease is up. Whereas if you own, and have a fixed-rate mortgage, you will be happy that your monthly payment won't increase as much in the long term (although they will still go up due to things like increases in property taxes and insurance rates). Regardless, it's important to be prepared for what your costs will be when you own. Here are a few to consider:

- Property insurance: On a $350,000 home, this can range from $800 to $2,500+ per year. If you live in an area with a high risk of natural disasters like hurricanes or tornadoes, expect to pay higher rates.[1]
- Property tax: The median property tax ranges from about

---

1. https://www.forbes.com/advisor/homeowners-insurance/average-cost-homeowners-insurance/.

$650 in Alabama (lowest) to over $8,700 in New Jersey (highest).[1] (This fluctuates based on state law—some change them annually, while others do so in different increments, such as once every five years.)

- Repairs and maintenance, 1–2% of the purchase price of your home. Ex: if you paid $300,000 for your home, you should budget $3,000–6,000 for annual maintenance and repair costs.
- Changes in laws, ordinances, and building codes
- Capital gains (difference between the purchase price and the selling price, aka the taxable profit you make after selling your home)
- Fees (legal, tenant screening, accounting, property management, etc.)
- Vacancy costs
- Accidents and emergency repairs
- The biggest cost: your time!

While I'm grateful that I was able to purchase my first real estate investment, my experience taught me I was not ready for the landlord life at that stage financially, or emotionally. Back then, I couldn't afford to shell out thousands of dollars to fix a broken air conditioner or repair a roof. I've gone back to renting because during this time of my life, I value being able to move within thirty days and not having to worry about what's going to happen to my home. After living in apartments for my whole adult life, I choose to rent a single-family home because I want the experience of living in a home without the long-term commitment, and because I value peace and quiet and don't want to deal with the lack of privacy that comes with having tenants living in the same house as me. More than anything, right now, I value the freedom of

---

1. https://www.forbes.com/sites/andrewdepietro/2023/09/01/property-taxes-by-state-a-break down-of-the-highest-and-lowest-property-taxes-by-state/?sh=.

renting my primary home, because I'm not quite sure where and when I want to settle down.

One of my favorite personal finance educators, Ramit Sethi, is an avid fan of debunking the biggest "myths" of homeownership. "Homeownership is an expensive investment that shouldn't be taken lightly, yet the idea that property is always a great investment has become a 'religion' in the US," he says.

Dasha Kennedy, financial activist and founder of the educational platform Broke Black Girl, echoes this experience: "A lot of people push the idea of buying a home.[1] But for ten years, I stayed in a very small two-bedroom apartment, even when I could afford to move. I didn't leave until it absolutely made sense. And when I did move, I chose to rent again. As a single mom, raising two sons on my own, I value flexibility. I'm very open about that, because homeownership is not something that you have to buy into. Renting makes sense for me, and for a lot of people it is a good and safe option."

"For many people, buying simply doesn't make sense, especially now, when the price of housing has gone way up and the effect—especially on young people, people without money, minorities—is to make them feel that they are failures," Sethi says. "You're not a failure if you rent." Thank you, Ramit!

## THINK TWICE BEFORE GOING FOR ADDITIONAL CREDS

Another area where people sometimes get caught up in **shoulds** versus **wants** is getting an advanced degree. A 2019 report from PayScale found that overall, roughly two-thirds of people with advanced degrees reported feeling regrets related to college. These degree-earners had high degrees of stress, especially millennials.

---

1. https://www.thecut.com/2022/09/what-if-i-never-own-a-home.html.

Most felt regret about their student loans. While 24.6% of those who earned bachelor's degrees regretted their student loans, that percentage jumped to 31.5% of those with a master's or doctorate degree. Those with non-MBA master's degrees reported the highest response rate in this category: 33.3%. Talk about an expensive lesson to learn!

## You Do You

Mujer, it's nobody's business but yours what you do with your money. It's up to YOU to define your financial priorities. Before making a big money decision like buying a house, or getting another degree, take some time to pause and reflect on your core values. Ask yourself questions like:

*Do I truly need this?*
*Do I actually want this, or do my parents/friends/loved ones want this for me?*
*Will it bring long-term value or happiness?*
*Does it align with my values and financial goals?*

Taking this pause allows you to evaluate your motivations and make more-intentional choices.

### Understanding the True Cost

Practicing delayed gratification is another way to avoid wrecking your budget. Resist the temptation of impulsive buying by giving yourself a cooling-off period. Delay gratification and wait at least twenty-four hours before making a purchase, particularly for non-essential items. If you're thinking of making a bigger purchase, like a home or a car, take the time to fully understand the true cost of ownership. This involves looking beyond the initial purchase price of an item and considering all the expenses associated with owning and maintaining it over its lifetime. By doing this exercise, you gain a more comprehensive understanding of the expenses associated with owning and maintaining an item. This allows you to make informed purchasing decisions, budget effectively, and plan for long-term expenses.

Here's a step-by-step process to help you calculate the true cost of ownership:

1. **Identify the item:** Start by identifying the specific item you want to evaluate. This could be a car, a home, an appliance, or any other significant purchase.

2. **Initial purchase price:** Determine the initial purchase price of the item. This is the amount you pay up front to acquire it. If you're considering a used item, include any additional costs such as taxes, registration fees, or delivery charges.

3. **Calculate financing costs:** If you're financing the purchase, consider the interest charges and any additional fees associated with the loan. Use loan calculators or consult with financial institutions to estimate the total cost of financing. For example: You purchase a car for $25,000 with a loan that has an 8% interest rate and a repayment term of 60 months. Over those five years, you will pay $5,414.59 in interest, so the total cost of the loan is actually $30,414.59.

4. **Maintenance and repairs:** Estimate the ongoing maintenance and repair costs over the expected life span of the item. Consider routine maintenance expenses like oil changes, tune-ups, inspections, or software updates. Also, account for potential repair costs that may arise due to wear and tear or unexpected breakdowns.

5. **Insurance:** Determine the cost of insurance required to protect the item. This could include auto insurance for a car, home-

owner's insurance for a house, or warranty coverage for electronic devices. Obtain insurance quotes or consult with insurance providers to estimate the annual or monthly premiums.

6. **Fuel or energy costs:** For items that require ongoing fuel or energy consumption, such as vehicles or household appliances, calculate the average fuel or energy costs. Consider factors like fuel efficiency, energy ratings, and prevailing prices of fuel or electricity in your area.

7. **Depreciation:** Evaluate the potential depreciation of the item over time. Research historical data or consult experts to estimate the average depreciation rate for the specific item. Depreciation is particularly relevant for assets like vehicles, electronics, or certain equipment.

8. **Resale or salvage value:** Estimate the potential resale or salvage value of the item at the end of its useful life. This applies primarily to items that can retain some value after use. Factors such as condition, market demand, and depreciation rates influence the resale or salvage value.

9. **Sum up the costs:** Add up all the costs determined in the previous steps—initial purchase price, financing costs, maintenance and repairs, insurance, fuel or energy costs, depreciation, and potential resale or salvage value. This sum represents the true cost of ownership over the item's life span.

10. **Compare alternatives:** If you're considering multiple options, repeat the above steps for each item and compare the true cost of ownership. This comparison can help you make informed decisions and choose the option that best aligns with your financial goals and budget.

Being mindful with your money also involves reflecting on what you have, instead of focusing on what you don't. Cultivating a sense of gratitude for what you already have can take you far. Instead of dwelling on what you lack or what you wish you had, focus on what you do have. Recognize the abundance of resources, opportunities, and experiences that are already present in your financial life. Embracing gratitude and contentment can help you curb unnecessary spending driven by a constant desire for more. (For more on this, revisit chapter 1!)

## When You're Ready to Turn Your Dreams into Reality

After getting really clear on my value-based spending beliefs, I took the plunge into property ownership again in 2022, but this time, I did it on my terms. I've always dreamed of owning property in Puerto Rico, and I was able to do it after saving up enough money to purchase a dreamy oceanfront condo. Until now, I never would have imagined that I could own property on my beloved island. Unlike my first foray into property ownership, where I let the pressure to "stop wasting money on rent" be my driving factor, this time around, I allowed myself to get clear on what I wanted, setting my intention and practicing patience rather than desperation. I trusted that the right property would come to me at the right time, and that's exactly how it happened.

A few days before flying to Puerto Rico for my annual solo trip, my real estate agent on the island sent me a property that was not yet listed. The owners were ready to sell, and she was able to convince them to wait until I got to Puerto Rico before listing the condo publicly. I saw the property and instantly fell in love, made the offer, and had the keys to my dream vacation home nine days later! Talk about manifesting your dreams, mi gente! Sometimes we rush into our "dreams" when a bigger/better dream will become real if we slow down instead. Practicing value-based spending helped me become a proud Puerto Rican property owner! Mind you, I'm still renting my primary home—so yes, you can have investment properties and still choose to rent.

Before you spend your dinero, it's critical to be sure that the decision aligns with your personal values. Don't let society, friends, or family tell you what you should be doing with your money. There's nothing wrong with renting, or right about owning. There's nothing wrong with skipping a big wedding to elope in Vegas, or spending $100,000 on the nuptials of your dreams. There's nothing wrong with living in a huge mansion or a tiny house. There's nothing wrong with choosing to be child-free, or having a bunch of babies! Those are simply opinions, everyone's gonna have one. The one that matters? Yours, and yours alone. Decide what works best for your lifestyle, what you value, what you can afford—and do what feels right.

# Knowing Your (Net) Worth

One of the biggest mistakes I made was buying a house without understanding the overall impact that this decision would have on my finances. Homeownership was always a smart thing to do, according to my Latino parents, who never explained to me how interest works or how to determine what you could afford (probably because they had no idea how this works, even though they bought a home!). I remember my parents saying they were sweating bullets when they signed their mortgage paperwork, and prayed to God that they'd always be able to afford the monthly payment. I assumed that since I could afford the mortgage, that was the only information I needed to consider, but I quickly realized how wrong I was. When it comes to making good financial choices, we need to know where we stand. That starts with knowing your net worth.

### What Is Net Worth?

Your net worth is the total value of all your assets, after you deduct your liabilities. **Assets** are things that you can cash in, such as cash accounts, property, and investment accounts. **Liabilities** include credit card debt, personal loans, car loans, and mortgages, to name a few. If you have a *positive* net worth, it means your assets outperform or outweigh your liabilities. If your net worth is *negative*, your debt is higher than your assets combined.

### How to Calculate Your Net Worth

If the idea of doing math stresses you out, don't worry! Calculating your net worth is actually really simple.

$$\text{Assets} - \text{Liabilities} = \text{Net Worth}$$

Assets are anything of value, such as:
- Cash or cash equivalents
- Real estate
- Vehicles
- Businesses you own or have an ownership interest in
- Investments (stocks, bonds, cryptocurrency)
- Jewelry, art, or other collectibles

Liabilities are anything that you owe, such as:
- Loans (car, student, personal, medical, etc.)
- Credit cards or other lines of credit
- Mortgages
- Legal or tax debt

To calculate your net worth, you'll have to check your current bank and creditor statements for all your existing accounts. You can calculate your net worth manually by creating a spreadsheet, or you can download the free net worth calculation tool available at **yoquierodineropodcast .com/networth**.

If you prefer a more automatic way of tracking your net worth, there are many tools online, such as Empower, that will track and manage your net worth for you. The simplicity of this tool is that it allows you to safely link your accounts, including checking, savings, credit, loan, and retirement accounts. It removes the work of checking each of your accounts routinely. Instead, it is updated in real time to show you what your net worth is at any given time.

Your net worth takes into consideration all your resources and all your financial commitments or constraints (past, present, and perhaps even future). It helps you understand your financial strengths and weaknesses, identify areas that need improvement, and make informed decisions about budgeting, investing, and managing debt. With a clear understanding of your net worth, you can develop a comprehensive financial plan to achieve your short-term and long-term financial goals.

Whether your goal is to buy a house within the next three years, start building up your kids' college fund, or take a big vacation for a milestone birthday, having a complete picture of your financial standing will allow you to meet each of your goals seamlessly. Having this data over time also allows you to decide if your past money behavior is in line with what you'd like your future money behavior to look like. Net worth is key to goal-setting; it tells you if your goal is either too small or not yet achievable. Who knew you could get so much insight from a simple calculation!

Let's say you have $30,000 in student loans. You started investing this year and have maxed out your 401(k) at $22,500. You've been able to build up a cash emergency fund of $10,000. You are renting in an area with a high cost of living and want to purchase a home in the next year.

**Assets:** $10,000 cash savings + $22,500 401(k) = $32,500 total
**Liabilities:** $30,000 student loans
**Net worth:** $32,500 – $30,000 = **$2,500**

By periodically tracking your net worth, you can assess whether your financial strategies and decisions are effective. If your net worth is not growing as desired, it may indicate a need to reassess your financial habits, increase savings, reduce debt, or make changes to your investment approach. Regularly reviewing your net worth allows you to make adjustments and course corrections as needed.

I think we can agree that budgeting is the least sexy word in the English language, but it also happens to be the ultimate weapon to slay your financial goals. Despite the bad rap, budgeting is the secret weapon that will help you manage your money like a boss and achieve financial freedom. With a budget in hand, you become a money ninja, fully aware of every single dollar that flows in and out of your life. No more reckless spending or drowning in debt! A budget helps you take control of your finances like a queen, making sure you live within your means and avoid the dreaded overspending trap.

But that's not all! Budgeting lets you kick those debt monsters to the curb so you can get debt-free faster and focus on building wealth. You'll stash away money faster, building a fortress of savings for those rainy days and future dreams. Want that luxury vacation? You got it! Dreaming of launching your own business? Budgeting will make it happen. It's like having a magic money madrina granting your financial wishes!

Say goodbye to financial stress because you'll be strutting around with your budget plan. When life throws a curveball, you'll handle it with grace. No more guessing games with your money. Thanks to your budget, you'll be able to make strategic decisions like a champ. Budgeting is the foundation on which you will build your financial empire. Get ready meet your money goals and live your best life because with a budget, you'll be unstoppable!

# CHAPTER 5

# Sis, You Need a Side Hustle

I f you have a single income source, like a regular W-2 job, you're potentially one step away from a financial calamity. It sounds dramatic, but it's true. I found this out the hard way. I've been fired exactly one time in my entire life, and the experience taught me the importance of never relying on a single way of earning a living. It was a cold Monday morning in January 2014. Forecasters were predicting a blizzard, but my employer decided to wait and see before telling folks they could work from home that day.

For some reason, which I can only suspect was divine intuition, I checked my email before heading into the office—something I rarely did. I noticed a random meeting invite was sent to me on Saturday for a Monday morning meeting at nine o'clock. I thought, *Hmm, that's odd*. When I looked at the invite list, it was my manager and someone I'd never met before. When I looked up her job title, I saw she was in human resources. *Oh shit*. I knew this wasn't gonna end well.

I arrived at work, set down my things, and proceeded to the meeting, where I was swiftly presented with a severance package, some spiel about my position being eliminated, and a gracious thirty-minute timeline to pack my belongings while my ex-manager watched to make sure I didn't steal anything and vacate the premises. It was quite the out-of-body experience, and the icing on the cake was the ensuing blizzard that turned my normal forty-five-minute commute into a three-hour ordeal. When I got home, reality hit me. The severance package was enough to last three months, maybe four. The job market was still recovering years after the Great Recession. My skill set was specialized, so it would probably take me a while to find an equivalent position. WTF was I going to do?

That day, I decided I'd never allow myself to be in that position again. I decided to focus my full attention on a project I'd begun about six months earlier. Feeling exasperated with my career in general, I had started a food blog, DelishDlites.com, as a passion project. I've always been a foodie, and I've been known to travel just for food. My sorority sister Paola and I have traveled to San Francisco to eat sourdough bread and cioppino, New Orleans for gumbo and charbroiled oysters, and Portland, Maine, to taste lobster rolls and seafood chowder. This love for cooking and eating was the reason that I dove headfirst into my food blog, which would later become my first side hustle. This side hustle helped me pay off $39,000 of student loan debt in seventeen months. This side hustle helped me pay off $10,000 of credit card debt in less than a year. This side hustle helped me max out my 401(k) contribution for the first time and invest enough money to become financially independent by the time I was thirty-five. This side hustle helped me quit my job and generate over $100,000 in passive income in a single year. I hope this convinces you: Side hustles are the way to ensure you never allow a job to derail your financial future. In a world where women are paid less, we can use the power of side hustles to earn more.

Amiga, you're probably not getting paid enough. Thanks to systemic racism, gender biases in hiring, the exploitative nature of capitalism, and that ever-present bitch known as the pay gap, Latinas are making about half of what a white guy earns. Sucks, doesn't it? Studies show it will take 136 years to bridge the wage gap. We literally can't afford to wait to reclaim our earning power. While I'd love for us to live in a world where equal pay is a given, our wallets can't wait for politicians, talking heads, or corporate CEOs to give a damn about paying mujeres our worth. Yes, we can fight for higher wages and pay transparency, but until those things become a reality, you need to take matters into your own hands. And that starts by becoming your own money printer.

Maribel Francisco, immigrant money coach and founder of the educational platform Our Wealth Matters, told me that her mother came to the United States from Mexico and found work as a seamstress. One day someone told her, "You're always going to be a seamstress." So Maribel's mom decided she needed a side hustle, went to H&R Block to get trained as an income tax preparer, and after a couple years working for them, set up her own practice. Once Maribel turned eighteen, she also became a certified income tax preparer, and started helping her mom with the business on weekends.

No one is coming to save us, and if you ask me, corporate America doesn't have much of an incentive to pay you what you're worth either. They just want access to your skills for the lowest price possible. If you really think about it, an employer is a talent broker. They're an organization that connects you (who has certain skills) with an opportunity to use those skills to make money (a job). In exchange for giving you that opportunity, they turn your skills into a profit, and give you a small slice to keep you around. But what if you got rid of the middleman, started charging for the true value of your skills, and sold those skills directly to your customer? That's the gist of entrepreneurship, and it can start with a side gig. The most immediate way to put more dinero in your pocket right now is by creating it yourself by increasing your income with a side hustle.

## What Is a Side Hustle, Really?

My definition of a side hustle is something you do outside of your 9-to-5 job that brings you personal satisfaction, capitalizes on your high-value skills, and makes you extra income.

The personal satisfaction part is key. If you're doing something you don't enjoy for extra money, it's more likely a dead-end part-time job, and who has time to spend after working over forty hours a week on something you don't even enjoy? Unlike your day job, your side hustle should be something that you're excited AF to work on. It's an opportunity for you to experiment with being your own jefa without the pressure to build a full-time business right away. A side hustle is an excellent opportunity for you to:

- serve as a subject matter expert in an area that you don't get to use in your day job.
- leverage your existing professional skills to create your own consulting business.

When I first started side hustling, it was because I wanted to do something completely different from my super analytical career as an engineer. I love cooking, and so I started to dabble with different side hustles that I could do in the evenings and on weekends. I tried my hand at becoming a personal chef and catered a couple of small events by offering my services to some sorority sisters. The work was fun but the hours were grueling, and it didn't allow me to work from home, which is something I really wanted. Two gigs were enough for me to realize that being a personal chef was not something I wanted to pursue further.

That led me to the world of food blogging, and I instantly knew that this was the perfect side gig for me. I could share my passion for cooking and food and create content online from the comfort of my own casita. I started slowly, figuring out what kind of content I wanted to create and how to build an audience that would eventually turn this passion project into a successful six-figure business.

## My Side Hustle Timeline

**May 29, 2013**—$0: Started my food blog *Delish D'Lites*.

**January 2014**—$0: Started taking it seriously; invested in a food blogging workshop at a local culinary school ($90).

**April 2014**—$0: Went back to another engineering job, kept working on my food blog after hours. Continued refining my content and the quality of my work, focused on building my portfolio, and launched a website.

**2016**—$2,295: First real earnings from my blog. I was hooked at this point!

**2017**—$10,589: My first five-figure year! I also started diversifying my income streams to include affiliate marketing and sponsored content creation.

**2018**—$21,860: Finding my rhythm! I started using this extra money to pay down my student loan debt.

**2019**—$46,033: The blog income keeps growing. This is the year I launched *Yo Quiero Dinero*.

**2020—$101,000:** Between *Delish D'Lites* and *Yo Quiero Dinero*, I'm officially a six-figure side hustler! This year I was able to pay off all my debt, thanks to side hustles.

**2021—$443,000:** I became financially independent, quit my job, and became a full-time business owner.

**2022—**My businesses have officially hit the half-million-dollar mark in annual revenue, and I've been able to hire my sister and mom. Entrepreneurship has allowed me to achieve incredible financial milestones and create real generational wealth, and it all started with a side hustle and a dream.

## My Six-Figure Side Hustle Secrets

Did you know that starting your own business is the fastest path to becoming a millionaire? In 2024, money expert Tom Corley set out to find out how millionaires become millionaires. His findings are fascinating! He spent five years interviewing and researching the daily activities, habits, and traits of 233 wealthy individuals.

Each of the 225 millionaires Corley interviewed fell into one of four categories:

**Saver-Investors:** No matter what their day job is, they make saving and investing part of their daily routine. They are constantly thinking about smart ways to grow their wealth.

**Company Climbers:** Climbers work for a large company and devote all of their time and energy to climbing the corporate ladder until they land a senior executive position—with an extremely high salary.

**Virtuosos:** They are among the best at what they do, and they're paid a high premium for their knowledge and expertise. Formal education, such as advanced degrees (e.g., in law or medicine), is usually a requirement.

**Dreamers:** The individuals in this group are all in pursuit of a dream, such as starting their own business, becoming a successful actor, musician, or best-selling author. Dreamers love what they do for a living, and their passion shows up in their bank accounts.

Guess which group became millionaires fastest? If you guessed the dreamers, you'd be right. About 28% of the individuals in the study were Dreamers. They had an average net worth of $7.4 million—far more than any other group in my study—and they were able to accumulate that wealth over a period of roughly 12 years, faster than any other group. The Dreamers path, however, also happens to be the hardest, riskiest, and most stressful one. I want to keep it real with you…cracking the code to entrepreneurship takes time and work, but when you get it right, it can totally change your life, just like it changed mine.

But how do you actually begin? Let's get into it.

## 1. Find Your Secret Sazón (aka Identify Your Skills and Areas of Interest)

Your business will only be sustainable for the long term if it is centered around something you love to do and something you're good at. So what are you good at? What do you love to do? Start by making a list of the professional and personal skills that you've picked up along the way in your life. Your side hustle idea will likely come from one of those lists.

What are those topics that people always ask you about?
- Are you the person that everyone looks to for the latest fashion trends and how to style their wardrobe?
- Are you the go-to foodie in your friend circle who always gets asked for restaurant recommendations?
- Do people scan your travel pics on Insta and slide into your DMs asking for trip itineraries?
- Are you the uber-organized friend who lives for Pinterest-worthy pantry labeling?

Those things you think aren't valuable skills actually ARE! Think about all the services and products you pay for. *Someone* created those things. And so now, it's your turn to find your sazón, that secret something—something that you do oh so well. You may well be able to turn it into some money-making magic.

Maybe you work in a bank in customer service, but dream of one day having your own certified financial planning firm where you can help mujeres get their coins and plan their financial future. In some cases, your side hustle may require formal credentials, certifications, and/or a license to practice. Find out what knowledge and credentials you will need to pursue your side hustles. If you find that you currently lack the skills you'd like to monetize, now's the time to learn them.

There are so many potential side hustles you can begin, so if you're still stuck, here's a list of twenty side hustles to begin exploring—maybe one in particular speaks to you, and if not, find a few more at my website, yoquierodineropodcast.com/blog.

| | | |
|---|---|---|
| Copywriter | Project Manager | Career Coach |
| Editor | Musician | Beauty |
| Data Analyst | Business Coach | Consultant |
| Content Marketer | Marketing | Investment Coach |
| Graphic Designer | Consultant | App Developer |
| Illustrator | Life Coach | |
| Web Designer | Social Media | |
| Photographer | Consultant | |
| Videographer | Fitness Instructor | |
| Transcriber | Leadership Coach | |
| Book Reviewer | Family Coach | |

## 2. Get Ya Mind Right (aka Work On Your Mindset)

Amiga, starting a business is scary AF. And that's exactly what you're doing when you create a side hustle. So before we talk about choosing your business name and designing your logo, we have to tackle the biggest thing you'll face…those shitty thoughts that start to show up whenever we decide to do something new. You'll inevitably start thinking thoughts that go something like this:

- I'm a freakin' fraud and there's no way I'm qualified to start a business.
- Why would anyone pay *me* to provide a product or service to them?
- This is stupid / no one cares / no one will ever pay me for my time or skills.

I'm willing to bet one or more of the above ideas came to mind as soon as you started reading this chapter. The biggest obstacle you will face when starting a side hustle is getting past the limiting beliefs you may have about your abilities and/or your business idea. Maybe you think the market is oversaturated and there's no way you'll ever be able to stand out. Maybe you have fears around asking people to pay you for your services. Maybe you just don't have faith that you have what it takes to pull it off. Fear is expected, but you have to push past it and start. The first step is asking yourself, "How badly do I want to succeed?"

If the answer is anything other than "LET'S DO THIS!" then you might not be ready for this yet (and that's OK). Relax—being scared about putting yourself out there is totally normal! Doing scary shit is, well…scary! The beauty is that you can feel the fear, acknowledge its presence, and do it anyway. But getting past your fears will take some work.

If fear is holding you back, it's time to do some serious self-assessment about whether or not this is something you're willing to make sacrifices for in order to achieve. These sacrifices will include time, money, and energy. One question to ask yourself: Am I excited about how my daily life might look once the business is up and running? In other words, is there excitement mixed in with your fears? Try focusing on letting the excitement push you forward. It might also be a good idea to talk to other women who have started their own businesses—bonus points if their product or service is similar to yours. What have their experiences been? Are they happy that they took the leap? Once you have your answers to these questions, you'll know if you have to continue working through your fears, or if you're ready to proceed to step 3.

### 3. Show Me the Money (aka Conduct Market Research and Validate Your Offer)

A successful business offers a valuable solution to a unique problem. Think about the businesses you're a consumer of: What problem do they solve for you? Amazon allows me to avoid leaving my house and have unnecessary human interaction, and that's why I'm a loyal customer. You have to figure out what problem your business is going to solve; this becomes important when you think about how to begin marketing yourself.

Next, you must perform market research. This starts by identifying your potential competitors.

- Who are they?
  * Make a list of five to ten competitors who stand out to you and who inspire you.
- How long have they been in business?
  * Find out as much as you can about them by visiting their brick and mortar spaces, talking to consumers of their product, or just finding out as much as you can about them.
- What are they selling and for how much?
  * Take a look at their product offers and price points to get an idea of where you can begin to set your own prices.
- How do they market themselves?
  * Scope out their website, social media, podcast, blog, etc. Do they offer freebies, use paid ads, text, or email marketing?
- What are people saying about them?
  * Look for clues in their social media comments, reviews, testimonials, and other customer-driven feedback.

Once you know what problem you're solving and how others have carved out their place in your niche, it's time for you to determine who your ideal client is. Start talking to people to get a sense of who you can best serve with your skills.

You can start by doing a survey of your network or polling strangers on the internet in Facebook groups, Reddit threads, or other online forums. Some important questions to ask include:

- Demographics: age, geographical location, ethnic background, gender identity, occupation, life stage
- Pain Points: What problems are they currently struggling with and how will your solution help them? How would their life change by investing in your offer?
- Where to Reach Them: Do they read blogs or listen to podcasts? Do they hang out on TikTok or Pinterest?
- Willingness to Invest: Are they currently paying for help in this area and not getting what they need? If so, what's missing? If they're not currently investing to fix the problem, how come? What are they looking for from the proposed solution?

It may sound like a lot of work (and it is), but who said starting a business was easy? If we're going to do this, let's do it right. All of this upfront research will ensure that you're not creating a solution to a problem that doesn't really exist.

Once you've secured your first clients, make sure to get feedback! Testimonials are such an important way for you to build trust and authority as you grow your brand. You can use surveys, emails, Google forms, or even social media DMs to gather feedback from your clients to bolster your brand.

## 4. Own Your Special Sabor (aka Differentiate Yourself from Competitors)

Once you start doing some market research, you may begin to believe that the market you're looking to enter is supersaturated and there's no way in hell you can possibly stand out. This is common, but I want you to ponder this: Contrary to popular belief, no one can do what you do in the way that you do it. Imagine if Bad Bunny said, "I'm not gonna pursue a music career cuz there's already too many música urbana artists from Puerto Rico." Sounds ridiculous, right?

You are one of one, a divinely gifted human with a unique personality and set of skills that cannot be duplicated. So tell that bitch imposter syndrome to shut it, and let's figure out your special sabor.

Nicole Nieves, digital marketing expert and founder of the award-winning marketing firm The Brand Vibe, told me that as a WOC, when she set up her own business after years of "code-switching" in corporate America, she was finally able to focus on the question "Who am I?" Nicole told me: "I felt like I couldn't be myself in corporate America...As a woman of color, you've had to go above and beyond to fit in and prove yourself. Now I can find myself again, I don't need to worry about how I'm being perceived." For so many Latina women, leaving the corporate world behind to start their own business allows them the opportunity to find themselves in a meaningful way.

The thing that makes you *YOU* is known as your competitive advantage. That is that "thing" that makes customers choose you and keep coming back for more. In order to harness that, you'll have to revisit your own history and reconnect with the journey you've taken to get to where you are today.

This is known as your founder's story, the reason why you were inspired to do what you do. Vulnerability is a huge part of how we connect as humans, so make a list of the challenges you've faced, and how you've overcome them. Don't forget to also share your triumphs. People connect with stories, not products. When someone invests in your business, it's because they found something about you that they relate to and they want more of it. You want your ideal client to see themselves in your own story. This builds trust, and when people trust you, they're much more willing to pay for your help.

Don't shy away from declaring exactly who your desired client is and weaving that messaging into your marketing plan. Be clear about who you serve and why so that you don't attract the wrong people. It's not your job to serve everyone—you are not a buffet, honey!

## 5. Trabaja SMARTer, Not Harder (aka Make SMART Goals)

As you consider your side hustle, you may find yourself feeling really excited, and that's great! You've got big goals, but then the overwhelm starts to set in. You start to think to yourself, "How the F am I going to do all of these things?" Being busy and being productive are not the same thing, so let's make sure you're setting yourself up for success. If you only state your goals verbally, it's easy to blow them off and forget what it was that you hoped to achieve. When you put your words to paper, they exist in a much more real, tangible way—and that can be frightening.

If you struggle with reaching your goals, they might not be SMART enough. Setting SMART goals helps you to clarify your ideas, focus your efforts, use your time and resources productively, and increase your chances of achieving exactly what you envision.

**SMART Goals Are:**

**S**pecific
**M**easurable
**A**chievable
**R**elevant
**T**ime-bound

When creating a SMART goal, there are several questions to ask yourself that will help you define a clear road map to success. By putting these specific boundaries on your goals, it becomes much easier to create an actionable plan to achieve them.

**Specific:** Who will be working on this? Will you be working with a business partner? Hiring employees? What do you want to achieve? Why is this important?

**Measurable:** What metrics are you using to determine success? How will you know you've reached your goal?

**Achievable:** Is this goal realistic? Are you giving yourself enough time and resources to make this goal attainable?

**Relevant:** How is this related to your overall plan professionally and otherwise? How does this get you closer to the vision you have for your life?

**Time-Bound:** How long will it take you to accomplish this? When will you do periodic check-ins to stay on track? Are you willing to hire someone to keep you accountable if needed?

Without applying SMART goals, you might say, *I want to start a side hustle where I can help people.* Working with SMART goals, you might adjust that and say, *I am launching a coaching business where I help overwhelmed moms learn how to prioritize their physical health while balancing motherhood. I'm purchasing my website domain and I will give myself thirty days to set it up so that I can start inviting clients to apply for my 1:1 program. My measure of success is securing my first ten 1:1 clients within six months of launching my website.*
Notice how much more concrete and focused the second goal sounds.

**Specific:** Launching my coaching business and setting up my website

**Measurable:** Signing up ten clients within six months of launching my business

**Achievable:** Giving myself a reasonable amount of time to set things up

**Relevant:** Starting my own business because I want to be self-employed

**Time-Bound:** 30 days to set up and launch + 30 days to market = 60-day timeline

## 6. Put Yourself on Blast (aka Set Milestones That Will Force You to Launch)

Any fellow perfectionists here? Listen, I get it. We want all the logo and graphics and color schemes and the website to be flawless before we tell a single soul about what we're doing. But perfectionism is just another form of imposter syndrome, aka thinking that you are only acting or pretending to be *All That*, versus truly believing you have what it takes to succeed. It's an excuse we use to justify why we haven't done what we said we'd do. Fact is, if you wait for everything to be perfect, you'll be waiting forever. Don't get stuck in the cycle of procrastination and delays. If you're ready to start your side hustle, it's time to tell everybody about it, and stop looking for reasons why you're not ready. Set some real deadlines and stick to them. Tell all your friends and family about what you're doing. Hold yourself accountable and don't allow yourself to make any more excuses. Let everyone in your circle know what you're doing. Send an email blast, post about it on social media, or text your besties. Reach out to your network and ask them to be your first paying customers. All it takes is one yes for your side hustle journey to begin!

## 7. Stop Doing All the Things (aka Delegate, Delegate, Delegate!)

I'm not sure if you've heard, but according to societal expectations, you're supposed to be:

- the world's best mom, who makes customized bento box lunches for each of your children.
- the planet's hottest wife, who's always ready to pounce on your partner.
- America's next top chef, who cooks up three-course meals three times a day.
- in the best shape of your life—no excuses.
- the best friend anyone's ever had, available at the drop of a hat.
- a well-rested boss babe goddess who's slaying your career.

AND now you're supposed to start a mother%$#&!@* business, too? The patriarchy is trash. You're tired. You want to feel more fulfilled in your life, but you're having a very hard time filling your own cup. In order to give yourself the room you need to reach your biz goals, you're going to have to learn how to put the "self" back in selfish. I'm here to grant you permission to do it. You are worthy of asking for help and voicing your opposition to being all things to all people.

Outsourcing certain tasks in my life allowed me to pursue my side hustle and still (somewhat—I gotta be real) maintain my sanity. While I was juggling my 9-to-5 and building my food blog business, I started outsourcing my laundry and hired a housekeeper to visit my home every two weeks. It was a win-win scenario. I hate laundry and cleaning, so I no longer had to do either myself, and I got hours of my week back I could use to work on my business, go to the gym, spend time with my family, or do nothing at all! This simple act of taking things off my plate also made me realize that the most valuable thing I own is my time, and it's definitely worth spending some money to get it back.

One of the keys to successfully managing your side hustle (and your life) is to free up as much time as you can and to look for things you can eliminate from your to-do list. You can't be good at everything all the time and you shouldn't want to be. It's impossible, so let's trash the idea that we must do all the things, all the time. Focus on doing the things you are good at and that you enjoy, and work to outsource everything else.

Your goal is to automate or delegate as much as you possibly can. The more time you free up by having a tool or another person do things, the more you have opened up to work on your business. There are two broad ways to start approaching delegation: you have to look for tools and/or people that you can start outsourcing tasks to.

**Tools** allow you to automate repetitive tasks, both at home and in business. If you're spending three hours grocery shopping every week and you'd prefer to use that time to work on your side hustle, a grocery delivery app like Instacart can save you time and potentially money, since you see your bill before checking out. Many grocery stores offer this service for free if you're ordering a certain amount of product. If the time you have available on weekends is consumed with meal prep, hiring a meal delivery service may be the right solution to buy your time back. The same goes for your business. One of the first things I teach in workshops is to outsource repetitive tasks like booking meetings with potential clients and business partners with an app like Calendly or Acuity Scheduling. If you are running into a time-sucking roadblock, there's probably an app for that, so do some research into what options exist.

**People** allow you to free up your own time and headspace so you can focus on the highest ROI (return on investment) tasks. A software program won't be able to clean your house, buy your groceries, or take care of your children while you work on your business. When it comes to hands-on tasks, you'll have to find a person who can take these things off your task list. Delegating to another person requires more research and due diligence on your part. Talk to your network and ask for recommendations for service providers who can help you around the house. Post your needs on social media. Check out websites like Care.com or

TaskRabbit for help with childcare or household chores. The goal is to find another person who can help you do things that you don't want to do.

You can decide to outsource home tasks or work tasks, or both! It can be hard, so start slow. A virtual assistant can be a game-changer for freeing up your time in your business. You can find them on places like Fiverr or Upwork, or ask your friends and family if anyone is looking for some extra work. My first hire was a recent college graduate who was looking for some experience in digital marketing, and I found her through Instagram! I find that the hardest part of outsourcing for most women is acknowledging that they need help, and admitting that it doesn't make them a bad person/woman/mom/wife.

Also, don't be afraid to ask for help—friends and family are often happy to help with support, but you need to let them know what you need. Reach out to your friends individually or in a group setting and express your interest in skill swapping. Let's say you've got a friend who needs their child picked up, and they're a great cook. You can offer child pickup in exchange for meal-prep services. Share the skills you can offer and the ones you are seeking in return. Make it clear that this is a mutually beneficial arrangement. The best part is that both asking for help and doing skill swaps are free!

## 8. Community over Competition (aka Build Your Network)

If I had to attribute my business growth and success to any one specific thing, I'd have to credit my network. I've made tens of thousands of dollars hosting collaborative events with other creators. I got my first paid media feature because my Instagram amiga tagged me in a Twitter thread with an editor from *Time* magazine. As someone who's very independent, it took me a while to warm up to the idea that working with others was better than working alone. As I've allowed myself to reach out to others and expand my network, it's had a direct impact on my net worth, in a good way.

It's important to surround yourself with people who are also on the same path. Having a network of like-minded people around me helps me recenter and refocus when I feel like giving up.

Social media is a great place to connect with people, so don't be shy! Slide into those DMs! When reaching out to someone via DM, avoid generic or automated messages. Take the time to personalize each message by mentioning something specific about the person's profile, recent work, or shared interests. This demonstrates your genuine interest in connecting. Clearly state why you are reaching out and express your interest in connecting. Share what you admire about the person's work, achievements, or industry knowledge. Highlight any common ground or shared interests to establish a connection. Show that you are willing to offer something of value in return for their time and attention. It could be sharing an interesting article, providing insights on a specific topic, or offering assistance with a relevant project. Offering value up front increases the chances of a positive response.

Before you know it, you will have curated a tribe of badass mujeres who inspire you to continue your progress. Schedule regular connection opportunities like networking sessions, coworking sessions, or skill-swap sessions; this can keep you motivated to move forward with your goals.

### 9. Paciencia y Fe (aka Scale & Create Your Exit Strategy)

Building a sustainable business takes time, so don't put unnecessary pressure on yourself to create a six-figure business in two weeks. That's not realistic, despite what social media may tell you. Make a plan to grow and scale your business by identifying what improvements you need to make to take things to the next level.

And please, don't get fired from your day job. If your goal is to make your side hustle your main hustle, practice quiet quitting: Do what you have to do at work so you can avoid the stress of making your side hustle profitable right away. Quiet quitting is just like it sounds: Quietly (but methodically!) move toward your goal of exiting without making any noise. In other words, do the job and do it well, but conserve energy wherever possible—don't sweat the small stuff. And whatever you do, don't perform side hustle work with company equipment or on company time. The last thing you want is to be let go before you're ready to take the plunge.

As you grow your business, it's so important to KNOW YOUR NUMBERS. I used to use basic spreadsheets to reconcile my side hustle income and expenses, and I usually only did this at year-end, so I had no idea what was happening throughout the year. When I made the decision to grow my side hustle into a full-time business in 2020, I invested in accounting software that allowed me to track my income on a daily basis. Having this information at my fingertips helped me stay in touch with my progress. Use an expense-tracking software like QuickBooks, Wave, or Xero to record your expenses. Once you start doing it regularly, you can cut out unnecessary expenses that are draining your bottom line in real time. And make sure your business finances and personal finances are separate.

Setting up your business finances involves several important steps to ensure that you can effectively manage your income, expenses, and overall financial health. Here's a guide to help you get started:

**Separate personal and business finances:** Establish separate bank accounts for your business to keep your personal and business finances separate. This separation is crucial for accurate bookkeeping and tax purposes.

**Choose an accounting method:** Decide whether you'll use cash or accrual accounting. Cash accounting records transactions when money actually changes hands, while accrual accounting records them when they occur, regardless of when payment is received. Consult with an accountant to determine which method is suitable for your business.

**Create a bookkeeping system:** Establish a system to record and track your business transactions. This can be done using accounting software like QuickBooks or a spreadsheet program of your choice. Set up categories for income and expenses to make it easier to analyze your financial data.

**Track income and expenses:** Record all sources of income and track your expenses diligently. Keep receipts, invoices, and any other relevant financial documents organized. Regularly review and reconcile your financial statements to ensure accuracy.

**Develop a budget:** Create a budget that outlines your projected income and expenses. This will help you plan and make informed financial decisions. Review your budget periodically and adjust it as necessary to reflect changes in your business.

**Manage cash flow:** Cash flow management is vital for the financial health of your business. Monitor your cash inflows and outflows to ensure you have enough liquidity to cover expenses and maintain operations. Consider implementing strategies such as managing receivables and payables, negotiating favorable payment terms with suppliers, and having a cash reserve for emergencies.

**Plan for taxes:** Understand your tax obligations and deadlines. Consult with a tax professional to determine the appropriate tax structure for your business and ensure you comply with all tax laws. Set aside funds regularly to cover your tax liabilities. A good benchmark is putting aside 25 percent of your business revenue for tax purposes, but this number will vary widely based on what state your business is registered in, whether you need to collect sales taxes, and whether there are state or local income taxes in your operating location.

**Monitor financial performance:** Regularly review financial reports such as profit and loss statements, balance sheets, and cash flow statements. These reports will provide insights into your business's financial performance, identify areas for improvement, and help you make informed decisions.

As you go through this process, it will be crucial to consult with accounting and legal professionals who are familiar with your specific business needs and local regulations. They can provide personalized advice tailored to your circumstances and ensure compliance with all financial and legal requirements. Setting up a robust financial management system will save your sanity *and* your business. You will thank me during tax time!

## The Ebb & Flow of Business Income

Receivables and payables are two fundamental terms in accounting that relate to money owed to and owed by a business, respectively. Receivables, also known as accounts receivable or trade receivables, represent the money owed to your business by customers or clients for goods sold or services rendered on credit. When you provide goods or services to a customer on credit, you create an account receivable. The customer is expected to pay the amount owed within a specific period, usually outlined in an invoice or sales agreement. Accounts receivable are recorded as assets on your business's balance sheet.

Managing receivables effectively is crucial for maintaining a healthy cash flow. It involves monitoring and tracking outstanding invoices, following up on overdue payments, and implementing strategies to minimize the risk of bad debts, such as credit checks and collection efforts.

Payables, also known as accounts payable or trade payables, refer to the money your business *owes* to suppliers, vendors, or service providers for goods or services received on credit. When you purchase goods or services from a supplier and agree to pay later, you create an account payable. Accounts payable are recorded as liabilities on your business's balance sheet.

Managing payables involves keeping track of your outstanding bills, ensuring timely payment to maintain good relationships with suppliers, and taking advantage of any early payment discounts offered. It's important to carefully manage payables to avoid late fees, penalties, and strained relationships with vendors.

Both receivables and payables play a significant role in your business's working capital management, cash flow, and overall financial health. Keeping a close eye on these accounts, maintaining accurate records, and effectively managing payment and collection processes are essential for successful business operations.

## 10. Stack That Dinero (aka Build a Sustainable Biz Before Quitting Your Day Job)

I decided to leave my 9-to-5 when I was earning enough income to cover my expenses without having to rely on the salary from my day job, and when it was starting to get in the way of opportunities for Delish D'Lites and Yo Quiero Dinero. This is why it's so important to know your numbers. Knowing how much you are bringing in on a monthly basis and how much you're spending is critical for you to understand your business's cash flow. Tracking your income will help you track how consistent your income is, and maintaining a cash cushion can help you manage months when business may be slower.

In order to prepare my finances for full-time self-employment, I worked with a certified financial planner to create an exit plan so I could feel confident that I was making all the right moves before taking the leap. I saved up an emergency fund that would cover eight months of expenses in a high-yield savings account. I opened a solo 401(k) through my business to save for retirement, put myself on payroll, took out a workers' compensation policy, set up life insurance, created an estate plan, and talked to my then spouse about joining his company's health-care plan (we'll talk about all this below).

Then, three months before quitting my job, I started paying myself a salary through my business and used my entire corporate paycheck to max out my 401(k) at work and bulk up my savings. I wanted to make sure I could pay myself entirely through my company. I also worked with my CPA to elect S-corporation status for my LLC so that I could save money on taxes. When you're thinking about quitting your job to become a full-time business owner, it's important to work with financial professionals—like a CPA, tax attorney, financial planner, or other licensed professional—to make sure you're establishing a strong financial foundation, so that you can leave your 9-to-5 in a good spot.

# It's Time to Classify Your Business!

This is also a good time to begin to legally formalize your business structure if you haven't already done so. Which business model you decide to go with can have a major impact on legal and tax issues associated with running your business. Here is a look at the two options and what their implications might be for your particular situation.

### Sole Proprietor

Most side hustlers start as sole proprietors, which is the default status for anyone who operates a business. On the most basic level, sole proprietorship means that you and you alone own and operate the business. As a sole proprietor, there is no line between your personal and business assets and expenses—they are considered one and the same from a legal and tax perspective. Legally, this means that you are personally responsible for all your business's debts and obligations. In a sole proprietorship, if your business is sued and loses, your personal assets—real estate, cars, bank accounts—can be targets for the parties seeking to collect damages. The same can be said, in some cases, if you default on a business loan and you signed a personal guarantee, or the lender placed a lien on your assets. The lender can attempt to recover its investment from your personal property.

Freelancers, consultants, and solopreneurs often choose to file their taxes as sole proprietors. If you are just beginning to build your business, you might want to take a little time to let it grow before exploring the idea of setting up an LLC, as—for one thing—setting up an LLC can be pricey, as we'll discuss in the next section. Depending on how your business develops and/or the type of business you run, it might even make sense in the long run to stay a sole proprietorship.

## LLCs, Corporations, and S Corps, Oh My!

As your side hustle grows, you may want to consider creating a Limited Liability Company (LLC) or a corporation to shield yourself from the risk of lawsuits, as one of the main perks is that an LLC helps separate your business assets from your personal ones. For example, if you were to have to file for bankruptcy, it would only apply to your business and not to your personal finances. Another added benefit of an LLC is that, if you have employees, it safeguards you from being legally liable for their actions. Perhaps the biggest perk of an LLC is that it allows you to start taking advantage of additional tax benefits available to entrepreneurs. An LLC is set up by filing paperwork with your state.

Starting an LLC involves various costs, and the total amount can vary depending on several factors. The most basic expense is the filing fee required by the state to officially register the LLC, which can range from around $40 to $500 or more, depending on the state. For example, an LLC that is doing business or organized in California must pay an annual franchise tax of $800! That's no small peanuts. In some states, there might be an additional fee to reserve the chosen LLC name before forming the business. A few states also require LLCs to publish a notice of their formation in a local newspaper, incurring an extra cost. Furthermore, having a registered agent, a person or company that receives legal documents on behalf of the LLC, comes with an annual fee of around $50 to $300. Creating an operating agreement, which outlines the rules and structure of the LLC, could also add to the expenses if you use an attorney or a template. Additionally, depending on the location and nature of the business, obtaining specific licenses or permits might be necessary, incurring further costs. It's essential to research the specific requirements and fees in your state or consult with a local business advisor or attorney to get a more accurate estimate of the costs involved. Keep in mind that some ongoing costs, such as annual report filing fees and taxes, will be incurred after the initial formation.

An accountant may recommend that you consider electing S corporation status, also known as an S corp, which is a legal structure for a business that provides certain tax benefits while still offering limited liability protection to its owners. The "S" designation comes from Subchapter S of the Internal Revenue Code in the United States, which outlines the rules and regulations for this type of corporation. They may also mention forming a C corporation instead of an LLC. A C corp is a type of big and formal business structure. It's like a big group of people working together to run a company. The people in the group are called shareholders because they own "shares" of the company. Like an LLC, a C corporation is separate from the people who own it. This means that if the company gets sued, the shareholders' personal stuff, like their money or homes, is protected and safe. One unique thing about C corporations is that they pay their own taxes, and the shareholders also pay taxes on the money they get from the company, which is known as double taxation. This type of business has more rules and paperwork to deal with compared to other types, but it's good for bigger companies or those planning to have many shareholders from the public. Talk to a CPA or business attorney to understand the business laws in your state to make sure you're setting up the right entity for your needs. Here's a quick breakdown of the differences between these business entities.

| Feature | Limited Liability Company (LLC) | C Corporation (C Corp) | S Corporation (S Corp) |
|---|---|---|---|
| Liability Protection | Your Personal Stuff Is Safe If The Business Has Problems. | Your Personal Stuff Is Safe If The Business Has Problems. | Your Personal Stuff Is Safe If The Business Has Problems. |

| Ownership | The Business Is Owned By People Called "Members." | The Business Is Owned By People Who Have "Shares" Of The Company. | The Business Is Owned By People Who Have "Shares" Of The Company. |
| --- | --- | --- | --- |
| Taxes | The Money You Make Is Just Added To Your Regular Income Taxes. | C Corps Face Double Taxation Because They Are Taxed On Their Profits, And Then The Shareholders Are Taxed Again On The Dividends They Receive From The Corporation. | An S Corp Does Not Pay Federal Income Taxes Itself. Instead, The Profits And Losses "Pass Through" To The Individual Shareholders, And They Report These On Their Personal Income Tax Returns. This Can Result In Significant Tax Savings. |
| Management | Members Or Managers Run The Business. | A Group Called The Board Of Directors Makes Important Decisions. | A Group Called The Board Of Directors Makes Important Decisions. |
| Formalities | Fewer Rules And Paperwork To Deal With. | More Rules And Paperwork To Deal With. | More Rules And Paperwork To Deal With. |
| Number Of Owners | Can Have Any Number Of Owners, Including Just One (That's You!). | Can Have Many Owners, Including Shareholders From The Public. | Can Have Up To 100 Owners. |

Remember, these are just general comparisons, and the details might vary depending on the specific laws and regulations in your location. It's always a good idea to consult with qualified tax professionals and do your research before making a decision about starting a business.

## Tax Tips: Navigating the Self-Employed Jungle

Being self-employed has its perks, including tax benefits! Let's start with the self-employment tax deduction. It's a relief to be able to deduct the employer portion of the Social Security and Medicare taxes you pay! That means less money coming out of your pocket.

But wait, there's more! One of the best parts of being self-employed is that you can deduct a bunch of legitimate business expenses—from office supplies, equipment, advertising costs, professional fees, and business insurance, to necessary travel expenses for your business. All of that can be subtracted directly from your income and reduce your tax liability.

Now, let's talk about home sweet home. If you use part of your house exclusively for your business, you're entitled to a home office deduction. This means you can deduct a portion of your rent, mortgage interest, property taxes, and utilities. Imagine saving money while working from your favorite corner of your home.

But that's not all. As you plan for your future, retirement plans designed for self-employed individuals, like SEP IRAs, solo 401(k)s, or individual 401(k)s, can save you more and have tax benefits. There's no reason to let the golden shackles of corporate retirement benefits be the reason why you don't start a business.

And let's not forget about medical expenses. If you don't have employer-sponsored health insurance, you have the opportunity to deduct your health insurance premiums as a business expense. That means tax relief and more money in your pocket to invest in your business. Tax-favored savings accounts like Health Savings Accounts (HSAs) or Flexible Savings

Accounts (FSAs) are also within your reach. You can deduct contributions to these accounts and use the funds to cover eligible medical expenses. It's like having a magic formula to reduce your taxes and take care of your health at the same time!

Quarterly estimated taxes are a way for entrepreneurs to pay their taxes throughout the year instead of all at once; instead of waiting until the end of the year, entrepreneurs make smaller payments every few months. Here's how it works: As an entrepreneur, you have to estimate how much money you think you'll make in a year. Based on that estimate, you need to figure out how much you should pay in taxes.

Quarterly estimated tax payment schedule:

| Payment Period | Income Earned | Self-Employed Individuals (Sole Proprietors, LLCs) | Corporations |
|---|---|---|---|
| January 1–March 31 | January, February, March income | April 15 | April 15 |
| April 1–May 31 | April, May income | June 15 | June 15 |
| June 1–August 31 | June, July, August income | September 15 | September 15 |
| September 1–December 31 | September, October, November, December income | January 15 (following year) | December 15 |

When it's time to make a quarterly payment, you send the money to the IRS through their website. It's important to make these payments on time because if you don't, you might have to pay extra money in penalties and interest. Keeping track of your income and expenses and estimating your taxes can be a little tricky, but it's an important responsibility for entrepreneurs. Online accounting software like QuickBooks, Xero, or Wave will help you keep track of these important business metrics.

If you're not sure how to calculate your estimated taxes, you can always ask a tax professional like a Certified Public Accountant (CPA) for help. They can guide you and make sure you're doing it right. Tax laws can change, and a professional can help you optimize your tax strategy and make sure you're getting the most out of all these benefits.

So, side hustle queen, seize these tax advantages that are rightfully yours. You have the power to succeed in the business world and conquer the world of taxes! Rise up, Latina entrepreneur!

## Health Insurance and Retirement Options for the Self-Employed

As your business grows, the time will come to start making a plan for your health insurance and retirement benefits, which are usually what chains us to corporate jobs. The United States needs to do much better when it comes to offering affordable healthcare, but until that happens, here are your best options.

### Some Options for Self-Employment Health Insurance

- Obtain coverage through your spouse or domestic partner's plan if possible. This is usually the most affordable option.
- COBRA (short term for 18 months only). Because your employer is no longer splitting the cost of insurance with you, this will be expensive. You could end up spending thousands of dollars per month to insure yourself and your family.
- Health insurance marketplace (healthcare.gov), also known as Affordable Care Act Plans or Obamacare. The health insurance marketplace is an online platform established under the Affordable Care Act (ACA) in the United States.

It serves as a centralized marketplace where individuals and small businesses can shop for and enroll in health insurance coverage. The marketplace offers a range of qualified health plans (QHPs) that meet certain standards set by the ACA. These plans provide essential health benefits and must cover preexisting conditions without charging higher premiums or denying coverage based on health status. A useful site to explore your health insurance options is HealthSherpa.com.

- Private health insurance (United Healthcare, Aetna, Cigna, Blue Cross Blue Shield, etc.). This isn't cheap! Expect to pay at least $300 a month in premiums for a very basic plan.

- Medicaid. This is a government healthcare program in the United States that provides medical coverage to low-income individuals and families. Generally, Medicaid is available to individuals and families with limited income and resources, including children, pregnant women, parents, adults without dependent children, seniors, and people with disabilities. This is a potential resource if you're a new business owner who isn't making a ton of money yet.

- Professional associations (Freelancers Union, Writers Guild of America, Affiliated Workers Association, etc.). These organizations offer memberships that can then give you access to negotiated rates for insurance.

- Pay cash for healthcare services. If you don't have health insurance, you can choose to pay for medical services directly using cash or other forms of payment. This may allow you to negotiate fees directly with your healthcare providers or use facilities that offer discounted cash prices. Reduced fees for paying cash are more common for diagnostic procedures, such as CAT scans, X-rays, and ultrasounds, but cash payers can also often get a better deal for certain lab work, prescription drugs, outpatient surgeries, and therapeutic services, such as physical therapy. Note that this can be pricey. For example, if you need an X-ray or imaging procedure, with insurance, you may be required to pay a copayment or a percentage of the cost. The insurance company negotiates discounted rates with imaging centers or hospitals, which can significantly reduce the overall cost. The amount you owe will depend on your plan's coverage and cost-sharing requirements. Without insurance, the cost of an X-ray or imaging procedure can range from $200 to $1,000 or more, depending on the type of imaging and the facility. You would be responsible for paying the full amount up front.

- Move to a country with universal healthcare, like Canada (seriously!).

## Retirement Plan Options for Self-Employed

- Individual/Solo 401(k)—This is a retirement plan that's very similar to a workplace 401(k), with a few exceptions:

    You can't have any employees other than you and your spouse (contractors don't apply).

    Just like a 401(K), there is an annual cap on how much you can contribute as an employee. In 2023, your total employee contributions cannot exceed $22,500. (Remember: These cap contributions change annually, so you'll want to stay up to date by visiting the IRS website at http://www.irs.gov.)

    On top of this employee contribution, your business can also contribute 25% of your net adjusted self-employed income (i.e., what your business earns after expenses and deductions), with a max income limit of $330,000 (for 2023) annually that you can consider. If you're an S corp, you can contribute up to 25% of your salary/compensation.

- SEP IRA—A simplified employee pension (SEP) IRA is an account designed for side hustlers and business owners, similar to a Traditional IRA, but it differs in a couple ways:

  The first is that you as an employee cannot contribute. Instead, your employer funds this account. But remember, as the business owner, you are both the employee and the owner.

  The second difference is that your contribution limit is significantly higher: $66,000 or 25% of your compensation as an employee of your business, whichever is lower (for the year 2023). The max income limit for SEP IRA contributions is $330,000, the same as for an Individual 401(k). These contributions are also tax-deductible, but you will have to pay taxes upon withdrawal upon retirement. Keep in mind that your personal cap to contribute may fluctuate year to year based on your adjusted income.

- Traditional and/or Roth IRA—These tax-advantaged retirement accounts are available to anyone with earned income, whether it's from corporate wages or self-employment income.

  There is a $6,500 annual cap (2023) on contributions for anyone under age 50; you can contribute $7,500 if you're 50 or older.

## Side Hustle, Simply

Becoming a full-time entrepreneur is one of the scariest things I've ever done, but it's the best fucking thing I've ever done for myself. For the first time in my life, I feel like limits don't exist. I am in full control of my schedule and my earning potential. I no longer have to request time off or accept mediocre pay raises. I no longer have to justify my value to an employer that doesn't appreciate me. It has grown my confidence and helped me get a clear vision of what my ideal life looks like. I now get to work with my mom and my sister and distribute wealth among my family. I've been able to create generational wealth, and it all started with a side hustle and a dream.

If you're looking to turn your side hustle into your main gig, my best advice is to start today, commit to the journey, and prepare to work. Trust me, when you're on the other side, you'll realize it was totally worth it.

# CHAPTER 6

# Investing Ain't Just for White Dudes—You Can Do It, Too!

Growing up in a Latino household, I thought the only way to become a millionaire was to win the lotto. I watched my family members diligently make their way to the bodega each week, $20 in hand, ready to pick the winning Powerball numbers that would surely change our lives. I'm still waiting for the call from my mom that they've won the big jackpot. Now that I'm an investor, I realize becoming a millionaire is very much possible, without having to play the lottery. But when I first tried to convince my parents that they should be doing it too, they didn't want to hear it. "That's too risky," they said, "Eso es para los blanquitos." Well, this Latina has built over half a million dollars of wealth in the stock market, and if I can do it, so can you!

Our fear of losing it all holds many of us back from participating in one of the most powerful wealth-building tools that exists. If you're not currently investing, you're not alone. According to investor resource platform Morningstar, more than two-thirds of Latino households aren't investing, much less putting aside anything through workplace savings vehicles such as 401(k) plans.[1] As of 2020, Hispanic families had a median wealth of just $52,190—substantially lower than the median household net worth for the population of non-Hispanic individuals ($195,600). If we're going to build wealth, stuffing money under the mattress or collecting coins in the plastic water jug isn't going to cut it.

Another ever-present factor that affects your ability to build wealth is inflation. Inflation is the increase in prices of goods that we experience as consumers over time. When you were a child, getting a bag of chips and a drink at the local bodega might have cost you $1. Now, those same chips and soda will cost you $3 if you're lucky. That's inflation at work. The same item (a bag of chips, a car, a house, etc.) will cost you more in twenty years than it does right now. So how do we help our money grow and keep up with inflation, if simply saving more might not cut it? That's where investing comes in.

Many Latinas I work with and speak to are overwhelmed with the burden of having to support multiple generations—kids and parents—at the same time. This puts a lot of pressure on those of us trying to save for retirement while also planning to help send our kids to college or financially support aging parents and family members living overseas. In order to break the cycle of generational poverty, we must invest. It's the best way to make your money work harder, so that you don't have to. Maribel Francisco, whom we met in chapter 5, told me that although her mother had eventually set up her own business as a tax preparer, she was still wary of risking her hard-earned money in the stock market. This changed one day when she showed her mom her investment account. In just a year, she'd earned $11,000. Maribel said, "My mother was surprised by how much was in there. This was just an index fund.

---

I took the middle path, but I was still up thousands of dollars. Investing has allowed me to go back to school and I used money that I didn't have to work for." Maribel's advice for her coaching clients: "Just start. There's never going to be a right time."

In order to understand why more of us aren't investing, we first have to be empathetic to our families' circumstances of origin. Culturally, in the United States at least, there is an overall lack of trust in financial institutions because many older generations of Latino immigrants hail from countries and territories where government corruption, failed economic policies, and social unrest are common. They may have even experienced abuse at the hands of the US financial system with racist banking practices like redlining—the practice of denying creditworthy applicants housing loans just because they live in certain lower-income neighborhoods—or predatory lending scams that targeted them.

On top of feeling a general mistrust of financial institutions, there is also a lack of representation in the licensed financial professional space. In 2020, the Certified Financial Planner Board reported that only 2.46 percent of CFPs identified as Hispanic, despite Hispanic individuals comprising 18.9 percent of the total US population. According to 2020 census data, there are 62.1 million Hispanics living in the United States. No wonder you feel like investing isn't something for you! The fact is that we Latinas face different financial pressures than other demographics, and most of the financial advice and assistance isn't targeted to our needs and circumstances. And yet (and this bears repeating): You can't save your way to wealth.

It's totally normal to be fearful of investing, especially because so many of us don't learn about it. Taking the time to educate yourself about different investment options, strategies, and risk management techniques is key. Reading books (like this one) and articles, attending seminars or webinars, and seeking guidance from financial advisors are all good places to start. The more you learn, the more confident and informed you'll feel about investing.

Understanding a bit of the stock market's overall history for the past hundred years may also help you feel better about investing. The stock market goes up and down, but it's returned an annual average of 9.6 percent since 1928. Although this isn't a prediction of future growth, it's good to know what the overall performance has looked like over time. Visit https://www.macrotrends.net/2324/sp-500-historical-chart-data to get an idea of trends over the past thirty years.

Historically, simply saving your money leads to much lower amounts of growth than investing over the long term. Investing is so powerful because it makes your money work for you without you having to actively exchange time for that money...which is also a form of passive income. When your money is invested in things like stocks, real estate, or even certain types of businesses, you can generate passive income that can help you diversify your income sources, build wealth, and achieve financial independence, as it provides the potential for ongoing earnings and financial stability.

It's important to note that passive income does not necessarily mean "no work at all." Initial effort, time, and investment are often required to set up and establish passive income streams. However, once they are in place, they can provide a steady source of income with less active involvement compared to traditional employment.

So, if you want to build real wealth, investing is a must. My best advice? Start small. Begin with small investments that you are comfortable with. This allows you to dip your toes in the water and gain experience without significant financial risk. Maybe you open a brokerage account with $20 and start doing monthly $20 auto-investments. As you become more confident and knowledgeable, you can gradually increase the size of your investments. Remember, investing is a long-term journey, and it's normal to experience some fear or apprehension along the way. Be gentle with yourself.

Now let's get down to it.

# Investing Terminology (Fancy Words Meant to Confuse You)

Before we get into what investing is, let's first review some investing lingo—aka unnecessarily complicated language intended to confuse you and make you feel like an idiot. The world of investing is intentionally designed to gatekeep people like us out, and it starts with all the jargon that can feel like another language.

**Investing**—When you purchase something of value (an "asset") with the hope that it increases in value over time. At some point in the future, you intend to sell the asset for a higher price than you bought it for, making you money!

**Asset**—Anything that can be utilized to produce value (stocks, bonds, real estate, cash, crypto, a business, intellectual property, collectibles, etc.).

**Appreciation**—The increase in the value of an asset over time.

**Asset allocation**—This is a fancy phrase for your investment strategy. Your asset allocation is the different percentages of asset classes you have in your portfolio, such as cash, stocks, and bonds. These percentages are determined by assessing your risk tolerance and your investing goals.

**Bond**—A debt instrument that represents a loan made by an investor to a borrower. Bonds are commonly issued by governments, municipalities, and corporations as a means of raising capital. When you buy a bond, you are essentially lending money to the issuer in exchange for regular interest payments and the return of the principal amount at maturity. Bonds provide a way for issuers to borrow money from investors and for investors to earn a fixed income over a specific period. They are considered relatively safer investments compared to stocks, as they typically offer regular interest payments and the return of the principal amount upon maturity. However, it's important to note that all investments carry some level of risk, including the risk of default by the issuer. Typically, bonds that are lower risk pay lower interest rates; bonds that are more risky pay higher interest rates.

> **Low-Risk Bonds** are things like government bonds, which are issued by stable governments with strong credit ratings. These bonds are considered the safest. Examples include **US Treasury bonds** and bonds issued by financially stable countries. **Investment-grade corporate bonds** are issued by large, financially sound corporations with good credit ratings; these bonds are relatively safe. They offer slightly higher yields than government bonds but still maintain a low default risk. Low-risk bonds are like lending money to safe and trustworthy people or companies. When you lend them money, they promise to give it back later and pay you some extra money (interest) for using your money. These bonds are considered safer because the people or companies you lend to are less likely to have problems and not pay you back.

> **High-risk bonds** can be **high-yield** or **junk bonds**, which are issued by entities with lower credit ratings or less established track records. They carry a higher risk of default but offer higher yields to compensate investors

for the added risk. They can also be **emerging-market bonds**, which are issued by governments or corporations in developing countries and can be riskier due to political instability, currency fluctuations, and economic volatility in those regions. High-risk bonds are riskier because you are lending money to people or companies that might have some financial problems. They might still pay you back with interest, but there's a higher chance that they won't. Because of this risk, they offer more money (higher interest) to attract people to lend them money. The thing about high-risk bonds is that they can make you more money, but there's also a bigger chance that you could lose some or all of your money. S—so, it's like a riskier, but potentially more rewarding, way to make money.

Which type of bond you choose depends on how comfortable you are with taking risks and how much money you want to make. If you want to play it safe and have a steady income, low-risk bonds might be a better fit. But if you're OK with taking more chances and potentially making more money, high-risk bonds could be an option. Just remember that all investments have some level of risk.

**Brokerage**—A financial institution or company that facilitates the buying and selling of various financial securities on behalf of its clients. Brokerages act as intermediaries between buyers and sellers in the financial markets, executing trades and providing related services. Brokerages typically offer online or electronic trading platforms that allow investors to place buy and sell orders for a wide range of financial instruments, including stocks, bonds, options, futures, and commodities. You open an investment account at a brokerage.

**Capital gain**—The profit from the sale of an investment. This difference is what you pay taxes on.

**Commodity**—Raw material or agricultural product that can be bought and sold in the global market. Commodities are used as investments to diversify portfolios. You can invest in oil and gas, metals like silver or gold, or farm products like wheat, corn, cocoa beans, or even livestock!

**Compound interest**—In the context of investing, this is the interest you *earn* on interest. In the context of borrowing, it's the interest you *pay* on the interest. In other words, compound interest is what helps your money to grow faster, and it's also what makes credit card and other variable-interest-rate debt so expensive. Think of it like a little snowball that rolls down the mountain, continuously collecting more snow and growing bigger. Eventually, you've got an avalanche on your hands. When it comes to wealth, that's great...with debt, not so much.

**Cryptocurrency (crypto)**—Refers to digital or virtual currencies that use cryptography for security and operate on decentralized networks called blockchains. Cryptocurrencies are not issued or regulated by any central authority like a government or financial institution, making them decentralized and independent of traditional banking systems. Cryptocurrencies are used for various purposes, including online purchases, as an investment, to send money to other people, and as a store of value, similar to gold. The first and most well-known cryptocurrency is Bitcoin. Visit yoquierodineropodcast.com/crypto to learn more about crypto.

**Diversification**—The process of spreading and mitigating your investing risk by investing in lots of different types of assets. The more diversified you are, the less risk you face in the event of a financial downturn.

**Dividend**—A (usually) quarterly payment that a company makes to its shareholders from their profits. This is used to incentivize shareholders to hold on to their stocks (and buy more!).

**Dividend investing**—An investing strategy where investors focus on selecting and holding stocks or other investments that pay regular dividends. The goal of dividend investing is to generate a consistent income stream from these dividend payments.

**Dollar cost averaging**—Dollar cost averaging (DCA) is an investment approach where you regularly invest a fixed amount of money into a specific investment at scheduled intervals, such as monthly or quarterly, regardless of how the market is performing, whether the stock market is going up or down.

Here's how it works: Let's say you have $100 to invest every month. Instead of putting all $100 in at once, you invest $25 each week for four weeks. This means you buy more shares when prices are low and fewer when they're high. Over time, this helps you get a lower average price for your investments. Why is this a good idea? Well, it takes the stress out of trying to pick the perfect time to invest because you're doing it regularly. Plus, it helps you stay calm when the stock market goes up and down because you know you're getting a deal when prices are low. DCA offers advantages such as eliminating the need to time the market precisely, instilling discipline in your investment strategy, helping you manage emotions during market fluctuations, and mitigating downside risk.

**Exchange-traded fund (ETF)**—Very similar to a mutual fund, this is a type of investment that pools together investor funds to purchase assets. Similar to an index fund, ETFs are professionally managed baskets of many securities, so they're diversified (meaning that they contain a lot of different types of securities that all behave differently). Unlike mutual funds, which are only traded once at the end of the day, ETFs can be traded throughout the day. They trade like stocks—you can buy or sell your investment in an ETF whenever the markets are open. This gives you more flexibility to buy and sell ETFs, but also means their price fluctuates just like a stock.

**Expense ratio**—The percentage of your money that goes to the managers of the mutual fund you're investing in. This is the price you pay in exchange for them to do the work of finding "good" investments. For example, a fund may charge 0.30 percent. That means you'll pay $30 per year for every $10,000 you have invested in that fund. You'll pay this on an annual basis if you own the fund for the year.

**Forex**—Forex, short for "foreign exchange," refers to the global marketplace where participants exchange one currency for another with the goal of making a profit based on the changing exchange rates. Forex trading involves buying one currency while simultaneously selling another. Traders speculate on whether a currency pair's value will rise (appreciate) or fall (depreciate). Forex trading can be very risky. Prices can change rapidly, and you might lose money if you make the wrong decisions. It's essential to only use money you can afford to lose and to have a good strategy in place. TL;DR: Forex is like a big online game where you exchange one country's money for another with the goal of making a profit by buying low and selling high. But remember, it's a game with real money and real risks, so you need to be careful and learn the rules before you start playing.

**Futures**—A futures contract is the agreement to buy an asset at a set price and amount at a future date. Businesses use futures contracts to hedge risk, and traders may use them to place speculative bets. For example, a corn farmer can use a futures contract to lock in a certain price for their corn months ahead of time. An airline can use futures to protect itself against the risk of rising fuel prices.

**Index fund**—This is a type of mutual fund built to mimic a market index or specific sector of the economy (healthcare, tech, energy, etc.), so its composition is created by a computer algorithm versus a human. These funds typically have lower expense ratios than mutual funds, which have actual humans who decide which stocks go into the fund. Index funds typically have investment minimums (like $3,000 at Vanguard), which can make them inaccessible to beginner investors.

**Leverage**—Leverage involves using borrowed funds or debt to increase the potential return on an investment or to control a larger amount of assets with a smaller amount of your own capital. In simpler terms, it's like using borrowed money to amplify your ability to make gains or losses when investing or trading. Leverage allows you to control a more significant position in an investment or trade than you could with your own money alone. However, it also increases the level of risk because losses are also magnified when using leverage. It's an essential tool in various financial markets, including stocks, real estate, and Forex, but it should be used cautiously and with an understanding of the associated risks.

For example, if you have $100 and you use 10x leverage, it's as if you're trading with $1,000. This can be helpful because it gives you the potential to make more money if your trade goes well. However, it's important to know that leverage works both ways. While it can magnify your profits, it can also magnify your losses. So, if your trade goes the wrong way, you could lose more money than you initially had.

Think of it like a tool: It can be helpful, but you need to be careful how you use it. It's a bit like driving a fast car—it can be exciting, but you need to know how to control it to stay safe.

**Market capitalization**—Also known as market cap, this is how much a publicly traded company is worth. This number is calculated by multiplying a company's stock price by the number of shares currently held by shareholders. The bigger the number, the larger (and more established/less risky) the company tends to be.

> **Large cap**—total market capitalization value of more than $10 billion
> **Mid-cap**—total market capitalization value of about $2 billion to $10 billion
> **Small cap**—total market capitalization value of between $300 million and $2 billion

**Market index**—This is a group of companies whose performance is tracked and used to measure the overall strength of the economy. For example, the Dow Jones Industrial Average (DJIA) is an index of thirty large publicly traded US companies; this index is one of the oldest, and one of the most frequently monitored by investors. There are hundreds of different indexes, and they can track publicly traded companies in specific sectors (like technology, healthcare, energy, etc.), or a specific group of companies based on size, geographical location, and more.

**Mutual fund**—A pile of money that comes from a lot of investors like you and is then invested in assets like stocks and bonds. A mutual fund may hold hundreds or thousands of stocks, with the purpose of spreading the level of risk for investors. In most cases, money managers make buy and sell decisions for the mutual fund for you.

**Non-fungible token (NFT)**—A digital asset that represents ownership or proof of authenticity of a unique item or piece of content. NFTs use the same blockchain technology that powers cryptocurrency. When someone purchases an NFT, they acquire a unique token that represents ownership or access rights to a specific digital asset. This asset could be a piece of artwork, a video clip, a music track, a virtual item in a video game, or any other form of digital content. While the digital content itself can often be freely copied and shared, the NFT serves as a certificate of authenticity and ownership, allowing the buyer to prove that they hold the original or authorized version of the asset. *Check out episode #124 on the* Yo Quiero Dinero *podcast to learn more about NFTs.*

**Option**—An option is a contract providing you the option (hence the name) to purchase something at some time in the future for some specified price, called the strike price. For example, Saida buys an XYZ Company stock option, and the strike price is $75. Then the market value of XYZ Company's stock shoots up to $150 per share. If she wants, Saida can "exercise" her option and buy that stock for $75 per share, instead of paying the market rate of $150.

An important note here is that these are advanced-level invest-ments, as options trading involves risks and complexities. It's important to have a good understanding of options and their associated risks before engaging in trading activities.

**Passive income**—Earnings generated from sources that require minimal effort or ongoing involvement once the initial setup is complete. It is income that continues to be generated even when you're not actively working or exchanging your time for money. Passive income streams can come from various sources, including investments, business ventures, or creative endeavors.

**Private equity**—A form of investment in which funds are raised from various sources, such as high-net-worth individuals, pension funds, and institutional investors, then used to acquire ownership stakes in private companies or take existing public companies private. Private equity firms typically pool together significant amounts of capital from investors to create a fund.

**Real estate**—Property consisting of land and any structures or improvements attached to it, such as buildings, houses, apart-ments, and commercial properties. Real estate is a tangible asset class that holds value and can be bought, sold, or rented for res-idential, commercial, or investment purposes. Besides owning physical real estate, there are investment opportunities available on the stock market that give you a chance to invest in real estate without owning the property yourself:

**Real estate investment trust (REIT)**—REITs are companies that own and manage income-generating real estate properties. They allow individual investors to invest in a diversified portfolio of properties without directly owning them. REITs are traded on stock exchanges, making them accessible to investors through the stock market. Investing in REITs can provide a way to participate in the real estate market without dealing with things like collecting rent and screening tenants, and you potentially earn dividends.

**Real estate mutual fund or exchange-traded fund (ETF)**—Mutual funds and ETFs focused on real estate investment in a portfolio of real estate–related securities, including REITs, real estate development companies, and mortgage-backed securities. These funds are traded on the stock market, providing investors with exposure to real estate assets through a diversified investment vehicle.

**Real estate companies:** Some real estate development, management, or construction companies are publicly traded on the stock market. Investing in these companies allows investors to indirectly participate in the real estate industry. However, it's important to note that the performance of these companies may not necessarily reflect the broader real estate market.

**Rebalancing:** Rebalancing your investments is like adjusting the ingredients in a recipe to maintain the right taste. Imagine your investments are like ingredients in a meal, each with its own flavor. Over time, some ingredients (or investments) might become more prominent than others due to their performance. Rebalancing involves adjusting the proportions of these ingredients to ensure the dish (or your investment portfolio) tastes just as you intended. By periodically checking and readjusting your investments, you can keep your financial "recipe" well balanced and aligned with your goals. Yum.

**Risk tolerance**—Risk tolerance refers to an individual's willingness and ability to endure fluctuations in the value of their investments or the potential for financial loss in pursuit of their goals. It's a personal trait influenced by factors such as financial objectives, time horizons, current financial situations, knowledge and experience in investing, emotional temperament, and the degree of diversification in their investment portfolio. Understanding your risk tolerance is crucial in making sound investment decisions that align with your comfort level. It helps you choose investments that match your willingness to take on risk, whether you prefer safer options like bonds or are open to riskier assets like stocks.

**Stocks**—Companies issue stocks to shareholders as a way to raise capital to grow their operations. When you buy stock, you're purchasing a tiny bit of ownership in the company that issues the stock. Someone who owns stock is known as a shareholder.

**Share**—A share, also known as a stock, represents ownership in a company. When you own a share of stock, you become a partial owner or shareholder of that company. Shares are typically issued by publicly traded companies that are listed on stock exchanges, allowing investors to buy and sell ownership stakes in the company.

**Target Date Fund**—A target date fund, also known as a life-cycle fund or a retirement date fund, is a type of investment fund designed to simplify long-term investing, particularly for retirement planning. These funds are often offered by financial institutions like mutual fund companies or retirement plan providers such as 401(k) plans. The primary characteristic of a target date fund is that it automatically adjusts its asset allocation (aka the percentage of stocks and bonds) over time based on a specific target retirement date.

Now that we have the right lingo, you may be thinking you're ready to start investing, right? Not so fast. Rushing into anything you don't understand can lead to lots of overwhelm and some bad decision-making. As a first-generation wealth-builder, you may not have anyone available to answer all your investing questions. Perhaps you've done a lot of research already, googling financial questions, following a bunch of personal finance "finfluencers," reading a ton of blogs, or scrolling through more TikToks than you care to admit. Whatever your level of familiarity with the world of finance, if you're here, you're taking a powerful first step toward your wealth-building journey.

If this isn't your first foray into personal finance and wealth building, you've probably done plenty of research already. The differences between a 401(k) and a Roth IRA or among your investment options or different brokerages are all important to learn about, but the single most important concept to understand is compound interest.

## The Power of Compound Interest and Your Investment Road Map

Compound interest is the interest that is calculated on the initial principal of the loan or deposit. In other words, it is the interest you earn on interest over time.

It's easier to understand when you see it at work, so follow this example:

You have $1,000 (this is your principal or starting amount) and it earns 10% interest each year in your investment account.

After the end of the first year, you'll have $1,100.

1,000 X 0.10 = $1,100.00

At the end of the second year, you'll have $1,210.

1,100 x 0.10 = $1,210.00

Let's see what happens after 20 years...

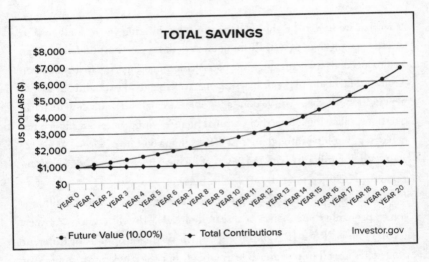

As your principal grows, so does the amount of interest you earn on it.

This is the power of compound interest. It's pure magic and why investing is so powerful.

Nothing beats this. Not high APYs (annual percentage yields), not low APRs (annual percentage rates), not even cutting your budget. The earlier you start and the longer you're in the market, the more your investments will have time to experience the power of compound interest. Check out our favorite compound interest calculator at Investor.gov.

Now let's create an investing road map. These are five essential questions I want you to ask yourself to help you create your investing strategy.

## 1. What Are Your Investing Goals?

"I want to invest" is not a goal. Remember our SMART goals from chapter 5? Start with this:

- Are you investing for traditional retirement or early retirement?
- Do you have a specific goal that investing can help you achieve, like buying real estate?
- Are you investing to pass along wealth to your parents, children, or a charitable cause?
- Do you want to invest funds to use for a specific purpose, like medical or educational expenses?

Once you're clear on why you're investing, this will help you choose the appropriate account to help you reach your goal.

## 2. How Much Risk Are You Comfortable With?

Investing always comes with some level of risk and reward; that's why we do it. How much risk you're willing to entertain is a part of determining your investing strategy. You can think of risk like a ladder. Near the ground, you can easily step off the ladder without risking a broken ankle. But as you climb higher up the ladder, your risk of falling off and hurting yourself increases, so you need to make sure you're really aware of what's going on around you before you keep going. This is how we can envision risk.

## THE LADDER OF RISK

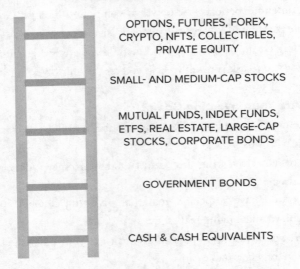

OPTIONS, FUTURES, FOREX, CRYPTO, NFTS, COLLECTIBLES, PRIVATE EQUITY

SMALL- AND MEDIUM-CAP STOCKS

MUTUAL FUNDS, INDEX FUNDS, ETFS, REAL ESTATE, LARGE-CAP STOCKS, CORPORATE BONDS

GOVERNMENT BONDS

CASH & CASH EQUIVALENTS

The technical term for assessing your risk as an investor is known as your **risk tolerance**.

Knowing your risk tolerance will help you decide on the right investments that match your personality. Once you know how much market risk you can stomach, you can create an investment strategy that aligns with your values and comfort level, and build a portfolio that matches that.

To determine your risk tolerance, investment management company Vanguard has an excellent investor questionnaire online at: https://investor.vanguard.com/tools-calculators/investor-questionnaire. This questionnaire asks you several questions in order to recommend a good asset allocation for you based on your goals, time frame, risk tolerance, and financial situation. Some examples:

1.   How do you feel about investments that go up and down frequently? Would you ultimately prefer to have less gain

overall if it meant less volatility, or are you comfortable with market fluctuation?

2. If you saw a 30 percent loss in a span of three months for a certain investment in your portfolio, would you buy more of the investment, sell all, or just hold on to it?

It's also a good idea to return to the questionnaire periodically to rebalance your allocations based on changes in your financial circumstances.

## 3. What's Your Investing Budget?

This may be the most important question you ask yourself: How much can you feasibly contribute per month toward your goals?

Before you know that number, you have to understand what your overall budget looks like—as we discussed in chapter 4.

- **Do you have an emergency fund?** If not, focus on saving at least one month's worth of expenses before you begin investing. There's nothing that will derail your wealth-building plans like a financial emergency that requires using a costly credit card. Once you've hit this number, start investing consistently with a small amount that you can manage, and continue building your emergency fund to six months' worth of expenses.

- **Do you have a plan to pay off debt like high-interest credit cards?** Another guaranteed way to nullify the power of compound interest as an investor is having that same thing work against you with high-interest-rate debt. If you're getting 10 percent returns in your investment portfolio, but paying 20 percent interest on your credit cards, you're doing a whole lot of nothing. Make a plan to get rid of your most expensive debt as fast as possible. Refer back to chapter 4 for debt payoff strategies.

Once you nail down a budget, you will get a better idea of what a sustainable investing strategy can look like for you. Maybe at first you start off with random lump-sum contributions when you can afford to; that's OK! The goal, however, is to develop a strategy around it and build up to investing on a consistent basis.

## Choosing Your Investments

I can't tell you how devastating it is to hear from my coaching clients who started investing...or so they thought. They'll say things to me like "I don't know what's going on, but my money isn't doing anything." On closer inspection, I realize the problem...they haven't actually purchased any investments! If you transfer money into your investment account without actually buying investments, you're essentially using your brokerage account as a glorified bank account. In order to build wealth, you must actually buy investments once your investment account is funded. Investing requires a three-step process:

1.  Open the account.
2.  Transfer funds.
3.  Buy your investments (and automate!).

### Mutual Funds vs. Index Funds

Many new investors are overwhelmed by the idea of choosing investments. What if you don't make the right choice? There's no need to fear; you don't have to pick an individual stock and hope that that one goes to the moon. Most investors can benefit from taking the lazy approach by letting other people (or computers) do the work of choosing the best investments for you. Why choose just one investment when you can invest in hundreds or even thousands of companies with a single purchase? This type of diversified investment is a mutual fund in action.

Mutual funds have a specific investment objective, such as growth, income, or preservation of capital. They are operated by active fund managers, who need to get paid for their work. As a result, mutual funds usually come with higher expense ratios (this is a percentage-based number, so the more you buy, the more they get paid). Many people are sold into mutual funds by people like Dave Ramsey (I have my own opinions about him), and because active fund managers sell promises of "beating the stock market." However, data suggests that they're not very good at their jobs. In fact, *79 percent* of fund managers underperformed the S&P 500 in 2022.[1] Why pay someone to do a bad job when you pay way less and get a better performance with an index fund?

Index funds are managed not by a money manager, but by a computer algorithm. In exchange for outsourcing the investment decisions to a computer instead of a human, index funds are cheaper, too. Let's see it in practice:

You open an investment account with $1,000 and contribute $1,000 per year for 30 years, at 10% return.

In the first scenario, your only investment is into an actively managed mutual fund that is attempting to outperform the entire US stock market. They charge a 0.8% expense ratio. After 20 years,

Ending value (net with fees): $168,533.13

Ending value (gross): $198,392.83

Cost of fees: **$29,859.70**

Now let's choose a low-cost index fund with a 0.04% expense ratio, like Vanguard's VTSAX. What happens then? After 20 years,

Ending value (net with fees): $196,773.56

Ending value (gross): $198,392.83

Cost of fees: **$1,619.27**

---

1. https://www.cnbc.com/2022/03/27/new-report-finds-almost-80percent-of-active-fund-managers-are-falling-behind.html.

In this scenario, you've saved $28,240.43 by choosing a low-cost index fund. That's a serious wad of cash! You can see how choosing high-quality investments with the lowest expense ratio possible is a good overall strategy, one that offers you the opportunity to invest in lots of companies at once, for a low price. VTSAX, Vanguard's Total Stock Market Index Fund, tracks the CRSP US Total Market Index and is designed to allow you to invest in the entire US stock market with the click of a button. Crazy, right?

An indexing investment strategy seeks to mimic the performance of a particular market index, which is "a hypothetical portfolio of investment holdings that represents a segment of the financial market." In the United States, the three most well-known and closely followed indexes are the Dow Jones Industrial Average, the S&P 500, and the NASDAQ Composite Index. Each of these indexes measures a different "segment" of the overall market. The S&P 500 represents the 500 largest publicly traded US companies. The Dow Jones Industrial Average follows thirty specific companies across different sectors, and the NASDAQ is focused on technology companies.

Since an index investment strategy seeks only to mimic the performance of a given index, we can consider this a passive investment strategy. This means you will not be managing your own portfolio by trading. Essentially, you're letting the market do its thing and counting on it to keep going up. If history tells us anything, it's that the market will, over the long term (i.e., after twenty years or more),[1] always be up. This is even more true when we practice a buy-and-hold strategy, in which you purchase investments and just hold on to them (and buy more over time).

Index funds are a great way to purchase shares of hundreds or even thousands of companies with a single transaction. You can automate your

---

1. https://money.com/stock-market-chart-rolling-returns/#:~:text-Year-toyear%2C%20the%20S%26P%20500%20can%20fluctuate%20wildly%2C%20from,for%2020%20years%20they%20are%20all%20but%20nil.

investing with index funds. All the major brokerages that offer access to index funds will allow you to set up a recurring investment. Simply link your bank account, set your desired frequency (weekly, biweekly, monthly, etc.), choose the fund(s) you want them to auto-buy, and you're well on your way to reaching that bougie auntie life in no time.

## Exchange-Traded Funds (ETFs)

As we've learned, an exchange-traded fund represents a certain sector of the market. Think of a stock like a piece of fruit. An ETF is a basket of fruit. In this basket, you can have all kinds of fruits, meaning you can have a variety of stocks.

ETFs, like index funds, can track an index. But some are also investing in a certain sector. Examples of sector-based ETFs include:

- Stock ETFs
- Balanced ETFs, which are a blend of stocks and bonds
- Bond ETFs
- ETFs focused on specific industries, such as:
  *Real estate
  *Technology
  *Medical products
  *Cannabis

ETFs, like index funds, also have low expense ratios, because they're passively managed via a computer algorithm as well.

### Index Funds and ETFs—What's the Difference?

These investments are actually quite similar, but there are a few key differences you should be aware of.

1. **Method of purchase and selling.** While ETFs operate like any other stock you can buy and sell throughout the market day, index funds can only be bought and sold at the end of

each trading day (4 p.m. Eastern Time, when the New York Stock Exchange closes).

If you follow an indexing strategy, this won't really matter, since your strategy is to buy and hold. However, if you are a trader who sells and buys investments on a regular basis, then the price at which you buy matters. For this strategy, an ETF is better suited, as you have control over the price at which you choose to purchase an ETF.

For an index fund, the price you pay for a share is decided at the end of the trading day on which you placed your order.

2. **Minimum purchase requirements.** An index fund can sometimes require a minimum investment. Vanguard's pioneer index fund, VTSAX, has a $3,000 minimum investment. Once you buy in, you can make regular investments (minimum $100) to continue to purchase more shares. Any amount you contribute to this fund will get you the equivalent portion of a share. This, however, is becoming less common as investing has become more accessible. Fidelity, for example, offers zero-minimum-investment index funds, like FZROX.

With ETFs, you can get started with as little as a couple dollars. Thanks to fractional investing, in which you can buy a fraction of a stock or ETF at a time to eventually own whole shares, you don't have to start with a specific minimum investment at most major brokerage firms. Fidelity, Charles Schwab, and TD Ameritrade are just a few firms that offer fractional investing. Because you can start with a small amount of money, ETFs are popular for beginner investors.

3. **The ability to automate.** You can automatically invest into index funds after meeting your initial minimum amount

requirement. This is great if you want to take a set-it-and-forget-it approach.

You can't automatically invest into ETFs, so you'll have to remember to manually go in and buy them on a regular interval. If you're a long-term buy-and-hold type of investor, this choice is all about personal preference. There are many index funds that have equivalent ETFs, and vice versa.

## Target Date Funds—The Ultimate Set-It-and-Forget-It Investment

A target date fund is the lazy investor's guide to retiring in style. Seriously, it doesn't get easier than this. Imagine you plan to retire in, say, 2050. You pick a target date fund with that year in its name. The cool thing is, you don't have to worry much about managing your investments; the TDF does it for you.

While you're young, say in your twenties, thirties, or forties, the fund manager allocates your money into a predetermined mixture of stocks, bonds, and other investments. They decide how much of each based on how long until you retire and how risky you want your investments to be.

As the years go by and you get closer to retiring, the fund automatically shifts your investments from riskier stocks to less risky, into bonds and cash equivalents, so your money is less likely to go up and down and you can withdraw money in retirement with confidence.

You don't have to do much once you pick the right fund for your retirement year. The fund takes care of everything for you, like making sure you're not putting all your eggs in one basket by spreading your money out across different types of investments. Target date funds are a simple way for people who don't want to get too deep into the investing world and just want to put their retirement savings on autopilot. But remember, different funds might do things a bit differently, so it's important to check and pick the one that matches what you want for your retirement.

## Types of Investment Accounts

Now that you have determined your overall goals plan and your risk tolerance, it's time to make some decisions. The first? What kind of account you will use to begin investing—and you have several options to choose from. As you think through how to start investing, you should choose the account(s) that make the most sense for your goals. Factors like your income level and employment status will determine what kinds of accounts you have access to. So let's take a look at your options. There are two main categories of investment accounts:

- **Tax-advantaged accounts**
- **Taxable accounts**

Let's break down what each of these consist of.

### Tax-Advantaged Accounts

Tax-advantaged accounts are either tax-exempt, tax-deferred, or offer some other form of tax incentive. You may have heard of these types of accounts by another name, especially if you've worked in a larger company or institution that offers a retirement benefit:

- **401(k):** A type of tax-advantaged retirement option for corporate employees
- **403(b):** Offered to local and state public employees, such as teachers
- **457(b):** Offered to local and state government employees, such as law enforcement officers
- **Thrift Savings Plan (TSP):** Offered to federal government employees and military service members

Sound familiar? These are known as employer-sponsored plans, and they're a type of tax-advantaged account. An employer-sponsored plan is a type of benefit plan offered to employees at no or a relatively low cost. If you're self-employed, you have the option of offering one or more of these, like an Individual 401(k) or a SEP IRA, to yourself and your employees through your business.

Depending on the type of employer you work for, you may have access to one or more of these plans. In some cases, for example, certain public-sector employees may have access to both a 403(b) and a 457(b) plan. This enables you to save in two different retirement accounts at the same time. If you have a side hustle and a corporate W-2 job, you can open a self-employment retirement account like a SEP IRA and save there, while also contributing to your company's plan. This is a great hack for accelerating your investing for financial independence, and it's the path I took to get there.

There are many benefits to participating in an employer-sponsored retirement account. Let's review some of the most common features.

**Company matching.** Some employers will offer to match a certain percentage of your total contribution, which amounts to free money in exchange for participating in the plan. You heard me right…FREE MONEY! There aren't many places in life where someone offers you free money for any reason, so taking advantage of an employee matching program is a must. Most employers match 3 to 6 percent of your salary,[1] which can significantly boost your overall retirement savings. Imagine putting in 6 percent of your salary and getting an additional dollar-for-dollar match of that 6 percent from your job. You've literally doubled your investment contribution, and it didn't cost you anything extra. This can add up, so if you can, always try to contribute enough to your plan to get the full

1.https://www.investopedia.com/401k-without-employer-match-5443070#:~:textMost%20 traditional%20401(k)%20plans,employer%20match%2C%20including%20tax%20benefits.

company match. This money is part of your overall compensation package, so don't leave it on the table!

| Example of a 401(k) Plan Matching Program | | | | | |
|---|---|---|---|---|---|
| Annual Salary | Employee Contribution % | Employee Contribution | Employer Match % | Employer Match | Combined Contribution |
| $75,000 | 1% | $750 | 50% | $375 | $1,125 |
| $75,000 | 2% | $1,500 | 50% | $750 | $2,250 |
| $75,000 | 3% | $2,250 | 50% | $1,125 | $3,375 |
| $75,000 | 4% | $3,000 | 50% | $1,500 | $4,500 |
| $75,000 | 5% | $3,750 | 50% | $1,875 | $5,625 |
| $75,000 | 6% | $4,500 | 50% | $2,250 | $6,750 |
| $75,000 | 7% | $5,250 | 50% | $2,625 | $7,875 |
| $75,000 | 8% | $6,000 | 50% | $3,000 | $9,000 |

Source: Annuity.org

**A preset list of investment options.** The available investment options in your employer-sponsored plan are preselected by your employer, and typically consist of mutual funds, index funds, target date funds, and company stock options (if applicable).

Generally, your investment options are more limited in an employer-sponsored retirement account than in an IRA (we'll learn more about IRAs shortly). These accounts have annual contribution limits and are only accessible after reaching age 59½. Early withdrawal penalties are assessed on withdrawals from these accounts, with a few exceptions. If you leave your employer, you can roll over your 401(k) into an IRA.

## IRAs: Key Features

Perhaps you're reading this book and realizing that no one mentioned retirement accounts during your onboarding process. You contact your local human resources representative at work about opening a 401(k) and they say, *401 QUÉ? We don't have those.* So, does that mean you can't invest for retirement and you'll have to grind away at this job forever? Absolutely not! You can take matters into your own hands by opening up an IRA, another type of tax-advantaged account.

IRA stands for Individual Retirement Account, and these accounts are available to anyone with earned income. This means that you can open an IRA with W-2, 1099, or self-employment income. If your employer doesn't offer a 401(k), you can use an IRA to save for retirement, and you can even have a spousal IRA if you're a stay-at-home parent. No excuses, amiga: You have the power to build wealth, regardless of your employment situation.

- IRAs are available in pre-tax (Traditional) or post-tax (Roth) options for tax diversification.
- IRAs offer a variety of investment choices, such as stocks, bonds, ETFs, and index funds.
- IRAs have an annual contribution limit of $6,500 in 2023 if you're under age 50, and $7,500 if you're age 50 or over.
- You can withdraw Roth IRA contributions at any time, for any reason, without paying taxes or penalties.
- If you withdraw Roth IRA earnings before age 59½, a 10% penalty usually applies.
- Withdrawals before age 59½ from a Traditional IRA trigger a 10 percent penalty tax, whether you withdraw contributions or earnings.
- In certain IRS-approved situations, you may take early withdrawals from an IRA with no penalty.

## Why Does the IRS Set Contribution Limits?

The IRS (Internal Revenue Service) is part of the US Department of the Treasury and is responsible for enforcing and administering federal tax laws. This includes setting annual limits to how much you can contribute to tax-advantaged retirement accounts.

Contributions to a Traditional individual retirement account (IRA), Roth IRA, 401(k), and other retirement savings plans are limited by law so that highly paid employees don't benefit more than the average worker from the tax advantages that they provide.

You can find the latest contribution limits by visiting https://www.irs.gov/retirement-plans/plan-participant-employee/retirement-topics-contributions.

### Roth vs. Traditional

These terms refer to the tax strategy you will be taking advantage of as an account holder. You can't have a "Roth account" or a "Traditional account," but you can have a "Traditional IRA account" or a "Roth 401(k) account."

Traditional means that the money you contribute is tax-deferred, meaning the funds that you contribute are subtracted from your taxable income during the year you make the contribution. Let's break it down. Perhaps you earn $75,000 in gross annual income per year. You're thirty years old, single, with no children:

### With a Traditional IRA contribution of $6,000 (2022)

Taxable income $56,450
Effective tax rate 14.5%
Estimated federal taxes **$8,167**

### Without a Traditional IRA contribution of $6,000 (2022)

Taxable income $62,450

Effective tax rate 15.2%

Estimated federal taxes **$9,487**

You'd save $1,320 in taxes by maxing out your Traditional IRA. Taking care of future you while also saving money on taxes today? That's sexy stuff right there!

Contributing to a pre-tax account like a Traditional IRA or 401(k) can lower your tax bill in the present. However, since you have not paid taxes on this money, you will have to pay taxes on the money contributed and the gains you've earned when you withdraw from your account. (You can begin withdrawals at age 59½ without penalties. Anything before that will incur a 10% penalty from the IRS. This is essentially how they discourage you from touching the funds too often.)

With a Roth IRA, the money you contribute to the account is post-tax, so upon withdrawal, you will not be taxed on any gains and money withdrawn. Roth accounts are pretty incredible, because once you've contributed to them, you will never owe taxes again. Let's say you invest $10,000 in your Roth, and it grows to $10 million. The only money you will ever pay taxes on is that initial $10,000 investment. Pretty wild, if you ask me!

Roth IRAs come with a five-year rule. It states that a Roth IRA account must be open for at least five tax years before any earnings can be withdrawn tax-free and penalty-free, provided the account holder is under the age of 59½. This rule applies to the earnings on contributions as well as converted amounts. To avoid penalties and taxes, withdrawals of earnings must meet the five-year requirement and one of the following conditions: the account holder is 59½ or older, becomes disabled, is a first-time homebuyer (up to a $10,000 lifetime limit), or in the case of death, the beneficiary can withdraw the earnings tax-free. The five-year clock starts ticking on January 1 of the tax year for which the first contribution or conversion is made, and each conversion has its own five-year clock.

You can have both Traditional and Roth accounts. Many employers also offer a Roth 401(k) option, so check with your employer's retirement plan administrator to see if that's an option that you have available to you.

## Pre-Tax or Post-Tax: That Is the Question

"Pre-tax" and "post-tax" contributions refer to the way money is taxed before it is contributed to retirement accounts or other financial investments.

Pre-tax contributions, also known as tax-deferred contributions, refer to money that is contributed to retirement accounts before income taxes are deducted. The amount you contribute to your retirement account is subtracted from your gross income before your income taxes are calculated. This reduces your taxable income for the current year.

Examples: Traditional 401(k) and Traditional IRA contributions are typically made on a pre-tax basis. This means the contributions reduce your taxable income for the current tax year, potentially lowering your overall tax bill.

Post-tax contributions, also known as after-tax contributions, refer to money that is contributed to retirement accounts after income taxes have been deducted. Post-tax contributions do not provide an immediate reduction in your taxable income. The money you contribute has already been taxed at your regular income tax rate.

Examples: Roth 401(k) and Roth IRA contributions are made on a post-tax basis. While these contributions do not lower your taxable income in the year you make them, qualified withdrawals, including earnings, are tax-free in retirement.

## How to Decide

Some things to consider when deciding whether you should make Roth or Traditional contributions:

**Your current tax bracket.** This can influence how much you contribute to tax-advantaged accounts. In general, higher tax brackets benefit more from maximizing contributions to tax-advantaged accounts to reduce taxable income and potentially lower tax liabilities. Understanding your tax bracket can guide your contribution strategy, helping you take full advantage of the available tax benefits.

**Your future tax bracket.** By the time you retire, do you expect to be in a lower or higher tax bracket? Knowing your expectation helps you to evaluate which account type aligns best with your current and future tax situation. For example, if you're in a higher tax bracket now and expect to be in a lower tax bracket during retirement, a Traditional IRA or 401(k) may provide upfront tax deductions while deferring taxes to retirement. Conversely, if you're in a lower tax bracket now and expect to be in a higher bracket later, a Roth IRA or Roth 401(k) allows for tax-free withdrawals in retirement.

**Benefit now, or benefit later?** By understanding your tax bracket, you can strategically diversify your retirement savings between taxable and tax-advantaged accounts. This provides flexibility in managing your tax liability during retirement. For example, having a mix of taxable and tax-free accounts allows you to strategically withdraw from different accounts based on your tax bracket, potentially optimizing your tax burden in retirement.

**What's your income level?** If you earn more than $153,000 for single tax filers or more than $228,000 for those married and filing jointly in 2023, you don't qualify for a Roth IRA (these numbers change each year; you can check the IRS website for current limits[1]). Knowing your tax bracket allows you to make investment decisions that align with your tax situation. For example, if you're in a high tax bracket (high income), you may want to prioritize investments that generate long-term capital gains, which are typically taxed at lower rates.

If you anticipate having a lower income in retirement, and therefore anticipate being in a lower tax bracket, you may want to focus on lowering your tax liability today by contributing pre-tax income into a Traditional account. If you anticipate having higher income in retirement, thus being in a higher tax bracket, making post-tax contributions via a Roth account may make more sense. You may want to consider consulting with a licensed financial professional to determine your individual investing strategy. I recommend working with a fee-only fiduciary certified financial planner (CFP). More on this in chapter 8.

## Taxable Accounts, aka Brokerage Accounts

A taxable account, also known as a brokerage account, has no immediate tax benefits, but fewer restrictions and more flexibility than IRAs and

---

1. https://www.irs.gov/retirement-plans/plan-participant-employee-retirement-topics-contributions.

employer-sponsored accounts. You can withdraw your money at any time, for any reason, with no age restriction or early withdrawal penalty. You can open a taxable account at most major financial brokerages (see our list of recommendations below). Your investment options are unlimited; you generally have access to any kind of securities, such as stocks, bonds, target date funds, REITs, ETFs, and index funds. Taxable brokerage accounts offer certain advantages and disadvantages compared to tax-advantaged accounts like IRAs or 401(k)s. Both options have pros and cons.

## The Pros

**Flexibility:** Taxable brokerage accounts provide flexibility in terms of contributions and withdrawals. There are no contribution limits, and you can deposit or withdraw funds at any time without penalties or restrictions. This makes them suitable for short-term savings goals or emergency funds.

**No withdrawal restrictions or penalties:** Unlike retirement accounts, taxable brokerage accounts do not have early withdrawal penalties or required minimum distributions (RMDs), the minimum amounts you must withdraw from your retirement accounts each year, generally starting when you reach age 72 (or 73 if you reach age 72 after December 31, 2022). You can access your funds whenever you need them without incurring any penalties.

**Diverse investment options:** Taxable brokerage accounts offer a wide range of investment options, including stocks, bonds, mutual funds, ETFs, and more. You have the freedom to choose investments that align with your risk tolerance and investment goals.

**Potential tax advantages:** While taxable brokerage accounts are subject to taxes, they can offer some tax advantages. For example, long-term capital gains from investments held for more than a year are generally taxed at lower rates than ordinary income. Additionally, tax-loss harvesting allows you to offset capital gains with capital losses, reducing your overall tax liability.

# A CLOSER LOOK AT TAX-LOSS HARVESTING

Tax-loss harvesting is a savvy financial move that investors use to reduce the taxes they have to pay on their investments. Here's how it works:

Imagine you have a portfolio of different investments, like stocks or mutual funds. Some of these investments may not be doing so well at a given time, and their value may have gone down since you bought them. We call this a "loss" because they're worth less than what you paid for them.

Now, instead of holding on to these losing investments and hoping they'll bounce back, tax-loss harvesting involves selling them to lock in those losses. When you sell an investment at a loss, you can use that loss to your advantage when tax season rolls around.

Here's the cool part: The tax system allows you to use those losses to offset any gains you might have made on other investments during the year. Let's say you made some profits on other investments that increased in value. Those profits are called "capital gains," and you might have to pay taxes on them.

But when you do tax-loss harvesting, you can use the losses from the sold investments to "cancel out" or reduce the amount of taxes you owe on the gains. It's like balancing the scales—the losses bring down the amount of taxable gains you have, saving you money on your tax bill.

If your losses are more than your gains, you can use the extra losses to lower your taxable income. This means you could end up paying less tax overall, and get to keep more of your hard-earned money in your pocket.

It's essential to remember that tax rules can be a bit tricky, so it's always a good idea to work with a knowledgeable financial advisor or tax professional to make sure you're doing tax-loss harvesting the right way and making the most of your investment strategy. With tax-loss harvesting, you're playing the tax game smarter, and it can make a real difference in how much you get to keep from your investments!

## The Cons

**Taxation of investment gains:** One significant disadvantage of taxable brokerage accounts is that investment gains are subject to taxes. Any dividends, interest income, or capital gains generated within the account are typically taxable in the year they are earned, potentially increasing your tax burden.

**Capital gains taxes:** When you sell investments within a taxable brokerage account, you may be subject to capital gains taxes. Short-term capital gains (investments held for less than a year) are taxed as ordinary income, while long-term capital gains (investments held for more than a year) are taxed at lower rates, but still affect your tax liability.

**Limited tax advantages:** Taxable brokerage accounts do not provide the same tax advantages as retirement accounts. Contributions to taxable accounts are made with after-tax money, and there are no upfront tax deductions or tax-free withdrawals in retirement.

**Tax inefficiency of certain investments:** Some investments, such as actively managed mutual funds or investments with high turnover, can generate taxable events through capital gains distributions, even if you haven't sold the investment. This can lead to tax implications that reduce your overall returns.

**Impact on financial aid:** If you or your children are seeking financial aid for education, having funds in a taxable brokerage account may count against you, as it is considered an asset. This could potentially reduce your eligibility for certain need-based financial aid, like grants or scholarships.

It's important to weigh the advantages and disadvantages of taxable brokerage accounts in relation to your financial goals and individual circumstances. Consider consulting with a financial advisor or tax professional to assess the best investment and tax strategies based on your specific needs and objectives.

## Lump Sum or Dollar Cost Averaging?

Imagine you've saved up $1,000, and you want to invest it in the stock market. You have two options: Invest all $1,000 at once (lump sum) or spread it out over several months (dollar cost averaging). The decision between investing a lump sum or using a dollar cost averaging (DCA) strategy depends on your individual circumstances, financial goals, and risk tolerance. There is no one-size-fits-all answer, and both approaches have their advantages and disadvantages. Here's a breakdown to help you decide:

### Lump Sum Investment:

Advantages:

- **Potential for Higher Returns:** Historically, the stock market has generally trended upward over time. Investing a lump sum immediately may capture gains from market appreciation.
- **No Timing Risk:** You avoid the risk of missing out on potential market gains if the market moves upward after you invest.

Disadvantages:

- **Immediate Risk:** You're exposed to the full market risk from the outset. If the market drops shortly after you invest, you could experience significant losses.

### Dollar Cost Averaging (DCA):

Advantages:

- **Risk Mitigation:** DCA helps spread risk because you invest gradually over time, reducing the impact of market volatility.
- **Emotional Comfort:** DCA can be less stressful because you don't need to worry about timing the market perfectly. It can help you stay disciplined in your investing approach.

Disadvantages:

- **Potential Missed Gains:** If the market consistently goes up after you start DCA, you may miss out on some potential gains.
- **Higher Transaction Costs:** DCA involves multiple transactions, which can lead to higher brokerage fees.

So, which one is better? It depends on how comfortable you are with risk and how long you plan to invest. If you can handle some ups and downs and are investing for the long haul, putting all your money in at once might be better. But if you're a bit worried about the market, or if you're investing for a shorter-term goal, spreading out your investments using DCA can be a good strategy. Remember, there's no one-size-fits-all answer, and it's essential to think about what makes the most sense for your situation.

## Investing for Your Kids

When it comes to building generational wealth, it's never too early to start. Investing can and should be for kids, too! If you're a first-gen wealth builder, you know one of the main motivations that keeps us going is the goal of laying the blueprint for future generations to be able to reap all the rewards of our hard work. Started from the bottom, now we here, baby! We're not only trying to build wealth for ourselves, we also want to pass on financial education and capital to our families, including the children in our lives.

As I've mentioned, the true power of investing is allowing compound interest to work its magic. The longer you can invest, the longer your money has time to grow and grow some more. You can even start investing before your child is born. Depending on the type of account you use, you can also provide them with a head start for paying for school, buying their first place, and even early retirement. Lastly, investing with your kids is a great way of teaching them about finances.

When it comes to figuring out what type of investing accounts to use for your children, it's important to first think about your goal—it's always about your goal. Whenever you are weighing investment account options, you should have a clear goal in mind. That could be a specific number, but perhaps even more important is the outcome or purpose of the account. So, before you jump into investing for kids in your life, you need to make sure you have a solid understanding of the end goal, be that paying for college or giving your child an early start to their retirement.

Here are the most common investing accounts you can use to build wealth for your kids.

## The 529 Plan (College Savings Plan)

This investment account is specifically designed to save for tax-free spending on higher education expenses, like tuition and fees for college, university, vocational and trade school, and even public, private, or parochial elementary and secondary school. You can use these funds for virtual school options as well. A 529 plan works very similarly to a Roth IRA. You contribute after-tax money and can invest in a variety of mutual funds or ETFs, depending on the plan. A 529 plan offers tax-free growth on your investments and tax-free withdrawals, so long as it is used for qualified educational expenses. You can find a comprehensive list of expenses at savingforcollege.com.

What's great about this type of account is that it is easy for anyone else in your family to contribute. Think about it: Instead of gifts, people can contribute to the 529 account for your child. I love the idea of crowdfunding your child's education instead of buying them another toy that is going to end up in the trash.

Technically, the 529 does not have official contribution limits. However, contributions made to a 529 are limited by the annual federal gift tax exclusion, which in 2023 is $17,000 per donor. Each state offers its own 529 plan, and you are not limited to the state that you are a resident of. New York has a very popular 529 program because it offers the lowest account fees of any state. And if you're worried about your child deciding to opt out of college, 529 plans are transferable to another child, or even to yourself for your own higher education! A recent change to US law provides even more flexibility for 529 plan assets. Starting in 2024, owners of 529 accounts will be allowed to roll over up to $35,000 into a Roth IRA for the plan beneficiary.[1]

This option, which will take effect in 2024, may provide beneficiaries with tax-free retirement money. It's important to note that you still have to abide by the Roth contribution limits, which are $6,500–$7,500 per year (for 2023), depending on the age of the plan beneficiary. So, it might take five or six years to move all the money into the account. Additionally, you can only move contributions that have been in an account for more than five years.

Until the law is in effect, if beneficiaries use assets in a 529 plan for anything other than qualified educational expenses, the earnings portion of any nonqualified distribution is likely to be subject to ordinary income taxes and a 10% penalty. Note that every state is different and has their own 529 plan rules, so to follow the latest news on these changes, visit https://www.collegesavings.org/find-my-states-529-plan/.

## Custodial Brokerage Account

If you're looking for a bit more flexibility, you may want to consider a custodial brokerage account. With this account, the parent or guardian

1. https://www.ameriprise.com/financial-news-research/insights/new-529-plan-rules#:~:text =Lifetime%20maximum%3A%20The%20529%20transfer,subject%20to%20change %20every%20year.

of the account is the account's beneficiary—until the child turns 18 or 21, depending on state laws.

Contrary to a 529, where your investment options are limited, a custodial account offers more variety in terms of investments—from individual stocks to ETFs and mutual funds, you have plenty of options. However, this account does not offer the same tax benefits that a 529 plan offers. Any income from the investments will be taxed at the child's tax rate, which sometimes can be as low as 0% but may be higher if the child has other income.

You'll want to give some thought to how you want to incorporate the child themselves into the process. Involving kids in investing can be a great way to teach them about financial literacy, the power of compound interest, and long-term wealth building. Start with the basics: Begin by explaining the concepts of money and saving, and the importance of setting financial goals. Teach them about the different types of investments, such as stocks, bonds, and mutual funds, in a simplified manner appropriate for their age. For instance, you can talk about companies they are familiar with, like the brands they use or products they enjoy. This can make the idea of investing more tangible and relatable to their daily lives. And you as a parent will want to consider how and when your child will obtain access to this money. We'll talk more about wealth distribution in chapter 10.

With the rise of retail investors, many brokerages have also created account types that are targeted to youth, which come with unique features that can allow for more participation from the child. If you already have a preferred brokerage, find out if they offer any accounts for youth.

## Custodial Roth IRA

Roth IRAs are good for kids for the same reason we love them for anyone else: the tax benefits and the variety of investment vehicle options. However, the same limits apply for kids as they do for adults.

This account type is only an option if your child has taxable income or wages. While there are certainly ways your kids can legally qualify for this through income, typically this won't happen until they get their first job at age 15 or 16. That's still an extra two to three years before they turn 18 that compound interest can do its job. During this stage, the Roth IRA will function as a custodial account, with full ownership transferring over when the child turns 18.

Keep in mind that this is a *retirement* account. Although contributions can be pulled out at any time, there are stipulations for permissible uses of investment funds. Aside from things like education or a first-home purchase, if these funds are used before the beneficiary turns 59½, a penalty fee will accrue. If you open this type of account, it should be because you want to kick-start this child's retirement plan, not necessarily to help them pay for their education or buy their first home.

## Make Sure to Teach

Regardless of the account you choose to open, a fundamental piece of the process is involving the child you are wanting to invest for. On the podcast, we discussed this with Kevin L. Matthews, former financial advisor and best-selling author of *From Burning to Blueprint: Rebuilding Black Wall Street After a Century of Silence*. Kevin told me that it's essential to include kids in the conversation as early as possible, so we can begin to ensure there won't be a misuse of their assets when they are legally handed over, and so that we can pass down the financial education that is so often absent from first-gen communities.

Encourage your children to actively participate in investment decisions by discussing investment choices and involving them in the decision-making process. This can include researching and selecting stocks or funds together based on their interests or values. Use educational resources and books suitable for their age to enhance their understanding. In addition to investing, teach your kids about other aspects of personal finance, such as budgeting, saving, and debt management. Helping them understand the importance of financial responsibility and the role that investing plays in building long-term wealth will set them up for future success! By involving kids in investing at an early age, you can help them develop sound financial habits and set them on a path toward financial success.

Investing for the kids in our lives is not just about building a cash nest egg for them. It is also about making sure they know how to understand money, how to manage money, and how to grow it efficiently. That's how generational wealth becomes multigenerational wealth!

## WEALTH HACK: USING YOUR BIZ TO BUILD GENERATIONAL WEALTH

As a business owner, you can contribute to a Custodial Roth IRA on behalf of your child or another minor, provided they have earned income from your business. However, there are certain rules and limitations you need to be aware of:

**Earned Income Requirement:** The child must have earned income to contribute to a Roth IRA. Earned income includes wages, salaries, tips, and other forms of compensation. Income from investments or gifts does not count.

**Contribution Limits:** The contribution limit for 2023 is $6,500 or the child's total earned income for the year, whichever is lower. This limit applies to all IRAs the child may have.

**Tax Treatment:** Roth IRA contributions are made with after-tax dollars, meaning contributions are not tax-deductible. However, the earnings in a Roth IRA grow tax-free, and qualified withdrawals in retirement are also tax-free.

**Custodial Account:** Roth IRAs for minors are usually set up as custodial accounts, where a custodian (usually a parent or legal guardian) manages the account until the child reaches the age of majority (which varies by state).

Tax laws and regulations can be complex, especially for business owners. It's advisable to consult a tax professional or a financial advisor who is well versed in retirement planning for personalized guidance based on your specific situation.

## It's Never Too Late to Start Building Wealth

You may be feeling a lot of pressure right now to "make up for lost time" because no one in your family has invested up until this point. Perhaps you've thought to yourself, "I'll never be able to build wealth—it's too late for me." Maybe you've even cursed out your family in your head for not teaching you this stuff. Believe me, I get it. "To be [a first-generation American] is to feel like you're trying to fix and heal the financial scars of many generations before you and trying to catch up to the other folks who have been generations ahead of you, all in one lifetime," says Berna Anat, Filipina American financial educator, and author and creator of Hey Berna, a first-gen financial literacy platform. She's so right, mi gente! The pressure is real, but I need you to be compassionate with yourself and your loved ones. It's important to realize that your family couldn't teach you how to invest, because they weren't doing it themselves. And chances are, your school didn't teach you either. I encourage you to take a balanced approach in your generational wealth-building journey. It is not your responsibility to break the cycle of intergenerational poverty on your own. That's super stressful to think about! Just by deciding to invest as a first-gen kid, you are already setting strong financial foundations for those who come after you. In fact, you're changing their financial trajectory. That's giving serious bichota energy, if I do say so myself.

**CHAPTER 7**

# How to Become a Financially Independent Mujer, aka #Goals

As a Latina in the financial independence and early retirement space, I have experienced many times what a novelty my very presence in this space is. When people hear my story about saving and investing half a million dollars by my mid-thirties, their emotions range from skepticism to intrigue. They're even more shocked when they find out that as a Latina with no professional financial background, I was able to research my way to starting online businesses that enabled me to walk away from a six-figure corporate salary. The utter disbelief that someone from my community can build wealth, invest, or start a business speaks to how much the lack of representation in personal finance is hurting our progress. I'm here to encourage you to dream beyond the struggle.

We know what struggle looks like; we're all too familiar with it. What we need now is **financial liberation**. For generations, we've had to rely on boyfriends, husbands, fathers, and other male figures in our lives to decide what is best for us financially. You can thank the patriarchy and toxic machismo for that bullshit. Think about women in your familia who are stuck in shitty marriages or relationships because they don't have the safety net in place to walk away without falling into financial chaos, homelessness, or worse. I'm SO OVER the idea of us being at the mercy of people who may not have our best interests in mind. In this chapter, I will teach you **how to fight back, with FIRE**. The FIRE (Financial Independence/Retire Early) movement is a financial lifestyle whose practitioners aim to achieve financial independence and retire at an earlier age than traditional retirement timelines. Because contrary to what you've been told, amiga, retirement is not about reaching a certain age. It's about reaching a certain number.

Why should you care about FIRE? Because a financially independent woman is unstoppable.

## Wanna Quit Your Job? Light It on FIRE

While the primary goal of the FIRE movement is financial independence, it doesn't necessarily mean quitting your job. However, it can provide you with the flexibility to make choices about your work life.

The FIRE movement emphasizes saving a significant portion of your income and investing it wisely. By adopting a frugal lifestyle, reducing unnecessary expenses, and prioritizing savings, you can accumulate a substantial nest egg over time. Financial independence can provide you with the freedom to choose whether or not to continue working a job, start a business or new hobby, or just spend your days lying face down on the grass in your backyard. No judgment here. As Jamila Souffrant, founder of the popular FIRE podcast *Journey to Launch*, puts it: "It's not about more money, it's about more options."

In 2018, Jamila found herself packing up her cubicle and heading out the door of her 9-to-5 job for the last time. How? "Because I had finally achieved the financial freedom I needed to leave my job." She liked her job, but it required her to commute an hour and a half or more each way, depending on traffic, from her home in Brooklyn to her job in New Jersey. One day, when she was pregnant and the ride home took her three hours, she began to plan her exit strategy. She wanted to have more kids and she knew she would be stretched too thin juggling her 9-to-5 and her podcast, which was just beginning to take off. Jamila spoke to her husband about cutting their expenses way down and saving more than just their usual "what was left over." In two years they were able to save and invest $169,000 by focusing on maxing out their pre-tax contributions to their retirement plans. Ultimately, their efforts allowed her to walk away from her job to focus on raising her kids and building her business. She achieved true financial freedom.

Through diligent savings and investments, individuals following the FIRE movement can build passive income streams. Unlike "active income," which is earned by a job or a business venture that requires active participation, passive income is income that requires minimal effort to obtain. It can come from sources such as investment portfolios, real estate, or business ventures. By generating passive income that covers your living expenses, you can reduce your dependence on traditional employment income, giving you the option to quit your job.

The FIRE movement encourages individuals to explore alternative career paths or entrepreneurial endeavors that align with their passions and interests. Achieving financial independence through FIRE can provide you with a safety net while you transition into a career that may be more fulfilling or aligned with your goals. It can give you the freedom to explore new opportunities without the immediate pressure of relying on a steady paycheck.

By following the principles of the FIRE movement, you can prioritize a better work-life balance. This can involve working fewer hours, pursuing part-time or flexible work arrangements, or taking sabbaticals to recharge and pursue personal interests. This increased balance and reduced stress can contribute to overall well-being and satisfaction with your work life. Doesn't that sound incredible?! But wait, there's more!

## Wanna Leave That Toxic Relationship? FIRE Can Help.

Financial independence allows you to have control over your own life and make decisions that align with your personal goals and aspirations. It enables you to have a sense of autonomy and the ability to shape your own future, rather than being solely dependent on a partner for financial support.

Financial independence promotes equality within a relationship. When both partners have their own income and resources, it reduces the power dynamics that can arise when one person has greater financial control. It ensures that decisions within the relationship are made on equal footing and that both partners contribute to the financial well-being of the household.

Maintaining your financial independence provides you with the flexibility to make choices that best suit your needs and desires. It allows you to pursue YOUR own career goals, invest in YOUR personal development, and engage in activities that bring YOU fulfillment. Because despite the self-sacrificing behaviors you may have seen modeled by your mama or abuela, your goals and dreams matter too, mujer!

Relationships can be unpredictable, and financial independence provides you with a layer of protection and security. In the event of a breakup, divorce, or the death of a partner, a financially independent woman is better positioned to navigate these challenges. You have the means to support yourself, maintain your standard of living, and provide for your dependents if necessary.

When you maintain financial independence, you become a role model for younger generations. You can take an active role in breaking the cycle of financial dependency and encourage other girls and women to strive for independence, pursue their dreams, and achieve economic empowerment. By setting an example, you can inspire others to take control of their own financial lives and promote gender equality in broader society. Que cool!

Financial independence doesn't mean financial isolation or the absence of shared financial goals and responsibilities with your partner. It simply refers to having the ability to support yourself financially and contribute meaningfully to your relationship without money being a part of the power dynamic. It's living in a world where you call the shots. You make your own decisions instead of relying on someone else to make them for you. You know that you've got your own back, and if a relationship turns toxic or abusive, you can walk away without a moment's hesitation. We'll talk more about love and money in chapter 9.

## Be the Change

When you're financially independent, you're financially unfuckwithable! This is why I believe that being a financially independent woman is a revolutionary act that we must all strive toward. And more importantly, it's something we must prepare for, because at some point in our lives, we will be forced to manage our finances independently.

Statistically, US Latinas can expect a long life. At 84 years, Latina life expectancy is second only to Asian American women (85.8 years). While Latinas have the gift of longevity, Hispanic males do not, living to an average age of 79.2 years, according to the Centers for Disease Control and Prevention. Other communities fare even worse. Non-Hispanic white males live on average to 76.5 years, and non-Hispanic Black males to 72 years.

Men, as a general rule, are far more likely to be single when they're young, marry later (and/or rack up multiple marriages), and stay married until their deaths. The reverse is true for women: They're more likely to marry young but then end up divorced or widowed and living alone as they age. A longer life expectancy means that you will likely require more financial resources to support yourself throughout your life, particularly in your later years.

Due to lower earnings, career interruptions to raise children, and caregiving responsibilities, women often have lower retirement savings compared to men. This can leave you more vulnerable to financial insecurity and poverty in your later years. Pursuing financial independence isn't a matter of choice, mujeres. It's a matter of living a dignified life. So, knowing that, what do you need to do to become financially independent? The first thing is to understand what it actually means.

## What Is FIRE?

FIRE stands for Financial Independence/Retire Early, and the concept involves:

- Saving a massive amount of your income (usually 50 percent or more)
- Living well below your means
- Investing heavily in low-cost index funds

Using these principles, FIRE proponents are able to shave years, even decades, off the traditional retirement age, which is usually 65 (but officially, in terms of Social Security benefits, is not until 67).

### How Did It Start?

The main ideas behind the FIRE movement originated in the 1992 best-selling book *Your Money or Your Life* by Vicki Robin and Joe Dominguez. They popularized the idea of achieving financial independence rather than spending the best years of your life working in a 9-to-5 to make money.

The core concept of their book is that most of us float through life unknowingly exchanging our time for money. Time, as our most precious and scarce resource, is spent earning money so we can buy fancy purses, the latest electronic gadgets, the big house, and the new car. Robin and Dominguez made the argument that people are trading their lives to buy things that don't actually bring them value. *And thus, a movement was born.*

## The FIRE Community Today

While *Your Money or Your Life* fueled momentum as a grassroots movement, it was another twenty-five years before the FIRE movement began to really take shape, during and immediately after the Great Recession of 2008. During this time, many people lost their entire retirement savings, homes, jobs, and more. It was a huge cultural moment that caused many people to become disillusioned with the "American Dream" of going to school, getting a job, saving for retirement, and mindless consumerism.

Some folks began to realize most personal finance advice just encourages behavior that keeps you stuck on an endless treadmill of earning, saving, and spending until you're old and gray, with no option to opt out of the rat race entirely. What if you could accelerate your savings, lower your cost of living, and retire in your forties, or even earlier? The answer: pursuing FIRE. The FIRE movement became an antidote for those seeking to escape the capitalistic churn-and-burn grind of corporate America.

One of the most well-known FIRE advocates is Mr. Money Mustache, also known as Pete Adeney. After retiring at thirty, he started his blog with the same name, where he shares with his followers (known as Mustachians) his journey to FIRE and tips for his readers to get there themselves. He focused on the concept of extreme frugality to achieve financial freedom. He and his now ex-wife saved over 60 percent of their incomes in their twenties, and they both retired shortly before having a child.

The movement was initially led by a number of white men, many of whom were in high-paying careers in tech and as such, had large amounts of disposable income to funnel toward investing. Some other well-known white male influencers in the space are The Financial Samurai, Grant Sabatier, and The Mad Fientist. Some popular books on FIRE include *Financial Freedom, How to Retire Early with Real Estate, Work Optional, ChooseFI, Quit Like a Millionaire, The Simple Path to Wealth*, and *The Millionaire Next Door*.

As time has gone on, women and people of color have increasingly joined the choir of voices promoting the FIRE lifestyle as an alternative to the 24/7 hustle culture that many people of color saw their parents pursue. Latina, Black, and Asian women have been crucial in diversifying the space and adding more cultural relevance to the FIRE conversation.

## MY FAVORITE FIRE FRIENDS

**Delyanne Barros:** A former undocumented immigrant from Brazil, Delyanne began sharing her journey on Instagram using the handle @delyannethemoneycoach during the 2020 pandemic and scaled her passion for teaching POC about FIRE and investing into a multimillion-dollar coaching business.

**Jamila Souffrant:** The founder and CEO of the popular financial blog and podcast *Journey to Launch*, Jamila shares her journey to reach financial independence while helping others do the same. Her podcast was the spark that lit my own journey to financial independence!

**Julien and Kiersten Saunders (*rich & REGULAR*):** This husband-and-wife duo started their blog in 2017 after a stint in real estate investing led them to discover the FIRE movement. Today, *rich & REGULAR* has grown into a community of like-minded people inspired to have better conversations about money.

**A Purple Life:** An anonymous woman of color blogger who began blogging at APurpleLife.com in 2015 to document her journey to retiring by thirty. She accomplished it in 2020 (yup, during the pandemic) and now shares her post-retirement journey via social media. I love her cuz she gets really transparent with her numbers, and we need more transparency in personal finance!

**Shang Saavedra:** Shang is the creator of Save My Cents. She and her husband became work-optional by the time she was thirty-one (and while living in Manhattan!). She shares her knowledge in a no-nonsense way, and encourages pursuing financial independence holistically.

## What's So Great About FIRE?

Financial independence isn't easy to achieve. It's a long road, taking many people a decade or more to achieve. What do people get when they reach financial independence? What drives them to create a plan and stick with it?

**Freedom to pursue work you love.** For many in the FIRE movement, financial independence isn't actually about retirement, it's about having the ability to choose work that you enjoy doing. Financial independence gives you the chance to choose the work that you do, without worrying about how much you make. It provides you with the freedom to explore new opportunities, take risks, and create a life that aligns with your goals and aspirations. It's more about freedom than anything else.

**Freedom to spend more time with family.** Financial independence means you can spend as much time with family as you want.

You can stay home with your kids while they're young, enjoy time with your spouse, and spend extended time visiting your parents without worrying whether your boss will care. Financial independence allows you to have more control over your life. You can choose how you spend your time and make decisions based on personal values rather than financial constraints. FIRE followers are super cognizant that tomorrow is not promised, and they're determined to make the most of it.

**Freedom to travel, live, and work from anywhere.** The United States is the only advanced economy in the world that does not guarantee its workers paid vacation days and paid holidays. This means employees can work for months or even years without any break, lacking the work-life balance that is so important for their physical and mental well-being. The average American worker gets just eleven days of paid time off (PTO) per year. *TLDR: America's PTO policy is ghetto AF.*

This is why FIRE is so appealing to those of us who pursue it. With FIRE, you can travel as much as you want, with complete disregard for how much PTO your boss wants to give you. It provides you with the opportunity to explore, travel, and move around the world, without having to worry about being restricted by the normal constraints of a traditional 9-to-5 job.

## GEO-*WHAT*?

Some people who pursue FIRE take advantage of geoarbitrage. This is the practice of using geographical differences in costs of living, wages, or other economic factors to improve your financial situation. It involves relocating or leveraging location-independent work to live in a place with a lower cost of living while earning income from a higher-cost location.

The concept of geoarbitrage is rooted in the idea that different regions or countries can have significant disparities in living expenses, including housing, healthcare, transportation, and food costs. By strategically choosing to live in an area with lower expenses while earning income from a higher-paying job or business in another location, individuals can potentially increase their purchasing power, savings, or overall quality of life.

For example, someone working remotely for a company based in a high-cost city like San Francisco may choose to live in a more affordable location such as a rural area, small town, or country with a lower cost of living. They can maintain their job and salary while benefiting from lower housing costs and other expenses, allowing them to save more money or enjoy a higher standard of living.

Geoarbitrage can also be pursued by individuals who are not location-dependent in their work, such as digital nomads or freelancers who can work from anywhere with an internet connection. They may travel or live in different countries or regions, selecting those with favorable economic conditions that align with their financial goals. Some low-cost areas popular with people pursuing FIRE are Central and South America, Southeast Asia, and Eastern Europe.

And extended travel isn't just for people who have reached FIRE. Many people on the path to FIRE choose to take a sabbatical for an extended period of time (like a year) to travel and enjoy the FIRE lifestyle.

# Passive Income: The Engine Behind FIRE

*"If you don't find a way to make money while you sleep, you will work until you die."*—Warren Buffett

Most of us are familiar with **active income**, money you earn by working as an employee, independent contractor, or freelancer. You show up, do some work, and get paid a certain amount of money for your skills and time. That's what we saw our parents and grandparents do, so for many of us, that's the only type of income we know how to earn. The downside? If you stop working or providing the services, the income stops. That doesn't sound like freedom to me.

FIRE followers are all about that **semi-passive** and **passive income** life. Since the primary goal of pursuing FIRE is to achieve financial independence, this requires having enough income and assets to cover living expenses without relying on traditional employment. Passive income streams are a key component of achieving financial independence because they provide ongoing income without requiring active work or employment. Semi-passive income refers to a type of income that falls somewhere between passive income and active income. It requires a moderate level of ongoing involvement or management, but it doesn't require the same level of active effort as traditional active income sources. Passive income streams can continue to generate income even when you're not actively working. Can I get a hell yeah?!

Let's talk about the types of income and break down what makes them different.

## Active Income

Your **salary** comes from income earned as an employee, where you receive a fixed or variable compensation for the work you perform. If you aren't salaried, you receive **wages**, income earned by performing specific tasks or jobs on an hourly or per-project basis. Depending on your circumstances, you may also receive income from freelance or contract work, earned by providing services or completing projects on a contract or freelance basis. This can include professions like graphic design, writing, programming, consulting, or any other field where you work on a project-by-project basis. You might have business income earned from actively running and operating a business, whether it's a retail store, restaurant, consulting firm, or any other type of business where you are directly involved in the day-to-day operations. Or you may also receive commission-based sales, where you receive a percentage of the sales you make or the revenue you generate. And lately, the gig economy provides income through gig work, such as driving for ride-sharing services, delivering food, or performing tasks on freelance platforms.

## Semi-passive Income

This type of income requires your involvement, but not as much. You might receive it through a rental property with partial management, owning rental properties and being somewhat involved in property management while delegating certain tasks to others. For example, you might handle tenant selection and major decisions while hiring contractors or property managers for maintenance and day-to-day operations. Investing in real estate syndication allows you to passively invest in real estate projects led by experienced professionals. While you may have some involvement in decision-making or monitoring the investment, the primary responsibility lies with the project sponsor or general partner.

Peer-to-peer lending platforms, in which you lend money to individuals or businesses, can be considered semi-passive income. While you need to review and select loan opportunities, the platform manages the loan servicing, repayment, and collection processes. Engaging in affiliate marketing means you actively create content and promote products or services, but the income continues to be generated even when you're not actively promoting. This involves building a website or blog, producing content, and establishing a network of affiliate partnerships. Running an online business, in which you outsource specific tasks or aspects of the business, such as order fulfillment, customer support, or content creation, allows you to maintain oversight and make strategic decisions, but you rely on others to handle certain operations. Operating an e-commerce store where you use third-party fulfillment services to handle inventory management, order processing, and shipping allows you to focus on marketing and product selection.

## Passive Income

For those of us who want to be truly hands-off when it comes to making dinero, there are many options for generating passive income. You can invest in index funds or stocks that pay regular dividends, without actively managing the portfolio or conducting frequent trades. Interest income can come from investments in interest-bearing assets, such as bonds, certificates of deposit (CDs), or high-yield savings accounts. You might earn royalties, which are earnings generated from licensing intellectual property, such as books, music, patents, or software, where you receive payment without active involvement in creating or marketing the products. Real estate investment trusts (REITs) involve investing in publicly traded REITs, which allow you to earn passive income from real estate properties without direct ownership or management responsibilities. Automated online businesses are fully automated and require minimal ongoing effort, such as drop-shipping stores, automated e-commerce platforms, or digital product sales with automated delivery. You might also own a rental property but hire a property management company to handle all aspects of property maintenance, tenant management, rent collection, and repairs.

Please note that these examples do not cover all possible sources of income, and the classification of income can sometimes be subjective. The categorization of income as passive, semi-passive, or active depends on the level of involvement and effort required to generate and maintain that income stream.

## The FIRE Movement Is for Everyone

Just like personal finance, your FIRE journey is personal. Pursuing early retirement is not just for the ultra-rich. With the right level of planning and intentionality, you can also achieve FIRE and not have to work for the rest of your life. There are so many flavors of FIRE (we'll get into those below) that you can literally design your financial freedom plan to fit your desired lifestyle. Maybe you don't want to work full-time until you're sixty-five, but you don't have a high salary or your cost of living is high because of where you live. Complete financial independence isn't your only option; you can consider semi-retirement or a work sabbatical as an alternative goal to start with.

Pursuing some version of FIRE or semi-retirement is entirely possible no matter how much you make, but it's going to take some careful planning and dedication. By creating a detailed budget to understand your income and expenses, you can identify areas where you can save more. Embracing a frugal lifestyle and prioritizing essential expenses will help you avoid unnecessary spending. The single biggest factor that will influence your ability to reach FI is increasing your income. You can consider picking up side gigs, freelancing, or part-time work. Every extra dollar earned can make a difference. Saving aggressively, even in small amounts, can accumulate over time. If possible, explore opportunities to downsize your living expenses, such as finding a more affordable area to live or opting for a smaller home. Adopting a do-it-yourself (DIY) mindset and practicing minimalism can help reduce expenses and simplify your life. Invest in improving your skills and education, as enhanced qualifications can open up new opportunities for higher-paying jobs or freelance work.

Remember, achieving FIRE or semi-retirement is not solely dependent on your salary, but rather on your ability to save, invest wisely, and live within your means. With careful planning, smart financial decisions, and dedication to your goals, you can work toward financial independence and the option to retire early or transition to a more flexible work-life balance. It's a journey that requires patience and discipline, but the rewards of increased freedom and financial security are well worth the effort.

My framework gives you an overview of what the journey to FIRE looks like.

## My Six-Step FIRE Framework

While each person's FIRE journey will be different, these are the six key steps that I used to achieve FI in my mid-thirties. Depending on where you are in your journey, you may or may not have to start at step 1.

**Step 1—Confront your current financial situation.** To reach FIRE, you need a long-term success plan. Once you have your FIRE target, it's time to identify the biggest ROI (return on investment) areas in your budget by determining your current obligations, assets, and liabilities. Target paying off high-interest-rate debt while putting aside funds for emergencies to prevent falling into the cycle of recurring debt. Determining your overall net worth is also a part of this step.

**Step 2—Reduce your cost of living.** In order to free up funds to reach your FIRE goals, find areas in your life where costs can be reduced. Instead of focusing on clipping coupons or cutting your Netflix subscription, tackle the big three: housing, transportation, and food.

**Step 3—Increase your income.** You can only cut so much out of your budget, but your ability to earn more money is theoretically limitless. Whether you make a career change into a higher-paying field, get additional education to pursue a promotion, or start a side hustle, now is the time to create more money.

**Step 4—Increase your savings rate.** With more money comes the ability to save more. Avoiding lifestyle creep as you earn more will allow you to save and invest more over the long term. When you get a windfall of money, like a tax refund or a bonus at work, resist the urge to upgrade your lifestyle if you're comfortable. Use that extra money to bulk up your savings account or add more to your investment account.

**Step 5—Invest for generational wealth.** When I began investing, it was in a 401(k) for my own retirement. As I grew my proficiency as an investor, I dabbled in real estate, then other investment accounts, cryptocurrencies, my own business, and most recently, as an angel investor. As your investing knowledge grows, take steps to create wealth in various ways. After securing your own financial safety net, consider investing for multiple generations, like your children or aging parents.

**Step 6—Remain flexible in your methods but firm in your goals.** Life has an interesting way of throwing us curveballs from time to time. If your financial situation changes, be willing to shift your FIRE timeline until things become steady again. And reward yourself along the way. Celebrate your progress toward reaching FIRE. Creating wealth is a lifetime pursuit, so enjoy the journey.

# Wanna Test Trial by FIRE? You Need an FU Fund.

Imagine this: You have been working at a stable place over the past few years. You have benefits, a consistent salary, and you get along with your team. But then the company gets acquired, management changes, or the conditions at your job deteriorate, and you are no longer happy.

Maybe you want to pivot careers entirely. This is what Gianni LaTange, creator of First Gen Money Musings, did. When Gianni realized that she was no longer happy, she began to build her FU fund—a "fuck you" or "financially unfuckwithable" fund. (I made that second one up.) This account allowed her the freedom to quit her stable education job in the middle of the COVID-19 pandemic, enroll in a coding boot camp, and fully transition into the tech industry.

So let's talk about FU funds, what they are and how to use them. An FU fund is a savings account funded with money that allows you the freedom of choice. It is called an FU fund for a reason—with FU money, you can say "eff you" to anything that does not fit into your current life or is bringing you stress.

## FU Funds vs. Emergency Funds

The main similarity is that both of these accounts are savings funds. The key difference is that an emergency fund is generally for unplanned events, or emergencies.

An FU fund is a pool of money that you set aside for future use, such as when you decide to take a career break, change jobs, travel, or spend time with your loved ones. An FU fund lets you enjoy a sabbatical without the pressure of having to find a new job right away.

Let's consider an example scenario like a job loss. If you experienced a job loss with just an emergency fund, the timeline you'd have to find another job would be the number of months your emergency fund can sustain you for. If you had four months of emergency fund money saved, you'd have that much time to find a job and replace your income.

You could decide to use your FU fund to take some time off to travel, invest in learning a new skill, or pivot your career entirely.

## Why Should I Build My FU Fund?

Having an FU fund provides you with greater flexibility and independence. It allows you to make choices based on what is best for you and your family, rather than being forced into desperate financial decisions. Also, an FU fund gives you the ability to take advantage of opportunities that may arise. Whether it's starting a business, investing in a promising opportunity, or pursuing a career change, having financial stability gives you the freedom to take calculated risks.

If you have irregular income or work in a freelance or self-employed capacity, an FU fund helps smooth out fluctuations in income. It provides a buffer during periods of lower earnings and ensures that you can meet your financial obligations consistently. With an FU fund, you can:

- Quit and leave toxic work situations.
- Explore new career options.
- Go back to school.
- Take time off to be with your family.
- Plan that vacation you've dreamed of.

An FU fund means more options. You've given yourself a financial runway that can allow you to enjoy the freedom of choice.

## OK, How Do I Do It?

In theory, saving for your FU fund will not be much different from any other type of saving. The difference? The intention behind the saving.

To build an FU fund, first start by looking at your budget. This means knowing what your current cash flow (income) is, what your expenses are, and what amount of money you can save each month toward your FU fund. There are several ways to budget, but key to building an FU fund is making a plan and staying consistent until you reach your savings goal.

If you find it difficult to set aside money for an FU fund, a side hustle can help increase your income, if you have the bandwidth.

If you intend to wait several years before using your FU fund, you can consider leveraging the stock market as a place for you to save toward it. Going this route can not only enable you to save money on a consistent basis but also bring you returns on your investments, thereby growing your FU fund at a faster pace.

Note that retirement accounts like a 401(k) or an IRA will "lock" up your money until you retire, so plan accordingly. Your best option in this scenario is a brokerage account.

## The Trinity Study and the 4 Percent Rule

The principle of the FIRE number is the **4 percent rule**, which became popular after the publication of a 1998 paper titled "Retirement Savings: Choosing a Withdrawal Rate that is Sustainable," often referred to as the Trinity Study.

The 4 percent retirement rule refers to your withdrawal rate: the amount of money you might withdraw each year from the starting value of your portfolio of stocks and bonds in retirement. Should you have $1,000,000 when you retire, the 4 percent rule would allow you to withdraw about 4 percent of that amount—or $40,000—the first year of retirement.

You could then increase that amount with inflation and have a probability of almost 95 percent that your money would last for at least thirty years, assuming your portfolio allocation was 50 percent stocks and 50 percent bonds.

The Trinity Study has some limitations, mainly that it assumes a thirty-year-long retirement. If you are planning to retire in your forties, you could end up in a scenario where you run out of money in your seventies. While 4 percent (or [x] 0.25) is the traditional rate that FIRE-followers use, you may opt to use a more conservative 3 percent annual withdrawal rate, to make your money last longer.

It's important to consider things like:

- The length of your planned retirement
- Your risk tolerance (i.e., the mix of investments you are comfortable with)
- Your desired lifestyle in retirement
- Your preferred withdrawal rate

FIRE is totally customizable, so let the formulas give you a starting point, versus a final destination.

## Calculating Your FIRE Number

In order to calculate your FIRE number, the formula is as follows:

**Annual Expenses [x] 25 = FIRE Number**

Warning: The number will shock you.

If you spend, on average, $60,000 per year to sustain your life—an amount that represents your annual living expenses—the math works out to:

**$60,000 [x] 25 = $1,500,000**
**Your FIRE number would be $1,500,000.**

Once your portfolio hits that number, you would become financially independent, because now your portfolio would be providing you with the income you may need.

*Are you panicking yet?*

It's a completely normal reaction when many people first discover the FIRE movement and calculate their FIRE number. Relax, there's more to this story. You're not actually going to have to invest $1 million of your own money to reach your FIRE number. We're going to use an investing BFF known as compound interest to get to our goal much faster.

If you were to try to save $1 million in a savings account that's paying 1% interest, you'd have to save $2,383.06 each month for thirty years. That's a ton of money, and chances are you don't just have an extra few thousand dollars lying around each month. This is why we invest: The compound interest you receive in the stock market is ten times higher on average.

So instead of using a savings account, if you invest in a fund that mimics the performance of the S&P 500 (an assortment of the 500 largest publicly traded companies in the United States), you will only have to invest $442.38 a month for thirty years to reach $1 million invested. For the past 100 years, the S&P 500 has returned an average of 10% interest. This will make your money grow infinitely faster and will require much less of it coming out of your own pocket.

You should consider the 25x rule as a goal-setting tool, rather than a precise prediction.

The 25x rule can help you create your initial FIRE number, but you probably shouldn't hang your entire retirement on this formula alone. You'll want to ask yourself questions like:

- Where will I live and what does the cost of living look like?
- How will I pay for health insurance after leaving the workforce?
- Who else is relying on me for income?
- Do I expect to travel a lot or be a homebody?
- What does my post-FIRE life look like?
- Will I pursue other income sources once I'm FIRE?

This will help you determine if 25x is a good amount to save, or if you need more or less.

This is the standard approach to the FIRE movement, but there are now many different iterations that allow you to customize your journey toward the overall goal of financial independence.

## Other Types Of FIRE

**Lean FIRE**. Think FIRE, but on a budget. People who opt into Lean FIRE expect to spend $40,000 or less on their annual expenses. If your current expenses are low and you don't plan on increasing them by a lot in retirement, this might be the most fitting type of FIRE for you. This version of the FIRE movement also appeals to those opting for a very minimalist lifestyle as they are on their FIRE journey as well as during retirement.

*Example*: If you plan to spend $30,000 annually in retirement, your portfolio would need to reach $750,000, per the 25x rule.

**Coast FIRE**. You achieve Coast FIRE when you have enough money invested at an early enough age that you no longer need to invest any more to reach financial independence by the traditional retirement age of 65 to 69. This type of FIRE is great for (1) people who are not in a rush to retire early but want to ensure they are set financially for retirement, and (2) tracking your progress.

*Example*: If you could save $263,000 by age 35 and simply not touch that money for 32 years, then it would eventually grow to over $1 million by age 67, assuming a 5% annual rate of return after inflation.

**Fat FIRE**. This is FIRE, but ballin', meaning this is for people who want to live lavishly. People who pursue Fat FIRE expect a high annual expenditure, usually upwards of $100,000 per year. We're talkin' new cars on rotation, unlimited Uber Eats, YOLO style travel, and few to no restrictions on spending to live your best life. Fat FIRE is for folks who aren't about to start penny-pinching in their financially independent life.

*Example*: If you plan to spend $150,000 annually in retirement, then you would need $3.75 million to hit Fat FIRE.

With Fat FIRE, you are truly free to live like a boss bish. You can do whatever you want, wherever you want. And if you choose to earn supplemental income because it makes you happy, that's an option too. It's the hardest level of FIRE to achieve, but arguably the most fun.

**Barista FIRE**. Think FIRE, but hybrid. Under this type of FIRE, you are still saving for a specific amount following the 4 percent rule. However, you don't want to grind away at work during what some may call some of the best years of your life. Instead, under Barista FIRE, you'll have the option of quitting your day job, withdrawing 4 percent of the portfolio you have built up so far, annually, and supplementing the income that's left to be covered with your side hustle or a lower-stress job that you would enjoy—like, say, becoming a barista, hence the name.

To calculate your Barista FIRE number, you need to first figure out how much you will earn from your Barista FIRE job long term. Then you deduct this number from your annual living expenses.

As an example: $65,000 (annual expenses) – $30,000 (Barista FI job income) = $35,000

You then calculate your FIRE number based on this lower amount.

Barista FIRE number = (annual expenses – annual job income) x 25

So in our example case, the calculation looks like this:

$35,000 x 25 = $875,000

Barista FIRE also allows you to test-run early retirement, so you can get an idea of what life in FIRE could look like.

**Slow FI**. Coined by the Fioneers, Slow FI is the concept of incrementally taking steps to build more joy and freedom into your life, while pursuing FIRE. The Fioneers define Slow FI as:

> When someone utilizes the incremental financial freedom they gain along the journey to financial independence to live happier and healthier lives, do better work, and build strong relationships.

People pursuing Slow FI could retire early or could retire at the traditional retirement age. The ultimate goal is full financial independence (not having to rely on a job as your primary source of income and financial stability), but the focus is on making the journey as remarkable as the destination.

**Cashflow FIRE.** The idea of saving a seven-figure portfolio was daunting for me as it's not something that many people are able to realistically do, especially in their thirties or forties, so on my path to financial independence, I chose the Cashflow FIRE method. With this type of financial independence, you find ways to increase your cash flow through multiple streams of income (starting a side hustle, investing in real estate, dividend investing, etc.) until you reach your monthly income target. Once you reach that monthly cash flow number consistently, you're financially independent.

### PRACTICE: Wanna Pursue FIRE?
### Ask Yourself These Questions First

Take the time to reflect on your values, goals, and priorities to determine if pursuing FIRE aligns with your vision of a fulfilling life. Consider:

- What is my motivation for pursuing FIRE? Understanding your underlying motivations will help you stay committed to your goals throughout the journey.
- What does financial independence mean to me? Define what financial independence looks like in your life. Consider factors such as freedom from traditional employment, pursuing passion projects, or spending more time with loved ones.

- What is my current financial situation? Assess your current income, expenses, savings, and investments. Understanding your financial standing will help you determine how much work is needed to achieve FIRE.
- How much money do I need to be financially independent? Calculate your target financial independence number, taking into account your expected expenses and desired lifestyle in retirement.
- How long am I willing to work toward FIRE? Determine your desired timeframe for achieving financial independence and retiring early. This will influence your savings and investment strategies.
- What lifestyle changes am I willing to make to reach FIRE? Consider the sacrifices and adjustments you are willing to make in terms of spending, saving, and investing to accelerate your journey toward FIRE.
- How will pursuing FIRE impact my relationships? Reflect on how pursuing FIRE may affect your relationships with family, friends, and significant others. Discuss your goals and plans with them to ensure alignment and support.
- How will I maintain healthcare and other essential benefits after retiring early? Explore options for healthcare coverage and other benefits that will be crucial after retiring early, such as life insurance or disability insurance.
- What will I do with my time once I achieve FIRE? Envision how you will spend your days after retiring early. Consider hobbies, passions, volunteering, or potential side ventures to stay engaged and fulfilled.
- What are the risks and challenges associated with FIRE? Acknowledge the potential risks, such as market fluctuations,

unexpected expenses, or changes in personal circumstances. Prepare contingency plans to mitigate these risks.

Once you've answered these questions, you're ready to start your FIRE journey.

### How to calculate Coast FIRE

The formula for Coast FIRE is  A / (1+r)t where:

A = the amount you need to save to be financially independent (FIRE)

r = your annual rate of return after inflation

t = the number of years investments have to compound

Example: Let's say you are 25 years old and determine that once you stop working at the age of 65 you will need $75,000 a year from your retirement account for living expenses. Your expected rate of return is 6% and you hope to reach Coast FIRE by the time you are 45 (20 years).

Here's how the formula works for you:

A = $75,000 x 25 = $1,875,000 / (1+0.06)20 = $584,634 = Coast FIRE amount. You have 20 years to accumulate that amount. (Remember: Your savings will be helped by compound interest during this time.)

So, how much per month must you save over 20 years to accomplish Coast FIRE? A savings goal calculator, such as the one found at Investor .gov, provides the answer.

Starting at age 25, using a savings/investment goal of $584,634, 20 years to grow, and an expected interest rate of 6%, with annual compounding, you will reach Coast FIRE at the age of 45 by saving $1,325 per month.

At that point you can stop saving for retirement if you wish. With 6% growth your nest egg will increase from $584,634 to $1.875 million by age 65, providing you with $75,000 a year in retirement income (using a 4% per year withdrawal rate).

(Source: https://time.com/personal-finance/article/what-is-coast-fire.)

## Work Less, Live More

The FIRE movement is rooted in the desire to pursue an alternative lifestyle that focuses less on work and more on living. By optimizing your finances, prioritizing debt payoff, increasing your income, and investing in income-generating assets, you can shave years and even decades off the traditional retirement age. For Latinos, financial independence represents ending the cycle of "working till you die" that many of us saw our parents and grandparents model. It's the ability to use money as a tool for prioritizing rest, time with your loved ones, the ability to pursue your passions, and ultimately, freedom. Freedom that has often been denied to us as people of color. FIRE is a form of resistance. When you don't have to work for money, you can opt out of a lot of shit, like toxic relationships, abusive employers, and environments that oppress you.

Who doesn't want that?

# CHAPTER 8

# How to Create Your Dinero Squad

I hate asking for help. I don't know if it's because I'm the firstborn, or first-gen, or because I never saw my mom ask for help, but I'm definitely the type of person who swears that I can do it all alone. Cue "La Toxica" by Farruko. I think as women, we tend to think that asking for help is some sign of weakness. But the truth is, when you start building wealth, you're going to encounter a lot of questions that you may not be equipped to answer. Questions like:

- Do I need life insurance? How much?
- What happens if I buy or sell cryptocurrency?
- Do I need a Roth IRA or a Traditional IRA?
- What are the tax implications of providing financial assistance to my parents?
- How can I pay my child to work in my business and get a tax write-off?

This is why finding your dinero squad is a must! You can start for FREE by checking out the *Yo Quiero Dinero* podcast, where we talk to lots of different voices in the personal finance space. I know what it's like to be overwhelmed by debt, confused about money, and disillusioned with traditional employment. This is why I've made it my mission to help others find financial freedom like I did. Listening to personal finance podcasts gave me access to a slew of incredible money educators who could help me answer the questions that I didn't feel equipped to answer on my own. Talking to your amigas is a great way to start this process too! They may know more about dinero than you think, or at least know someone who does!

Knowing who can help you with money questions and how to find them can be daunting. For many Latino first-generation families financial planning isn't common, but it's an important aspect of building generational wealth. It's so important for us to work with trustworthy financial advisors, especially since we have faced systemic discrimination in many areas, including access to financial services. Many of us come from families that have been historically disadvantaged, and building wealth is an important step in breaking this cycle. A trustworthy financial advisor can help you create a plan to build wealth and pass it down to future generations. In addition, people of color are often targeted by financial scams and predatory lending practices. A trustworthy advisor can help you avoid these scams and make informed financial decisions. And the most important reason? They can help us close the wealth gap. Latinos have a lower median net worth than white Americans, and working with a trustworthy advisor can help you bridge this gap by creating a plan to build wealth and invest in your future.

When I began to hit new financial milestones I set for myself, I decided that I needed professional help to manage my money better. I hired a CPA (certified public accountant) when my tax return started getting complicated after starting a business and buying an investment property. I hired a CFP (certified financial planner) when I wanted to determine whether I could quit my job to become a full-time entrepreneur and also for help in creating a retirement plan for myself and my parents, since I do plan to provide some level of financial support to my parents in their retirement. I hired a registered investment advisory firm when I began to realize that my stock portfolio was not adequately diversified and I didn't feel qualified to re-allocate my existing investments on my own.

I want you to know that it's perfectly OK to ask for help on your financial journey. A trustworthy financial advisor can help you navigate the complex financial landscape and achieve your financial goals in a way that is tailored to your unique circumstances. When the time comes to enlist professional assistance, it's important to know what options you have.

## Financial Advisors—Everything You Need to Know

Financial advisor is a broad term for a variety of financial professionals who can support you in your money journeys at all stages. From budgeting to tax planning to income streamlining, there are different financial advisors for all kinds of situations and budgets. Their role is to support you in various aspects of financial planning, including investment management, retirement planning, tax planning, and insurance. There are several types of financial advisors, each with different areas of expertise and qualifications. Here are some of the most common types:

**Registered investment advisor (RIA):** An RIA is a financial advisor who is registered with the Securities and Exchange Commission (SEC) or a state securities regulator. RIAs are required to act in a fiduciary capacity, which means they are legally obligated to act in the best interests of their clients.

**Certified financial planner (CFP):** A CFP is a professional who has passed a rigorous certification process and has demonstrated expertise in financial planning. CFPs are trained in a wide range of financial topics, including investments, taxes, insurance, and retirement planning.

**Chartered financial analyst (CFA):** A CFA is a professional who has completed a rigorous program of study and testing in investment management and financial analysis. CFAs are experts in analyzing financial markets and investments. To become a CFA, a candidate must pass the three-level exam, build up work experience in a related field, provide letters of reference, and apply to join the CFA Institute.

**Certified public accountant (CPA):** A CPA is an accountant who has passed the CPA exam and has met other state-specific education and experience requirements.

**Insurance agent:** An insurance agent is a professional who sells insurance policies and provides advice on insurance-related matters. Insurance agents may specialize in certain types of insurance, such as life insurance, health insurance, or property and casualty insurance.

**Robo-advisors:** A robo-advisor is an automated investment platform that uses algorithms and computer programs to provide investment management services. Robo-advisors typically use algorithms to create and manage investment portfolios for clients based on their risk tolerance, investment goals, and other factors. They can also provide basic financial planning services, such as retirement planning and goal setting. Since they're not a real person, they're typically much more affordable, but more limited in their scope as well.

When selecting a financial advisor, it is important to consider their qualifications, experience, and areas of expertise, as well as their fee structure and approach to working with clients. It is also important to make sure that the advisor is a good fit for your specific financial needs and goals.

## What Is a Fiduciary?

A fiduciary is a person or entity that is legally and ethically obligated to act in the best interests of another party. In the context of financial services, a fiduciary is a financial advisor or other professional who is required to act in the best interests of their clients when providing financial advice or managing assets.

The fiduciary duty requires the advisor to put their client's interests ahead of their own, and to disclose any potential conflicts of interest that could affect their ability to provide impartial advice. Fiduciaries are required to act with a high degree of care, skill, and diligence, and to provide advice that is appropriate for their client's individual financial situation and goals.

Fiduciary duty is a legal obligation, and those who breach their duty can be held liable for any resulting losses or damages. Many financial advisors are fiduciaries, while others may be held to a lower standard of care, such as the suitability standard, which requires only that the advice is suitable for the client's needs but does not require that the advice be in the client's best interests.

It is important to understand whether your financial advisor is a fiduciary, as this can have a significant impact on the quality of advice you receive and the level of trust you can place in your advisor.

To know if your financial advisor is a fiduciary, you can ask them directly if they are held to a fiduciary standard. You can also ask to see a copy of their Form ADV, which is a document that registered investment advisors (RIAs) are required to file with the Securities and Exchange Commission. The Form ADV provides information about the advisor's business practices, fee structure, and disciplinary history, and should indicate whether the advisor is held to a fiduciary standard.

You can also look for certifications and designations that require a fiduciary standard, such as Certified Financial Planner (CFP), Chartered Financial Analyst (CFA), and Registered Investment Advisor (RIA).

## How Can I Tell if My Financial Advisor Is Legit?

There are plenty of examples of financial advisors who've betrayed the trust of their clients. Ever heard of Jordan Belfort? He is a former stockbroker who was convicted of fraud and securities violations in the 1990s, and is best known for his memoir *The Wolf of Wall Street*, which chronicles his rise and fall as a stockbroker and the illegal activities he engaged in, including securities fraud and money laundering.

Belfort founded the brokerage firm Stratton Oakmont in the 1990s and used high-pressure sales tactics and manipulated stock prices to defraud investors of millions of dollars. He was eventually caught by the FBI and pleaded guilty to securities fraud and money laundering in 1999. He served twenty-two months in federal prison and was ordered to pay restitution to his victims.

Bernie Madoff is another classic example of a financial advisor who was anything but trustworthy. Bernie Madoff was an American financier and former chairman of the NASDAQ stock market who was convicted of running the largest Ponzi scheme in history, defrauding investors out of an estimated $64.8 billion.

Madoff began his fraudulent activities in the 1970s and continued until his arrest in 2008. He attracted investors by promising high returns with low risk through his investment firm, Bernard L. Madoff Investment Securities LLC. Instead of investing the money as promised, Madoff used new investors' funds to pay off earlier investors, creating a classic Ponzi scheme.

Madoff's fraud was eventually uncovered during the financial crisis of 2008, when many investors began requesting their money back. He was arrested and later pleaded guilty to eleven counts of fraud, money laundering, and perjury. Madoff was sentenced to 150 years in prison, one of the longest sentences ever handed down for financial crimes.

The Madoff scandal is considered one of the biggest financial frauds in history and had a significant impact on the financial industry and the public's trust in the markets. It also led to changes in securities regulation and investor protection laws. So how do we prevent ourselves from becoming victims of unscrupulous individuals who, like Belfort and Madoff, pretend to be trustworthy advisors? There are several ways to verify whether the advisor you're considering working with is someone you can trust to give you solid financial advice. First, ask some questions:

- What are your qualifications and credentials?
- How long have you been in practice, and how many clients do you currently have?
- What is your approach to financial planning and investing?
- How do you typically work with clients, and what is your communication style?
- What is your investment philosophy, and how do you select investments for your clients?
- What is your fee structure, and how are you compensated?
- Do you have any conflicts of interest that I should be aware of?
- Can you provide references from current or past clients?
- Have you ever been disciplined by a regulatory body or professional organization?
- Can you explain how you will help me achieve my financial goals?

This will help you assess whether the advisor is a good fit for your needs and whether they are trustworthy and competent. Make sure to take the time to fully understand the advisor's answers and to ask follow-up questions if needed. Here are some guidelines for finding a legit financial advisor:

**Credentials:** Find out if the advisor has the appropriate licenses and certifications, such as a Certified Financial Planner (CFP), Chartered Financial Analyst (CFA), or other industry-recognized certifications. These designations often require extensive training, testing, and continuing education, which can be an indicator of the advisor's commitment to their profession and their clients.

**Experience:** Look for an advisor who has experience working with clients similar to you in terms of financial situation and goals. Consider the advisor's track record and whether they have a history of achieving positive outcomes for their clients. Look for an advisor with a longstanding reputation of providing quality advice and service.

**Reputation:** Research the advisor online and check their references and reviews. Ask for referrals from friends, family, or other trusted sources. Check to see if the advisor has any disciplinary history with regulatory bodies such as the Securities and Exchange Commission or the Financial Industry Regulatory Authority (FINRA). You can access this information on the SEC (sec.gov) and FINRA (finra.org) websites. You can also check LetsMakeAPlan.org to find a CFP in your local area. These directories allow you to search for advisors in your area and filter based on their qualifications and specialties.

**Fee structure:** Make sure you understand the advisor's fee structure and how they are compensated. Look for an advisor who is transparent about their fees and who has a fee structure that aligns with your financial goals and preferences.

**Communication:** Choose an advisor who communicates clearly and regularly, and who listens to your concerns and answers your questions in a way that is easy to understand. Make sure you feel comfortable working with the advisor and that they understand your financial goals and risk tolerance.

Ultimately, it is important to choose an advisor whom you feel comfortable working with, who has a track record of acting in their clients' best interests, and who can help you achieve your financial goals. A trustworthy financial advisor should be able to listen to your concerns and provide personalized advice that meets your needs. There's no need to rush the decision—consider interviewing the advisors you are interested in working with; this will give you a chance to ask questions, get a sense of their communication style, and make sure they are a good fit for you.

Remember, it's important to do your due diligence when choosing a financial advisor, as they will be responsible for helping you make important financial decisions.

## Do I Really Need an Advisor? Or Can I Just DIY?

Deciding whether to hire a financial advisor or do it yourself (DIY) depends on several factors, including your financial goals, level of expertise, and time commitment. Here are some factors to consider:

**Complexity of your finances:** If your financial situation is straightforward, such as managing a small investment portfolio or creating a basic budget, then you may be able to handle it on your own. However, if your finances are more complex, such as managing multiple investment accounts, creating a retirement plan, or managing a business, then it may be beneficial to hire a financial advisor who has expertise in these areas.

**Time commitment:** Managing your finances can be time-consuming, especially if you have a lot of investments to manage or complex tax-planning needs. If you don't have the time or desire to manage your finances, hiring a financial advisor can be a good option.

**Expertise and knowledge:** Financial advisors have specialized training and expertise in financial planning, investing, and tax planning. If you don't have this knowledge or expertise, it may be beneficial to hire a financial advisor to help guide you through the process.

**Emotional biases:** Emotions can impact financial decision-making, especially during periods of market volatility or financial stress. A financial advisor can provide a more objective perspective and help you avoid making impulsive decisions based on emotion.

**Cost:** Financial advisors charge fees for their services, which can range from a flat fee to a percentage of your assets under management. If you are comfortable managing your finances on your own and can achieve your financial goals without the help of an advisor, then it may be more cost-effective to DIY.

Before you decide what to do, weigh the costs and benefits of each option and consider seeking advice from a trusted financial professional to help make an informed decision.

## How Is Your Financial Advisor Paid?

Here are some common ways financial advisors are paid:

**Commission-based:** Some financial advisors receive commissions for selling financial products, such as mutual funds, annuities, or insurance products. This means they earn a percentage of the sale, which can create a conflict of interest if their recommendations are based on the products that earn them the highest commissions.

**Fee-only:** Fee-only financial advisors do not receive commissions or other forms of compensation based on the products they recommend. Instead, they charge a fee for their services, which can be based on a percentage of the assets they manage (known as AUM or Assets Under Management) or a flat fee. This means they have fewer conflicts of interest and may be more likely to provide objective advice.

**Hybrid:** Some financial advisors may be paid through a combination of commissions and fees. For example, they may receive a commission for selling certain products, but also charge a fee for their advice and ongoing services.

It's important to understand how a financial advisor is paid, as this can impact the overall cost of their services and the recommendations they make. You should also consider whether their payment structure aligns with your financial goals and preferences.

---

## DAMN, THESE FEES ARE ADDING UP!

Imagine you have $1,000,000 to invest. When you choose how to pay your investment advisor, there are two main options:

**Option 1: Flat Fee ($2,000 per year)**
With this choice, you pay your advisor a fixed amount of $2,000 every year, regardless of how much money you make from your investments.

**Option 2: AUM Fee (1% of your money per year)**
With this option, you pay your advisor a percentage of your total money, in this case, 1% of $1,000,000, which equals $10,000 per year. So, if your money grows, you pay more; if it shrinks, you pay less, but it's always a percentage of your total money.

Now, let's compare:
- If your money stays at $1,000,000, the flat fee of $2,000 is cheaper than the AUM fee of $10,000.
- If your money grows, you pay more with the AUM fee because it's a percentage of your growing money. For example, if your money grows to $1,200,000, the AUM fee becomes $12,000.

Think about how much your money might grow and how comfortable you are with paying more if it does.

## The Power of Familiarity

As people of color and first-generation wealth-builders, it's helpful to build a relationship with financial professionals who can at least be empathetic to our unique financial backgrounds. You want to ensure you have a relationship with your financial advisor that promotes honesty and transparency about your financial history. Finding an advisor who is culturally competent and who is compatible with your personality and communication style is super important.

You should feel comfortable working with the advisor and trust their expertise. During an initial consultation or interview, ask questions about the advisor's experience working with clients from your cultural background, their approach to financial planning, and their understanding of any unique financial challenges you may face. These people are meant to be your allies in the wealth-building process, so make sure to take the time to find a culturally competent advisor who can help ensure that you receive the guidance and support you need to achieve your financial goals. I want to leave you with some inspiration on the power of working with a financial professional by sharing Maria's story.

Maria had always been focused on providing a better future for her family and ensuring their financial stability. However, she knew that she couldn't do it alone. Maria was determined to find a financial planner who could guide her and her family toward a multigenerational retirement plan.

After researching various financial planners, Maria stumbled upon an exceptional professional named Gloria. Gloria, a Latina herself, specialized in helping families create comprehensive financial strategies that spanned generations. Intrigued by Gloria's expertise, Maria decided to schedule a meeting to discuss her family's unique financial goals and aspirations. During their first meeting, Maria shared her dreams of creating a secure future for her children and grandchildren. She spoke passionately about the importance of financial literacy and wanted to break the cycle of financial struggle that her family had experienced in the past. Gloria listened attentively, empathizing with Maria's desire to provide a solid foundation for future generations.

Impressed by Maria's determination and vision, Gloria crafted a tailored multigenerational retirement plan for the family. She took into account their current financial situation, income streams, and long-term goals. Gloria guided Maria through various investment options, tax-efficient strategies, and estate planning techniques. With Gloria's guidance, Maria and her family began implementing the multigenerational retirement plan. They established an emergency fund, started contributing to retirement accounts, and diversified their investments to mitigate risk. Gloria emphasized the importance of regular check-ins and adjustments to ensure the plan remained aligned with their evolving needs.

Over the years, Maria witnessed the power of the multigenerational retirement plan unfold. She saw her family's financial well-being improve significantly. As her children grew, they were instilled with financial literacy and responsible money management skills. Together, they discussed the importance of saving, investing, and planning for the future. As time went on, Maria's children became financially independent and started their own families. However, the legacy of financial stability and wise planning continued to be passed down through the generations, Maria's grandchildren grew up with a strong foundation of financial knowledge and were well prepared to navigate their own financial journeys.

Maria often reflected on her decision to seek the help of a financial planner like Gloria. Not only did Gloria's expertise provide her family with a solid financial road map, but she also became a trusted confidante and mentor. Gloria's guidance went beyond numbers and investments; she genuinely cared about Maria's family and their long-term well-being. Through their partnership, Maria's family achieved a newfound sense of financial security, breaking free from the financial struggles that had plagued previous generations. Maria proudly witnessed her family's ability to create a legacy of prosperity and financial independence.

The story of Maria and Gloria reminds us that seeking professional guidance, like that of a skilled financial planner, can make a profound difference in building a multigenerational retirement plan. With the right expertise and support, you can overcome financial challenges, create a lasting legacy, and provide a solid foundation for future generations. I hope this inspires you to not be afraid to ask for help and to create a squad that's gonna help you secure the big bag!

# CHAPTER 9

# Love & Dinero

Protecting Yourself from Financial Abuse,
Breakups, and Divorce

Love is complicated. Money is complicated. Mix them together, and you can be in for a serious shit show. The United States has the sixth-highest divorce rate in the world, with 40 to 50 percent of marriages ending in divorce. According to a SunTrust Bank survey conducted online by the Harris Poll, 35 percent of people blame finances for the stress they experience in their relationships—and, often, at the heart of many couples' financial strife is debt.

Did you know that almost 70 percent of divorces are initiated by women? I'm not surprised in the least. I believe that as women have gained economic mobility, our tolerance for inequality in our relationships has plummeted. More and more of us are no longer accepting the bare minimum effort from our partners when it comes to managing all the unpaid work of running a household and having kids, and the many other duties so many of us handle solo. More of us have the option to leave abusive relationships without worrying about the financial consequences. More of us are no longer accepting the toxic masculinity that is so prevalent in Latino culture and that trapped so many of our mamas and abuelitas in abusive relationships.

I've also experienced what it's like to be faced with the decision of leaving an emotionally abusive relationship; I actually got divorced while writing this book. I never could have imagined getting divorced in my late thirties, but that's exactly what happened to me in the summer of 2022. Like many decisions I made in my twenties, getting married was another item on the "adulting checklist" that I was hell-bent on achieving, but, looking back, I now realize what a mistake that was. I wasn't thinking about the long-term and potentially financially devastating consequences of choosing a bad spouse; I just needed to be married because that's what we're supposed to do, right? Many of our elders feed us the narrative that a Latina's main purpose in life is to get married and pop out some kids. In Puerto Rico, there's a word for a woman who's "past her prime," unmarried, childless, and with few prospects of achieving either of these "critical milestones." She's known as a *jamona*, which literally translates to a female pig or ham. Yikes!

In the 1994 memoir *When I Was Puerto Rican* by Esmeralda Santiago, this concept of a jamona is explored through the eyes of the book's protagonist and narrator, Negi. Negi's real name is Esmeralda; she was given the nickname Negi as an infant because her skin was nearly black (*negra* is a Spanish term used to describe a dark-skinned woman, and is often used as a term of endearment, albeit a very problematic one if you ask me).

Negi's interest in and interpretation of love and relationships changes over the course of the memoir. As a child, Negi believes that her parents' relationship is normal; she's raised to believe that all men have zero control over their sexual desires and therefore have affairs. However, as Mami and Papi's relationship grows more chaotic as a result of Papi's continued infidelity, Negi begins to escape the unpleasantness of watching her parents fight by daydreaming about fantasy boyfriends and lovers. She finds herself caught between the extremes of her family and her fantasies, and because of this, she struggles to form her own understanding of what love is and what makes a good or bad relationship.

In contrast to these idealized romances, Negi also learns that it's possible for a woman to be jamona, which equates to "spinster." Women who are jamona are defined by the absence of a relationship with a man, like it's a negative thing, while men who don't have a relationship with a woman are jokingly considered lucky, not defective. Though Papi insists that Negi will never become jamona, she later decides that being alone must be better than crying over men who are expected to disappoint the women in their lives. PREACH SIS.

Though *When I Was Puerto Rican* comes to no clear conclusions about true love or what makes a truly good and healthy relationship, Negi's adolescent daydreams suggest that she does at the very least aspire to a relationship that's more loving and reliable than what she witnessed of her parents' relationship. Further, her realization that being jamona is better than being abused suggests that Negi realizes the only person she can rely on to love her, care for her, and never leave her is herself. In Spanish, we have a famous saying that goes "mejor sola que mal acompañada," which means *better alone than in bad company*. Damn right, girlfriend.

In our culture, the word "divorce" is practically sacrilegious. Divorce has not become a part of the family structure among Latin American families and their cultural fabric. While almost half of all marriages in the United States end in divorce, divorce in the United States is not seen as a tragedy or surprise by the family when it takes place. In contrast, for Latino families, there is still negative stigma attached to divorce, which results in stress for everyone involved.[1] While things are changing with the younger generation of Latinas who are being raised in the US with American values, there's still a lot of stigma around divorce in our culture. Married a shitty partner? Sucks for you, hermana. You're supposed to stick it out for the sake of the kids, like we've seen so many mujeres before us do, no? Sacrifice your life for others. Shut up and take it. Calladita te vez más bonita, as they say.

My ex-husband was terrible with money since the day we met, and over our sixteen-year relationship and our nine-year marriage, none of that changed. He defaulted on his student loans, credit cards, and car loans. He racked up unpaid tax debts, multiple arrests for drinking and driving, and legal debt to deal with said issues. Debt collectors regularly sent letters to our home trying to recoup money that they were owed. He was utterly uninterested in learning anything about money and how to use it as a tool for building wealth.

Seeing my husband's irresponsible behavior around money early on in our relationship, I chose to not combine our finances when we moved in together in our mid-twenties. I didn't feel comfortable tying my money into his financial chaos. Looking back, I should have taken all this as a sign that I shouldn't be wrapped up in his chaos, period. This isn't always the case, but often the way a person handles money is the way they handle a lot of other things. But as they say, you live and you learn. In the last year of our marriage, I realized he took one of my credit cards and maxed it out to pay for legal fees that he couldn't afford, without me knowing! That's financial abuse, ladies (we'll talk about what that means and looks like in this chapter).

When I finally filed for divorce after finding out that he was also a serial cheater, I soon realized that the end of this toxic relationship had

---

1. C. G. Ellison, N. H. Wolfinger, and A. I. Ramos-Wada, "Attitudes Toward Marriage, Divorce, Cohabitation, and Casual Sex Among Working-Age Latinos: Does Religion Matter?" *Journal of Family Issues* 34, no. 3 (2012): 295–322, doi:10.1177/0192513x12445458.

been a long time coming. I was devastated emotionally but also very relieved. Here's why…

I didn't have to pay my ex-husband a single dollar out of my pocket, even though I was the primary breadwinner during the entire marriage. I built multiple six-figure businesses while I was married and had over $500,000 in investments and other assets at the time of my divorce. I got to focus on healing my mental health after leaving the marriage, without also worrying about my financial security. My God, what a blessing! So how TF did I manage to walk away from a toxic nine-year marriage with my financial dignity intact? Two words: *postnuptial agreement*. Never heard of one? I'm not surprised.

Prenuptial (prenup) and postnuptial (postnup) agreements have a huge stigma associated with them—I know many Latinas who won't even consider getting one or even bringing it up to their partners because of the weird vibes associated with them. You may have heard the following if you've ever tried to have this convo with your family, friends, or soon-to-be spouse about your desire to get a prenup:

*"Why are you thinking about a prenup? It's like you're planning to get divorced!"*

*"We don't need a prenup. I don't want your money, that's not why I'm here!"*

*"That's a terrible way to start a marriage, it's not gonna last."*

Um, with all due respect, fuck that. We're building more wealth than any other generation of mujeres before us even could, and many of us are putting it at risk by not having this critical conversation before tying the knot. The fact of the matter is simple: Sis, if you are thinking of getting married, you need a prenup. Or if you are already married and you didn't get a prenup, create a postnup. Because the reality is this: Marriage is a legal contract, and when that contract is irreparably broken, either you can decide how the assets you've acquired and built during the marriage get divided, or the courts will do it for you. And you're probably not gonna like how they divide things up, especially if you're the breadwinner.

## WHAT HAPPENS TO YOUR ASSETS WITHOUT A PRENUP?

Without a prenuptial agreement, the division of assets during a divorce typically follows the laws of the jurisdiction in which the divorce takes place. In community property states, such as California, Arizona, Texas, and several others, assets acquired during the marriage are generally considered community property, which means they are owned equally by both spouses. In the event of a divorce, community property is typically divided equally between the spouses, unless an agreement can be reached otherwise.

In equitable distribution states, which include most other states in the United States, assets acquired during the marriage are not automatically divided equally. Instead, the court will consider various factors to determine a fair and equitable distribution of assets based on each spouse's contributions, financial needs, earning capacity, and other relevant factors.

In both community property and equitable distribution states, assets considered separate property are typically not subject to division. Separate property generally includes assets owned by either spouse before the marriage, inheritances or gifts received by one spouse during the marriage, and certain assets obtained through personal injury settlements or judgments.

It's important to note that these are general guidelines, and the specific laws and regulations can vary depending on the jurisdiction. Additionally, certain types of assets, such as businesses or complex investments, may require additional considerations during the asset division process.

We've seen real-life examples of what it looks like when a woman builds an empire while married and then the marriage crashes and burns.

From 2016 until 2018, Grammy-winning singer and songwriter Mary J. Blige was ordered to pay $30,000 a month in alimony to her ex-husband Kendu Isaacs. Originally, his lawyers requested quadruple that amount to help him sustain his lifestyle. Isaacs claimed that he "has experienced physical manifestations of stress and emotional distress from this matter, which has caused him to become hospitalized." The singer's former manager further claimed that he had become "unemployable," and that without her financial support he would be "destitute" and paying rent had become "impossible."

The multi-time Oscar nominee says her finances were so stretched that she didn't have the resources to pay for housing. She had to go out on tour to pay her bills and recover from this financial catastrophe.

WTF.

## Prenup vs. Postnup

A prenuptial agreement is a legal contract signed by both parties before getting married that outlines how assets and debts will be divided in the event of divorce or separation. It can also address issues such as spousal support and property division.

A postnuptial agreement is a similar legal contract signed by both parties *after* they are already married.

Both can be useful tools for couples who want to protect their individual assets or financial interests in the event of divorce or separation. They can also be helpful in clarifying expectations and avoiding misunderstandings about financial matters.

To create a prenuptial or postnuptial agreement, both parties will typically need to hire separate attorneys to represent their interests. They will then work together to negotiate the terms of the agreement and ensure that it is legally binding and enforceable.

It is important to note that prenuptial and postnuptial agreements can be sensitive issues, and it is important for both parties to approach the process with honesty, transparency, and mutual respect. It is also important to ensure that both parties fully understand the terms of the agreement and that it is fair and equitable to both parties.

## Starting the Conversation

Bringing up the topic of a prenuptial agreement can be sensitive and potentially difficult, but it is an important conversation to have if you are considering getting married and want to protect your financial interests. I encourage you to bring up the prenup conversation well in advance of the wedding, ideally several months before the big day. This allows both you and your future spouse to have plenty of time to discuss and negotiate the terms of the agreement, and ensures that the process is not rushed or pressured. This is not the type of conversation that you want to delay.

I didn't get a prenup, but in 2021, I was talking to my CFP about quitting my day job to become a full-time entrepreneur, and she advised me to obtain a postnuptial agreement to ensure that my business (which I built during the marriage), my retirement accounts, and other assets would be protected in the case of a divorce. Boy, am I glad that I listened to her! About eighteen months after getting my postnup, I ended up filing for divorce, and didn't owe my ex a dime. No alimony. No splitting of assets. No money from my business. Nada. These documents can literally save your wealth.

But how to even bring up that you want a prenup? When I approached my ex-husband about getting a postnup, I mentioned that my financial planner recommended it, in order to protect both of our financial interests. When broaching the subject of a prenup or a postnup, it is important to be open and honest with your partner about your reasons for wanting one. Explain that you are not planning for the marriage to fail, but simply want to ensure that both parties are protected in the event of divorce or separation. Highlight the benefits of a prenup to your partner, such as the peace of mind it can provide both of you in case of unexpected circumstances, and the fact that it can help clarify financial expectations and prevent misunderstandings.

### Prenup Prompts

Even if you feel confident about your decision to ask for either a prenup or postnup, just the idea of starting the conversation, especially if you feel your partner won't be receptive, can be nerve-wracking. Here are a few prompts you can use to get started.

**Future financial goals:** "Let's talk about our long-term financial goals and how a prenuptial agreement could help protect those goals."

**Asset protection:** "Considering the assets we each bring into the marriage, how can we ensure their protection in the event of a separation or divorce?"

**Debt management:** "We both have student loans and other debts. How can we address these debts and protect ourselves individually?"

**Business ownership:** "If one of us owns a business or plans to start a business in the future, how can we safeguard it in case of a marital dissolution?"

**Inheritance and family assets:** "Let's discuss how we can preserve any family inheritance or assets that are important to us or our families."

**Income disparity:** "Given that our incomes might differ now or in the future, how can we create a fair financial agreement that addresses any income disparities?"

**Children from previous relationships:** "As we have children from previous relationships, how can we ensure that their interests are protected through a prenuptial agreement?"

**Alimony and spousal support:** "What are our thoughts on spousal support or alimony in the event of a separation or divorce? How can we address these issues in a prenuptial agreement?"

**Financial transparency:** "Let's discuss how a prenuptial agreement can encourage financial transparency and help us build trust in our relationship."

**Legal protection and peace of mind:** "A prenuptial agreement can provide legal protection and give us peace of mind in case of unforeseen circumstances. What are your thoughts on that?"

It will be important to listen to your partner's concerns and address any questions or reservations they may have about a prenup. Be patient and understanding and try to find common ground. Consider consulting with a family law attorney or financial advisor who can help guide you through the process of creating a prenup/postnup and ensure that it is fair and equitable to both parties. Approaching the prenup conversation with honesty, openness, and a focus on mutual benefit can help ensure a positive and productive discussion.

# Financial Abuse: It's More Common Than You Think

Studies have shown that in 99 percent of all domestic abuse cases, people report a level of financial abuse as well. In advocacy and policy spaces, financial abuse is known as "hidden abuse" because it does not show up in ways we expect abuse to appear. That is precisely why it's so dangerous and why we need to know what exactly this is.

## What Does "Financial Abuse" Mean?

Within the context of any relationship, financial abuse in its most basic sense is when one person is somehow forced to be financially dependent on another. Perhaps the abuser controls this person's financial resources. Perhaps the abuser uses their financial advantages as leverage in multiple scenarios. The different forms financial abuse can take will vary situation by situation, relationship by relationship.

The common thread across all different forms of abuse is an abuse of power, an exertion of control, and manipulation. Jennifer Toledo, financial educator and founder of the educational platform Talk Finances to Me, told me that her Puerto Rican parents raised her to be very financially responsible. Her mom was the first woman in their family to finish high school. Jennifer had her first job at the age of fourteen, moved out of her parents' home at age nineteen, and had her first son when she was twenty-one. She was taking care of herself and her son when she entered into a relationship that ended up being extremely toxic. She told me, "In the beginning I was so in love. He could do no harm. But in the end, he knew that I couldn't afford to handle our shared expenses by myself and so he used the threat of leaving me with all the expenses to keep me in the relationship. I knew I needed to save up money to get out of it." It took her some time, but she is so thankful she had the skills to build up the emergency fund necessary to do it.

On one level, like any form of abuse, financial abuse can leave people with pain, shame, and regret over having stayed in that relationship. On another level, the impacts can be very tangible, wreaking havoc on your livelihood for years to come.

Depending on what the financial abuse looks like, direct impacts can look like leaving you without access to basic necessities like housing, removing your ability to have any level of financial independence, or negatively impacting your financial power (e.g., harming your credit score, limiting your employment opportunities, or forcing you into bankruptcy or debt collection).

Because part of the intention behind abuse is to isolate people, it can be even harder for someone who is being financially abused to find someone for support. This further adds to the pattern of financial abuse by making it harder to leave the relationship, because of how dependent they have become on the abuser out of necessity.

## Signs of Financial Abuse

Financial abuse can come in many different forms. Here's a nonexclusive list of some red flags to look for:

### Direct Control over Financial Resources

- Taking your money without your consent
- Using your credit cards without consent

- Demanding control over your paycheck
- Forcing a budget onto you
- Micromanaging your income, expenses, and spending
- Demanding to know how you spend every cent of your money
- Forcing joint accounts onto you
- Opening your bank statements without your consent
- Requiring bailouts for every financial problem they might be in

### Sabotaging Access to Financial Resources
- Running up your credit card balances and not paying for them
- Placing all bills under your name
- Preventing you from opening bank accounts
- Limiting your ability to actually go to your job
- Pressuring you to quit your job
- Judging your job and career choices
- Using income disparities or financial privilege against you

### Coercion or Threats to Your Financial Security
- Threatening to leave the home knowing you can't afford to live on your own
- Forcing a budget you cannot realistically afford
- Threatening to cut you off financially

When you combine any number of these different warning signs, it becomes clear why it can be so hard to leave a financially abusive relationship. The power the abuser holds is that they are often the key to maintaining your standard of living, since they hold power over the financial resources. Being able to leave this type of relationship is a feat of its own, but going from a dual income to a single income can be a difficult process.

After I got divorced, life got a lot more expensive. Now all of a sudden I was paying rent, utilities, health insurance, and more on my own. As the female breadwinner in my marriage, I maintained my financial independence, but many women suffer financial setbacks upon divorce. For women who were financially dependent on their spouse, adjusting to a single-income lifestyle can be particularly challenging. According to a study published by the US Government Accountability Office, women's household income fell by an average of 41 percent following a divorce, while men's household income fell by only 23 percent. The facts are clear: A man is not a financial plan. You need to protect yourself and your wealth, and being a financially independent person can help you avoid becoming the victim of a financial abuser.

If you or someone you know is being financially abused or in danger, please visit nnedv.org or call the US National Domestic Violence Hotline at 1-800-799-7233 and TTY 1-800-787-3224, or 911 if it is safe to do so.

## How to Have Healthy Conversations About Money with Your Partner

Money can be a sensitive topic in relationships, and disagreements about finances can easily lead to conflicts. Many couples struggle to talk openly about money. It doesn't have to be that way. Healthy couples can agree to disagree about some things, but when each of you has financial responsibilities within the relationship and beyond, discussing financial goals and strategies is essential.

Dasha Kennedy, financial activist and founder of the educational platform Broke Black Girl, told me it wasn't until she found herself going through the process of divorce that she finally had important conversations about money with her ex that she wished she'd had early on in their relationship. "I learned very quickly that we had a combined financial life. I wish I had asked more questions in the beginning, like, 'Will we have separate accounts? Who is going to pay what bills? Do you have any debt?'" When she separated from her ex, she suddenly found herself a single mom with two young boys living on one income. The financial impact was immediate. Her advice: "Never take a backseat, stay involved with your household finances from the beginning."

If we ignore our money issues with our partners, we will be leaving space further down the line for even more problems. However, by establishing open communication, setting shared goals, and practicing financial responsibility, you can avoid money fights and build a healthier financial foundation for your relationship. Here are my best tips for navigating money convos with your boo.

**Watch your timing.** Five minutes after your partner comes home with an expensive new watch or struts by you in a new designer dress isn't the best time to talk about money. You'll be too worked up about it to avoid a fight. Choose a time to open the conversation when you are both well rested and not preoccupied with stresses from work or family.

**Discuss values and goals first.** It's important to understand each other's money stories. Some people grew up believing that all debt is evil, while others are fine with "good" debt, like mortgages and education expenses. Explain your internalized attitudes toward money and encourage your partner to do the same. That will help you understand each other when you talk about your values and goals. Do you have a long-term plan as a couple? Do you share a goal of buying a house or taking a vacation?

One way to talk to your partner about money without fighting is to use "what if?" scenarios—both positive and negative. What if you won the lottery? What if you lost your job? This will help you understand the goals that are important to you both, as well as your attitudes about how money factors into achieving those goals.

**Set shared financial goals and decide how to split your income.** Depending on your differences in income, you and your partner may decide to take one of the following approaches to dividing your income.

You may decide to each contribute an equal percentage of your income to shared expenses. For example, if one partner earns 60 percent of the household income and the other earns 40 percent, you can contribute accordingly to cover shared costs. This method ensures a fair distribution of financial responsibility based on income.

If you and your partner have significant income gaps, a proportional contribution may make more sense for your partnership. In this scenario, you contribute to shared expenses based on your respective incomes. For instance, if one partner earns $4,000 per month and the other earns $2,000, you might contribute to shared expenses in a 2:1 ratio. So, if rent is $1,200, partner A pays $800 toward the rent, and partner B pays $400. A great site to help you make this calculation quickly is https://split.rent/.

Work together to identify common financial goals, such as saving for a house, paying off debt, or planning for retirement. Having shared goals helps you prioritize your spending and make decisions that align with your objectives.

**Make a budget together.** Once you have an idea of your goals and of each other's money "personality" (saving and thrifting or spending and paying over time), you can drill down to the practical aspects of your financial situation. Make a budget together that shows how much comes in and how much goes out each month.

Sit down together, discuss financial goals, and allocate funds to different categories such as savings, bills, investments, entertainment, and debt repayment. Be honest with your partner about how much income you have and how much you're willing to contribute toward supporting your life together. If you hide income and assets from your partner and you someday split up, you may have to reveal them as a part of a spousal support order. Divorce is never easy, but it can get ugly when one partner discovers the other has been hiding money for years. (Note: This does not apply if you or someone you know is trying to escape an abusive relationship. In this case, having money that the abuser doesn't know about is a lifeline that can get you to safety, so keep it a secret if you can.)

**Decide on your money management system.** Managing money as a couple is an essential aspect of a healthy financial relationship. You and your partner have several options to choose from when it comes to how to manage your income together.

**Joint accounts:** You can choose to merge your finances by opening joint bank accounts. All income and expenses are shared, and both partners have equal access to the funds. This method promotes financial transparency and simplifies money management, but can lead to financial abuse in the wrong relationships.

**Separate accounts:** You and your partner may prefer to keep your finances separate by maintaining individual bank accounts. In this scenario, each partner is responsible for their own expenses and contributes to shared expenses through a predetermined agreement. This method allows for individual autonomy and can be useful when you and your partner have different spending habits or financial goals.

**A mixture of joint and separate accounts:** You can also choose to adopt a hybrid approach by combining joint and separate bank accounts. You can have a joint account for shared expenses, such as rent, utilities, and groceries, while maintaining individual accounts for personal expenses. This method allows for both shared financial responsibility and individual financial freedom.

**Maintain your individual financial independence.** While sharing financial goals and responsibilities, it's important to maintain some financial independence. Each of you should have a personal discretionary fund to spend as you please, without needing approval or causing conflicts. Yes, you should have shared money goals that you work on together, but don't let nobody tell you that you can't spend your hard-earned dinero on YOU.

**Play to your strengths.** Acknowledge which of you is better at paying bills on time, saving, investing, and managing debt. Then divide your financial responsibilities according to your strengths. Don't blame or shame your partner for making less money or for maintaining separate savings to fund personal dreams you don't share.

Perhaps one of you is rock solid in bringing in consistent income. The other may be an artist or musician with less dependable income but great resourcefulness with thrifty purchases. Maximize your efforts together by leveraging each other's gifts and talents.

**Make money dates.** Schedule periodic meetings to review your financial situation, track progress toward goals, and make adjustments if necessary. Find a quiet and comfortable environment where you can have an open and focused conversation. This could be at home, a favorite café, or a peaceful outdoor spot. Determine the topics you want to discuss during your money date. These could include budgeting, savings goals, debt management, investment strategies, or any other financial concerns you both have. Remember that a money date doesn't have to be all serious and formal. Incorporate elements of fun and relaxation into the date. Consider treating yourselves to a nice meal, enjoying a shared activity, or rewarding yourselves for your financial efforts. These money dates should be something you both look forward to and will create a ritual where you both can come together to address any concerns, reevaluate priorities, and make joint decisions together.

**Seek professional help.** If you're struggling to manage your finances or having recurring conflicts, consider seeking guidance from a financial planner, money coach, or a relationship/marriage counselor. They can provide an objective perspective and help you develop strategies to overcome challenges.

Remember, open communication, mutual respect, and a shared commitment to financial well-being are essential for avoiding money fights and building a strong financial foundation in your relationship. Talking about money without fighting is possible if you choose your time wisely and, most importantly, if you're honest with each other about your income, debts, and attitudes about saving and investing. Don't shy away from tough money convos—they're an opportunity to strengthen your bond, improve your financial literacy, and work toward a secure financial future together.

# CHAPTER 10

# Rich Mami Money Moves

Look at you go, sis! You're out here making serious money moves, building wealth, and slaying the game! You're well on your way to becoming the generational-wealth changemaker that your ancestors could only have dreamed of. Because we have been systemically barred from achieving generational wealth, it's so important to make what I call Rich Mami Moves. In this chapter we will cover legal protections you can put into place that will allow you to set out a plan for the wealth you've built and ensure it will be transferred to future generations in your family.

Talking about estate planning and, frankly, death can come with a lot of feelings that you may not want to confront. But the fact is there are only two certainties in life, taxes (unless you're Jeff Bezos or Elon Musk, apparently) and death. So we're not gonna ignore those realities, we're going to give the ultimate gift of love: a legally documented plan for our money after we are gone. But that's not all we'll be talking about in this chapter. As mujeres, we also have to protect ourselves from things that may happen when we are still alive, such as the loss of a partner, medical emergencies that require someone to act on our financial behalf, and much more.

## Estate Planning

How do you protect all the hard work you've done, and make sure that the wealth you've created lives on forever? This requires doing things that you thought were only for the super wealthy. What you've created is called an estate, and that baby needs protection. Yup, you heard right! You got a whole-ass estate! Wait...what's that?

### But First...What's an Estate?

An estate is simply all the things of value that you own. We're talking bank accounts, houses, stocks, crypto, your abuela's wedding ring, that car you're driving. Everything that you own is part of your estate. An estate may also refer to the legal entity created when a person passes away, which is responsible for managing and distributing their assets according to their will or the laws of intestacy (aka the state of dying without a will). In this context, the estate may also include any debts or obligations the deceased had at the time of their death. The process of settling an estate, including identifying and valuing assets, paying debts and taxes, and distributing remaining assets to heirs, is called estate administration. To make this process easier, you should have an estate plan.

"The general belief within the Hispanic community is that wills, and all financial planning topics, are only for rich people," says Maria Victoria Colón, a certified public accountant who teaches financial literacy on social media with Dinero en Spanglish. Colón's dad died without a will five years ago. She says that while estate planning can cost money up front, not having a plan can be time-consuming and even more costly for beneficiaries, who have to pay legal fees after their loved one has died.

Colón has spent more than $2,500 in legal fees to organize the documents needed for her to receive her father's assets, and she's not even done yet. Meanwhile, writing your own will can be as cheap as using a template found online and having it notarized, she says, though she recommends consulting with an estate planning attorney. Colón also notes that some employers offer legal services as part of employee benefits, and taking advantage of those can include drawing up a will. This is how I got my own estate plan. My employer offered access to legal insurance through Arag Legal as an employee benefit for $12 a month. Total out-of-pocket costs besides my $12 monthly paycheck deduction? Zero dollars.

You can also check out websites like trustandwill.com to create an estate plan online.

Still think you don't need an estate plan? Consider this: How many times have you been to a funeral or heard of family drama involving people fighting over who gets Mami's house? You don't need to repeat that mess. In fact, you can avoid a lot of drama by talking to your family about what they own, who they'd like it to pass on to once they're no longer here, and even who will take care of your children in the event something were to happen to you. It's important to find out if they have written their wills and go through the implications of not having one if they aren't aware.

## Why You Need an Estate Plan

Besides making things easier for your family, having an estate plan is important because it allows you to control how your assets and property will be distributed after your death, and it can help minimize the burden on your loved ones during a difficult time. There are so many reasons to create an estate plan, but here are some of the most important ones:

**You can avoid probate:** One of the main reasons to have an estate plan is to avoid probate, which is a legal process that takes place after someone dies to validate their will, pay off their debts, and distribute their assets. Probate can be a lengthy and costly process, and it can tie up your assets in court for months or even years. During this time, your loved ones may not have access to the assets they need to pay bills or cover expenses. Probate is a public process, which means that your will and other documents will become part of the public record. This can lead to privacy concerns and may make it easier for creditors and other parties to contest your will. Finally, probate can be unpredictable, as a judge may have the final say in how your assets are distributed, even if it is not in line with your wishes. Ain't nobody got time for that!

**You can protect your assets:** An estate plan can help protect your assets from creditors, lawsuits, and other potential threats. By creating trusts and other legal structures, you can ensure that your assets are passed down to your beneficiaries in a way that is protected from outside forces, like creditors, or that sleazy family member who's up to no good.

**You can provide for your loved ones:** By creating a will or trust, you can ensure that your loved ones are provided for after your death. You can name guardians for your minor children, provide for family members with special needs, and make sure that your assets are distributed according to your wishes.

**You can minimize your estate's tax liability:** With an estate plan, you can minimize the taxes that your estate will owe after your death. This can help ensure that your loved ones receive as much of your estate as possible. There are several ways this can happen.

- If your estate is valued above a certain threshold, it may be subject to federal estate taxes. However, there are ways to minimize or eliminate estate taxes through **estate planning**.

For example, you can make gifts during your lifetime to reduce the size of your estate, or you can set up a trust to hold your assets and reduce your estate's taxable value.

- If you plan to give gifts to your loved ones during your lifetime, you may be subject to **gift taxes**. However, there are ways to minimize or eliminate gift taxes through estate planning. For example, you can use the annual gift tax exclusion to give tax-free gifts up to a certain amount each year, or you can make tax-free gifts for certain purposes, such as paying for someone's medical or educational expenses.

- Your estate plan can also help you with **income taxes**. For example, you can use certain types of trusts, such as a grantor trust, to reduce your taxable income during your lifetime. You can also plan for the distribution of your assets to minimize income taxes for your beneficiaries.

- If you own a business, your estate plan can help you minimize taxes when transferring ownership to your heirs as part of your **business succession plan**. For example, you can set up a buy-sell agreement to transfer ownership to your heirs at a reduced price, or you can use a family limited partnership to transfer ownership while retaining control.

## HOW DOES AN ESTATE PLAN AFFECT THE PROBATE PROCESS?

The probate process can vary depending on whether the person had an estate plan or not. Let's consider both scenarios to see which one sounds better (*hint: it pays to have a plan*).

**Without an estate plan:** If a person dies without an estate plan (also known as dying intestate), the probate process can be more complicated and lengthy. In this case, the court will appoint an executor to handle the deceased person's assets and property. The executor is usually a family member or a close friend of the deceased person.

The executor will have to identify and gather all the deceased person's assets, pay any outstanding debts and taxes, and distribute the remaining assets to the deceased person's heirs according to the state's intestacy laws. Intestacy laws are laws that determine how assets are distributed when a person dies without a will or an estate plan.

The probate process can take several months to complete, and it can be expensive, as the executor will need to hire an attorney to assist with the process.

**With an estate plan:** If a person dies with an estate plan, the probate process can be much smoother and faster. The estate plan can include a will, a trust, or both. A will is a legal document that outlines how the deceased person's assets will be distributed after their death. A trust is a legal entity that holds the deceased person's assets and distributes them to the beneficiaries according to the terms of the trust.

If the deceased person had a will, the executor named in the will is responsible for handling the deceased person's assets and property. The executor will need to identify and gather all the deceased person's assets, pay any outstanding debts and taxes, and distribute the remaining assets to the deceased person's beneficiaries according to the terms of the will.

If the deceased person had a trust, the assets in the trust will be distributed according to the terms of the trust, and the probate process may not be required at all.

In general, having an estate plan can make the probate process much easier and less expensive for everyone involved.

# Estate Plan Essential Documents

So, you know you want an estate plan, but what does that actually look like? Well, as fancy as it all sounds, an estate plan is simply a set of legal documents and instructions that outline how a person's assets and affairs should be managed and distributed after their death. Here are the most important documents to include in your estate plan:

## Last Will and Testament

A last will and testament, also known as a will, is a legal document that outlines how a person's assets and affairs will be handled after their death. It allows the person, known as the testator, to specify who will receive their assets, how much each beneficiary will receive, and who will be responsible for carrying out their wishes.

In a last will and testament, the testator can name an executor, who will be responsible for managing the distribution of assets and carrying out the testator's wishes. The executor's duties may include paying off debts, taxes, and other expenses; collecting and distributing assets; and filing the necessary legal documents.

A last will and testament typically covers the distribution of assets such as money, property, and personal belongings. It may also include instructions for the testator's funeral arrangements and the care of any minor children or pets. You won't believe the wacky stuff some folks have put in their last wills and testaments!

In 2004, billionaire hotelier Leona Helmsley left instructions for her $4 billion fortune to be spent caring for dogs, having apparently rethought an earlier draft that left it to the poor. Her nine-year-old Maltese, Trouble, received $12 million in the will, with her grandchildren either cut out or ordered to visit their father's grave annually in order to inherit their share. Trouble's inheritance was later cut to just $2 million by a judge, although the dog still needed to go into hiding amid death and kidnap threats.[1] I literally can't even.

Oprah (who is still living, thank goodness) established a trust funded with $30 million for her pet dogs, so that they will continue to receive excellent treatment and care. She plans to give the bulk of her $3 billion estate to charitable causes. "When I'm gone, everything that I have is going to go to charity because I don't have children. And I believe that that's what you should do," she said. "To whom much is given, much should be given back."[2] Cheers to leaving a legacy that will live on long after she's left this earthly realm. We love to see it, queen!

However, it is important to note that a last will and testament only covers assets that are owned solely by the testator at the time of their death. Assets held jointly or those that are already designated to a beneficiary, such as life insurance policies and retirement accounts, may not be covered by a will.

To create a last will and testament, the testator must be of sound mind and at least eighteen years old. The document must be in writing, signed by the testator, and witnessed by at least two people who are not beneficiaries named in the will.

In order for a last will and testament to be legally binding, it must go through probate, which is a legal process that validates the will and oversees the distribution of assets.

## Trusts

A trust is a legal arrangement in which a person (known as the trustor or grantor) transfers ownership of assets to a trustee, who manages the assets on behalf of beneficiaries. The trustor creates the trust document that outlines the terms of the trust, such as who the beneficiaries are, how

---

1. https://www.theguardian.com/money/2015/aug/25/10-strangest-wills-finances-death.
2. https://www.pierchoskiestatelaw.com/19-weird-will-requests-inspiring-us-to-think-outside-the-box/.

and when they will receive distributions from the trust, and who will serve as the trustee.

There are several different types of trusts, each with its own unique characteristics and uses. Some common types of trusts include:

**Revocable living trust:** This type of trust is created during the trustor's lifetime and can be modified or terminated by the trustor at any time. The trustor typically serves as the initial trustee and retains control over the assets in the trust. Upon the trustor's death, a successor trustee takes over and distributes the assets to the beneficiaries named in the trust.

**Irrevocable trust:** An irrevocable trust cannot be modified or terminated by the trustor once it is created. This type of trust is often used for tax planning and asset protection purposes. The trustor gives up control of the assets and the trustee manages them on behalf of the beneficiaries.

**Testamentary trust:** This type of trust is created through a person's will and goes into effect upon their death. The trust can be used to provide for minor children or other beneficiaries who are unable to manage their own assets.

**Special needs trust:** This type of trust is designed to provide for the needs of a beneficiary with a disability without disqualifying them from receiving government benefits. The trust can be used to pay for expenses such as medical care and living expenses.

**Charitable trust:** A charitable trust is created to support a particular charity or cause. The trust provides income to the charity for a specified period of time or in perpetuity.

**Spendthrift trust:** This type of trust is created to protect a beneficiary's assets from creditors or from being squandered. The trust restricts the beneficiary's access to the assets and typically requires that distributions be made directly to service providers for the beneficiary's benefit.

The type of trust that is best for you will depend on your goals, the assets being transferred to the trust, and the needs of the beneficiaries. It's always best to talk to a licensed attorney in your state to determine which trust makes the most sense for you. See below for information on finding an attorney.

## Financial Power of Attorney

A financial power of attorney is a legal document that allows a person, known as the principal, to give someone else, known as the agent or attorney-in-fact, the authority to make financial decisions on their behalf. This can include tasks such as paying bills, managing investments, and buying or selling property.

To create a financial power of attorney, the principal must first choose an agent that they trust to manage their financial affairs. The principal then creates a document that outlines the scope of the agent's authority and any limitations on their power. To be legally binding, this document must be signed by the principal and notarized.

The financial power of attorney can be either **durable** or **nondurable**. A durable power of attorney remains in effect even if the principal becomes incapacitated or unable to make decisions, while a nondurable power of attorney is terminated if the principal becomes incapacitated.

Once the financial power of attorney is created, the agent can act on behalf of the principal as specified in the document. The agent has a fiduciary duty to act in the best interest of the principal and to manage their finances responsibly. The principal can revoke or modify the financial power of attorney at any time, as long as they are still of sound mind.

It is important to choose an agent who is trustworthy and capable of managing financial affairs. It is also important to keep the financial power of attorney document in a safe place where it can be easily accessed if needed. In the event that the principal becomes incapacitated and unable to manage their own finances, the financial power of attorney can provide peace of mind that their affairs will be handled by someone they trust.

Another aspect of power of attorney is a **healthcare power of attorney**, which is a legal document that allows a person (known as the principal) to appoint someone else (known as the agent or healthcare proxy) to make healthcare decisions on their behalf if they become unable to make these decisions themselves.

To create a healthcare power of attorney, the principal must first choose an agent they trust to make healthcare decisions in accordance with their wishes. The principal then creates a document that outlines the scope of the agent's authority and any limitations on their power. This document must be signed by the principal and notarized to be legally binding.

The healthcare power of attorney can also include instructions for the agent to follow regarding specific medical treatments or procedures that the principal does or does not want. These instructions are known as a living will or advance directive.

Once the healthcare power of attorney is created, the agent can act on behalf of the principal as specified in the document. The agent has a duty to make decisions that are in the best interest of the principal and in accordance with their wishes, as outlined in the document.

It is important to choose an agent who is trustworthy and who understands the principal's wishes regarding healthcare decisions. The healthcare power of attorney should be kept in a safe place and easily accessible in case it is needed. It is also a good idea to provide a copy of the document to the agent, the principal's healthcare provider, and any family members who may need to know about the document.

In the event that the principal becomes unable to make healthcare decisions, the healthcare power of attorney can provide peace of mind that their wishes will be followed by someone they trust.

---

## BENEFICIARY DESIGNATIONS

Many assets, such as life insurance policies, retirement accounts, and bank accounts, allow for the designation of beneficiaries. This means the asset will be transferred directly to the designated beneficiary after the owner's death, bypassing the probate process. Make sure that you have assigned beneficiaries for all your accounts. It's really easy to do online, and so important in terms of ensuring that your money goes to the family or loved ones you would most want to receive it if you were gone. And don't forget to update them regularly. The last thing you want is your ex-spouse inheriting your retirement accounts upon death because you forgot to change your beneficiaries after getting a divorce.

---

### Advance Directives

An advance healthcare directive (also known as a living will or healthcare directive) is a legal document that allows a person to make decisions about their medical care in advance, in case they become unable to communicate their wishes. It is a type of healthcare power of attorney that outlines the person's preferences regarding medical treatment and end-of-life care.

To create an advance healthcare directive, a person must first consider their values, beliefs, and wishes regarding medical treatment for terminal illnesses or end-of-life care. This can involve discussing these issues with family members, healthcare providers, or a lawyer.

The document should include instructions about the type of medical treatment a person wishes to receive or not receive, such as whether they want life-sustaining treatment, pain management, or palliative care. It can also include information about organ donation, funeral arrangements, and other end-of-life decisions.

The advance healthcare directive must be signed and dated by the person creating it, and witnesses may be required to sign the document as well. It is important to check the legal requirements in the person's state or jurisdiction to ensure the document is legally binding.

Once the advance healthcare directive is created, it should be shared with healthcare providers, family members, and anyone else who may be involved in the person's medical care. It is also a good idea to keep a copy of the document with the person's important papers and medical records.

In the event that a person becomes incapacitated or unable to communicate their wishes, the advance healthcare directive provides guidance to healthcare providers and family members about the person's wishes for medical treatment and end-of-life care. It can also provide peace of mind to the person creating the document, knowing that their wishes will be respected even if they cannot express them at the time.

## Letter of Instruction

A letter of instruction is a non-legal document that outlines a person's wishes and preferences regarding their funeral arrangements, the distribution of personal property, and other matters that may not be addressed in other estate planning documents.

## Securing Your Digital Estate

In today's digital world, it's not enough to make sure you have a plan for your physical possessions. Chances are you've got a whole lot of digital real estate you need to secure too! Many of us spend a significant part of our lives online. How will these accounts be managed or deleted? From social media accounts to online banking and even cryptocurrency wallets, it's important to create a plan for managing and securing your logins so that your loved ones can manage the corresponding accounts efficiently. Not doing this could be a nightmare.

Just take a look at the story of Gerald Cotten, co-founder and CEO of QuadrigaCX, a Canada-based cryptocurrency exchange. Cotten died suddenly on vacation at the age of thirty due to complications of Crohn's disease, and this is just the beginning of the tragedy. As a result of Cotten's sudden passing, investors were locked out of $190 million in cryptocurrency assets because he failed to share the password to a laptop that contained the business's records.[1] Holy shit. Please don't let this be your story.

To protect and pass on your login information as part of your estate plan, start by creating a comprehensive inventory of all your online accounts, including usernames and passwords. Using a reputable password manager like LastPass or Keeper can help securely store this information. Designate a digital executor in your estate plan, someone trustworthy and tech-savvy, who will manage your digital assets. Compose a detailed letter outlining how to access your password manager and the inventory of accounts. Keep this letter and any relevant access codes or keys in a secure location, such as a locked safe, and ensure your digital executor knows where to find them. Regularly update your information, consider encryption for added security, and review your estate plan periodically to keep it current.

Please note that this list of documents is not exhaustive and the specific components of an estate plan will vary depending on your individual circumstances and goals. It is important to work with an experienced estate planning attorney in your state to ensure that your plan is comprehensive and tailored to your needs.

---

1. https://www.cnet.com/tech/tech-industry/crypto-founder-dies-taking-only-password-and-190m-with-him/.

## FINDING AN ATTORNEY

To find a reputable estate planning attorney, you can ask friends or family members for referrals, or conduct a search on websites like Avvo or Martindale-Hubbell to find ratings and reviews of attorneys in your area. Check to see if they have any disciplinary actions or complaints filed against them with your state bar association. You'll want to make sure the attorney is licensed to practice law in your state and has experience in estate planning. Look for additional certifications or memberships in professional organizations like the National Academy of Elder Law Attorneys (NAELA). Ultimately, you should feel comfortable with the attorney you choose and trust that they have your best interests in mind. If something feels off, don't hesitate to continue your search for someone who is a better fit for you.

# Talking to Your Familia About Estate Planning

This can be a difficult topic, but it is an important conversation to have to ensure that everyone's wishes are respected and that their affairs are in order. No one wants to think about dying, right? But the fact is that until someone finds the fountain of youth and bottles a cure for aging, you have a 100 percent chance of dying at some point. Knowing that, the best thing you can do is to prepare for it and take the burden off your loved ones to make decisions on your behalf. They're already going to be grieving your loss; why complicate things by throwing them into legal matters without any guidance? California-based family law attorney Genoveva Meza Talbott says the kindest gift you can give your loved ones during the grieving process is an estate plan. That way, they know they're honoring your legacy, and you can spare them from having to make difficult decisions about your estate without guidance. Genoveva told me she has found that in the Latino community there can be a lot of resistance to having these conversations. "There is a lot of superstition about discussing death, as if by talking about it, something bad might happen." She recommends to her clients that they tell their families it's important to them to have the discussion because they see it as an act of love to ensure that their family is taken care of when they're gone. "I tell them it's a love gift."

I can't say enough about why estate planning is so important, but you don't have to just take my word for it. Take it from my amiga Ana. Ana recognized the importance of planning for the future and ensuring the financial security of her loved ones. With a strong desire to protect her family's legacy, she bravely decided to initiate an estate planning conversation. Gathering her family together on a warm Sunday afternoon, Ana chose a time when everyone was relaxed and open to discussion. Sitting around the dining table, she began by expressing her love and concern for each family member. Ana shared stories of her own experiences and the lessons she had learned about the importance of planning ahead.

With a compassionate and gentle approach, Ana explained how estate planning could bring peace of mind, preserve their assets, and ensure their wishes were carried out. She emphasized that estate planning was not just about finances but also about taking care of their loved ones and protecting their legacy. At first, Ana's family members were unsure and hesitant. The topic felt unfamiliar and uncomfortable. However, Ana's warmth, sincerity, and genuine concern created a safe and welcoming space for discussion. She encouraged them to share their hopes, fears, and aspirations, assuring them that this conversation was an opportunity to provide for their loved ones and maintain their family's unity.

As the conversation progressed, Ana introduced the concept of wills, trusts, and powers of attorney. She explained how these legal documents could safeguard their assets, designate guardians for minor children, and ensure their healthcare wishes were honored. Ana also shared stories of other families who had faced challenges due to a lack of planning, high-lighting the importance of proactive measures.

Recognizing that each family member had unique concerns and priori-ties, Ana encouraged open dialogue. She actively listened to their questions, fears, and suggestions, fostering a collaborative and inclusive environment. Together, they explored various estate planning options, seeking advice from professionals and educating themselves on the available resources.

As the weeks and months passed, Ana's family gradually embraced the idea of estate planning. With Ana as their guiding force, they sought the help of a skilled Latina estate planning attorney who understood their cultural background and values. Through thoughtful discussions and con-sultations, they crafted personalized estate plans that reflected their desires and protected their loved ones.

With the estate planning process complete, Ana's family experienced a profound sense of relief and empowerment. They had taken proactive steps to safeguard their assets, ensure their children's well-being, and maintain their family's unity. Ana's dedication to initiating the conversation had trans-formed their uncertainty into a shared commitment to their collective future.

As the years went by, Ana's family faced life's inevitable challenges with greater resilience and confidence. When difficult decisions arose, they referred back to their estate plans to guide them. The planning pro-cess had not only protected their assets but also strengthened their bonds, creating a deeper sense of unity and understanding.

That first conversation eventually made a lasting impact on Ana's family. With compassion and dedication, she had not only navigated a potentially difficult subject but also guided her loved ones toward a future filled with security, harmony, and a strong family legacy.

By initiating conversations around estate planning, you can be like Ana and empower your familia to navigate future challenges with confi-dence, unity, and a shared commitment to preserving your legacy.

To begin having these conversations in a productive way, find a quiet and comfortable place where everyone can sit and talk without distractions. Choose a time when everyone is relaxed and not stressed. Hint: Maybe don't choose to have this conversation during Noche Buena dinner after everyone's had entirely too much coquito to drink.

You'll want to explain to your loved ones why estate planning is important and why you want to discuss it as a family. You can use examples from your own experience, those of friends or family, or from news stories to illustrate the importance of having a plan in place. Leading by example can also be very helpful. Share your own plans for estate planning and explain why you made the choices you did. This can help open the conversation and make it easier for others to share their own thoughts.

Be open to feedback from your familia. This is a sensitive topic, so make sure you're creating an environment that invites an open dialogue. Ask for input from your family members about their wishes and concerns, listen carefully to their input, and be respectful of their opinions. If you get some resistance about discussing this topic, it may be helpful to mention the potential implications of not having an estate plan in place, such as legal battles and financial issues. And last but not least, consider bringing in an estate planning attorney or financial planner to help facilitate the conversation and answer any questions.

Remember that estate planning is a personal and sensitive topic, and it may take several conversations to fully address all concerns and come up with a plan that everyone is comfortable with. Be patient, respectful, and open to feedback, and keep the focus on ensuring that everyone's wishes are respected and their affairs are in order.

## Practical Prompts for the Estate Planning Convo

If you need a way into the conversation, here are some helpful prompts you can use:

- "I've been thinking about our family's legacy and how we can ensure that everything we've worked hard for is protected and passed down to future generations. Have you ever considered discussing estate planning?"
- "I've heard stories of families struggling with confusion and disagreements when a loved one passes away without clear instructions. It might be a good idea for us to discuss estate planning to avoid any potential conflicts and make things easier for everyone."
- "I know that discussing end-of-life matters can be challenging, but in our culture, it's important to look out for our family's well-being. Estate planning is a way of caring for our loved ones, even after we're no longer here. Let's talk how we can protect what you've worked so hard to build."

## What About Life Insurance?

According to Hispanic Market Advisors, 44% of Hispanic people have no life insurance coverage, compared with 37% of the non-Hispanic population. The main reasons are the cost of the insurance and the lack of knowledge about insurance. And of those with life insurance, 49% believe that they do not have enough coverage.

Experts say that some of the top reasons why Latinos have lower rates of life insurance coverage is trust issues with financial companies, language barriers, and cultural differences. According to Prudential financial planner Silvia Tergas, many Latino families have negative experiences with financial professionals, especially if financial ruin was the reason they left other countries. She says lack of education and an overarching mistrust are barriers for the community and its approach to financial services like insurance.

Life insurance can provide significant financial protection and support for your family in the event of your death. Knowing that there is a financial safety net in place can offer your family peace of mind, so that they can focus on emotional healing and supporting each other during a difficult time.

These are just a few ways life insurance can help your family:

- Income Replacement: If you are the primary breadwinner, life insurance can replace your income, ensuring that your family's financial needs are met even after you're gone.
- Debt Repayment: Life insurance can cover outstanding debts such as mortgages, loans, or credit card balances, preventing your family from inheriting your financial obligations.
- Education Expenses: Life insurance proceeds can be used for your children's education, ensuring they can pursue their dreams without financial limitations.
- Day-to-Day Expenses: It can cover daily living expenses, such as groceries, utility bills, and healthcare costs, maintaining your family's standard of living.
- Funeral Expenses: Life insurance can cover funeral and burial expenses, which can be substantial and unexpected costs for your family.
- Estate Taxes: Depending on the size of your estate, life insurance can help cover estate taxes, ensuring that your assets are passed on to your family without a heavy tax burden.
- Protecting The Family Business: Life insurance can provide the necessary funds to prevent the sale of the business to pay off debts or taxes after the owner's passing, preserving the family's source of income and wealth.
- Inheritance: Life insurance can serve as an inheritance, providing your heirs with a financial legacy.

- Charitable Contributions: If you are philanthropically inclined, you can designate a portion of the life insurance proceeds to go to charitable organizations or causes you support.

"Life insurance is something many people think about, but don't act on, especially in the Hispanic community," said Roselyn Sanchez, a Latina actress, producer, and dancer.

"My daughter is ten and I didn't get life insurance until she was two years old when my business manager mentioned that I needed it as a parent to protect my daughter," Sanchez told Yahoo Money. "There's a lack of education in the Hispanic community around life insurance, but once I read and learned about it, I knew it was necessary."

Life insurance is also a key wealth-building tool that we need to take advantage of as a community. Why? Because it's one of the few tax-free ways to build and transfer generational wealth.

In general, life insurance proceeds are tax-free to the beneficiaries. When a policyholder passes away, the beneficiaries receive the death benefit from the life insurance policy, and this money is typically not subject to federal income taxes. This means that the beneficiaries do not have to report the life insurance proceeds as income on their tax returns.

By leveraging life insurance policies strategically, we can protect our assets, provide for our families, fund educational aspirations, and leave a lasting legacy for future generations. Knowing this, let's talk about what life insurance is, and what your options are.[1]

## What Kind of Life Insurance Do You Need?

There are two types of insurance: term and permanent:

---

1. Source: https://money.yahoo.com/hispanics-life-insurance-192027136.html.

**Term life insurance:** This type of insurance provides coverage for a specified period of time, such as 10, 20, or 30 years. If the insured person dies during the term of the policy, the beneficiary receives the death benefit. If the insured person survives the term, the policy expires and there is no payout.

**Whole life insurance:** This type of permanent insurance provides coverage for the entire life of the insured person, as long as premiums are paid. It also has a cash value component that grows over time and can be borrowed against or used to pay premiums.

**Universal life insurance:** This type of permanent insurance is similar to whole life insurance, but it offers more flexibility in terms of premiums and death benefits. The cash value component can also be invested in different accounts, such as stocks or bonds.

**Variable life insurance:** This type of permanent insurance allows the insured person to invest the cash value component in a variety of investment options, such as mutual funds. The death benefit and cash value depend on the performance of the investments.

"Life insurance is a pretty broad product," says Laura Adams. Most people don't know where to start in making a decision between what are called "term" and "permanent" life insurance.

Adams says that the average consumer will only need term insurance but those with the need for a little added security should consider a permanent policy.

Say, for example, you have teenage children. You'd probably want to be certain they'd have support up until their early twenties, until they can become financially independent. In that case, a 10–20–year policy might be best. That changes a bit if you have a child with a disability and a need for lifelong care. For that family, a policy that covers you no matter when you die would be the best buy.

There are a lot of different things to consider when deciding how much life insurance coverage you and your family need, but overall, Adams says, you should factor in how much you'd need to replace your income. Also consider the cost of paying off your mortgage, debts, your funeral—which can be up to $20,000—and other expenses like putting your kids through school.[1]

When you're reaching the advanced levels of wealth building, it's important to protect all the hard work you've done by creating a robust financial parachute. The Rich Mami Moves we've discussed in this chapter—your estate plan, insurance, and more—are all critical parts of ensuring that the legacy you've built lives on for generations to come.

---

1. Source: https://farnoosh.tv/2013/03/your-life-insurance-buying-guide/.

# Unleashing the Latina Financial Revolution!

**W**ell, well, well, my fierce and fabulous Latinas, we've reached the end of this badass personal finance journey tailored specifically for us. Can we get a round of applause for the incredible transformations we've undergone? From budgeting like bosses to investing like Wall Street divas, we've conquered the financial world with style!

Now, as we conclude this groundbreaking adventure, let's take a moment to reflect on the awe-inspiring impact it's had on our lives. We've shattered the stereotypes and smashed the barriers that have tried to hold us back. We've embraced our unique challenges and used them as fuel to propel ourselves toward financial freedom. And damn, have we done it with style!

Throughout this book, we've soaked up the knowledge, strategies, and tips that will forever change our financial game. We've become masters of our money, slaying debt like it's nobody's business and building empires of wealth. And honey, we're not stopping there! We're using our newfound power to inspire and uplift our comunidad, ensuring that no Latina gets left behind on this journey to financial badassery.

Our Latina heritage is a vibrant tapestry that we proudly carry with us. From Abuelita's timeless financial wisdom to the fierce matriarchs who've paved the way, we've inherited a legacy of strength, resilience, and resourcefulness. So, let's wear our culture like a crown, infusing it into our financial decisions and using it to fuel our determination to rise above the limitations placed upon us.

But let's not forget the power of sisterhood and the bond we share. We're a tribe of unstoppable Latinas, and together, we're a force to be reckoned with! Let's create a network of fierce mujeres who empower, support, and cheer each other on as we slay our financial goals. We'll celebrate our victories with mojitos and margaritas, dance to the rhythm of our financial freedom, and show the world that Latinas mean business!

In our pursuit of financial independence, let's remember that money is just one part of our incredible worth. Our wealth encompasses the love we give, the dreams we chase, and the impact we make on our communities. We're not just building bank accounts; we're building legacies of empowerment, resilience, and Latina excellence.

As we bid farewell, know that you, my badass hermana, have the power to shape your financial destiny. Trust in your abilities, embrace the guiding spirits of the ancestors, and let your dreams guide you toward an abundant and extraordinary life. The road may have twists, turns, and the occasional speed bump, but with our fierce energy, we'll conquer anything that comes our way!

Keep shining, keep hustling, and keep rocking that financial crown like the queen you are! The world better be ready, because we're about to unleash the Latina financial revolution!

Con mucho cariño y puro fuego…cheers to becoming unfuckwithable, reina!

Stay Poderosa,

Jannese

# ACKNOWLEDGMENTS

I am filled with deep gratitude as I reflect on the completion of this groundbreaking personal finance book specifically crafted for Latinas. I can't believe we did this! The support and contributions of numerous individuals have been vital in bringing this project to life. I would like to express my heartfelt appreciation to the following:

My parents, Marga and Confe: Thank you for standing by me, celebrating my successes, and lifting me up during the challenging moments I faced while writing this book. The pages within are a testament to the values and support you have instilled in me.

My little sister Lianne: Thank you for being the unsung hero behind the YQD brand. From working the backend of our website, to coordinating podcast guests, to keeping my calendar up to date, you're the order to my chaos. I literally couldn't do any of this without you.

Richelle Fredson, my magnificent book proposal coach: My sincerest thanks for your unwavering belief in the importance of empowering Latinas through financial knowledge. Your friendship, guidance, and encouragement throughout the writing process have been invaluable. Because of you, this crazy idea of mine has actually come to life!

Farnoosh Torabi, my badass money mentor: I am constantly inspired by your courage and willingness to share your story as a pioneer in the personal finance space. Your mentorship as a fellow woman of color has inspired and enriched the pages of this book. I am immensely grateful for your wisdom and expertise in the world of money. Your insights and guidance have fueled my journey to make relevant and impactful content for Latinas and people of color who are seeking financial empowerment.

Sara Carder, my talented editor: Thank you for your unyielding support and encouragement throughout the writing process. Your belief in the transformative power of financial knowledge for Latinas has been a constant source of motivation. Your commitment to ensuring the accuracy and clarity of the content is deeply appreciated. Thank you for your meticulous editing and proofreading, which have significantly enhanced the quality of this book. I can honestly say this book wouldn't exist without you.

Wendy Sherman, my brilliant literary agent: I am indebted to you for your support and advocacy along this journey. Your guidance, wisdom, and mentorship have shaped not only this book but also my growth as a writer and individual. Your patience and belief in my abilities have fueled my determination to see this project through to fruition.

Nana K. Twumasi, my incredible publisher: My heartfelt appreciation for your commitment to amplifying diverse voices and perspectives in the publishing industry. Your support in bringing this book to the readers has been instrumental in reaching Latinas who are hungry for financial empowerment.

Adam Kirschner, my awesome talent manager: Thank you for helping me keep the lights on while writing this book! Anyone who takes on a project like this knows that it can have a real financial impact on your bottom line, and you've done a great job of finding new and exciting projects for me to work on throughout this time.

To all my phenomenal podcast guests, who've inspired so many stories shared throughout this book: Thank you for your vulnerability, honesty, and transparency. I'm so grateful that you're a part of this beautiful community that's working to uplift nuestra gente with inspiring money stories.

I want to express my gratitude to the readers, podcasters, listeners, social media followers, and supporters who have embraced this book. Your enthusiasm and love give purpose to my work, and I am humbled to be a part of your journey toward financial empowerment. It is for you that I have poured my heart and soul into these pages. I hope this book empowers, inspires, and guides you on your own financial journey.

I extend my deepest thanks to my loved ones for their unwavering support and understanding during the writing process. Writing a book involves a lot of sacrifice, and you all graciously understood why I had to hibernate and focus during this process. I've missed you all, so thank you for your patience! Your love and encouragement have been my anchor throughout this endeavor.

And to all those whose names may not be mentioned but have offered their support, encouragement, and belief in me, thank you. I am forever grateful. Your contributions, whether big or small, have played an integral role in the creation of this book. Please know that they are acknowledged and deeply appreciated.

Writing a personal finance book for Latinas has been a profound experience, and I am honored to have had the opportunity to empower and uplift my community through its pages. I'm looking forward to this being the start of an influx of diverse voices that talk unapologetically about dinero, because our voices matter so much.

Thank you all for being a part of this financial revolution.

With profound gratitude,

Jannese

# GUIDE TO PODCAST EPISODES

**W**ant to dive deeper into the topics we've covered in the book? Here's a list of podcast episodes from *Yo Quiero Dinero* that correspond to some of the stories in the book to help you keep the momentum going. To find the full *YQD* podcast archive, visit yoquierodineropodcast .com/podcast. Make sure to subscribe on your favorite podcast platform so you never miss an episode!

| NAME | EPISODE # | EPISODE TITLE | CHAPTER |
|------|-----------|---------------|---------|
| Anna N'jie Konte | 45 | How To Stop Letting Money Create Stress In Your Life | 2 |
| A Purple Life | 58 | How To Retire Early And Live An Intentional Life | 6, 7 |
| Bernadette Joy | 77, 150 | How To Crush Your Money Goals, How To Manage Wealth Guilt | 2, 4 |
| Cindy Zuniga-Sanchez | 66 | How Cindy Paid Off $215,000 In 4 Years | 4 |
| Dasha Kennedy | 132 | How To Maintain Your Financial Independence In A Relationship | 9 |

| | | | |
|---|---|---|---|
| David Auten & John Schneider | 156 | How Money Affects The Queer Community | 1, 4 |
| Delyanne Barros | 13 | How Delyanne Is Pursuing FIRE To Retire By 45 | 7 |
| Evie Prete | 125 | How To Negotiate Your Salary | 3 |
| Farnoosh Torabi | 96, 219 | Why We Need Wealth In The Hands Of Women, Becoming A Breadwinning Woman | 7 |
| Genoveva Meza Talbott | 95 | How Marriage, Divorce & Death Affects Your Dinero | 9 |
| Gianni Latange | 93 | How FU Money Can Help You Pivot Your Career | 7 |
| Jamila Souffrant | 76 | How To Buy Back Your Freedom With FIRE | 6, 7 |
| Jannese Torres | 140 | How To Create 10k Months In Your Business | 5 |
| Jannese Torres | 143 | How To Hire Your First Employee | 5 |
| Jannese Torres | 160 | How To Make Money As A Blogger | 5 |
| Jennifer Toledo | 108 | How To Overcome Financial Abuse | 9 |
| Kevin L. Matthews | 126 | How To Build Generational Wealth | 10 |
| Kirsten & Julien Saunders | 31, 153 | Why Achieving Financial Independence Matters For Communities Of Color, How To Redefine Your Relationship With Work | 1, 7 |
| Lynne Alfaro | 222 | Why The Future Of America's Economy Depends On Latinos | 1 |
| Nicole Nieves | 194 | How To Market & Grow Your Brand | 5 |
| Selma C. (Bitch I'm Budgeting) | 173 | How To Stop Hating Budgets | 4 |
| Shang Saavedra | 193 | How To Become Financially Independent As A Family | 6, 7 |
| Soledad Fernandez-Paulino | 218 | How To Self-Care Your Way To Financial Freedom | 2 |

# INDEX

# ABOUT THE AUTHOR

Jannese Torres is an award-winning Latina money expert. Her English-language personal finance podcast and platform *Yo Quiero Dinero* empowers Latinas and people of color on personal finance topics like entrepreneurship, financial independence, building generational wealth, investing, and money mindset through guest interviews and solo episodes. *Yo Quiero Dinero* is a recipient of the 2022 Plutus Award for Personal Finance Podcast of the Year.

Jannese became an accidental entrepreneur after a job loss inspired her to turn her food blog into a six-figure business. Throughout the years, her passion for entrepreneurship led her to notice a gap in the conversation around money. Inspired by the J.Lo & Cardi B song "Dinero," in 2019 she decided to start teaching marginalized communities about topics like entrepreneurship, investing, and financial independence through her award-winning personal finance podcast and platform, *Yo Quiero Dinero*. Jannese is an expert in the areas of digital entrepreneurship, content creation, financial independence, creating multiple income streams, and passive income. With over a decade of experience in digital entrepreneurship, content creation, and multicultural marketing, she is now a highly-sought-after business expert who helps her clients monetize their skills and pursue financial independence. You can learn more about Jannese and YQD at yoquierodineropodcast.com.